The History and Traditions of Islington.

Thomas Coull

The History & Traditions of Islington.
Coull, Thomas
British Library, Historical Print Editions
British Library
1861
124 p. ; 8º.
010349.bb.13.(1.)

The BiblioLife Network

This project was made possible in part by the BiblioLife Network (BLN), a project aimed at addressing some of the huge challenges facing book preservationists around the world. The BLN includes libraries, library networks, archives, subject matter experts, online communities and library service providers. We believe every book ever published should be available as a high-quality print reproduction; printed on- demand anywhere in the world. This insures the ongoing accessibility of the content and helps generate sustainable revenue for the libraries and organizations that work to preserve these important materials.

The following book is in the "public domain" and represents an authentic reproduction of the text as printed by the original publisher. While we have attempted to accurately maintain the integrity of the original work, there are sometimes problems with the original book or micro-film from which the books were digitized. This can result in minor errors in reproduction. Possible imperfections include missing and blurred pages, poor pictures, markings and other reproduction issues beyond our control. Because this work is culturally important, we have made it available as part of our commitment to protecting, preserving, and promoting the world's literature.

GUIDE TO FOLD-OUTS, MAPS and OVERSIZED IMAGES

In an online database, page images do not need to conform to the size restrictions found in a printed book. When converting these images back into a printed bound book, the page sizes are standardized in ways that maintain the detail of the original. For large images, such as fold-out maps, the original page image is split into two or more pages.

Guidelines used to determine the split of oversize pages:

• Some images are split vertically; large images require vertical and horizontal splits.
• For horizontal splits, the content is split left to right.
• For vertical splits, the content is split from top to bottom.
• For both vertical and horizontal splits, the image is processed from top left to bottom right.

[PRICE EIGHTEENPENCE.]

THE

History & Traditions

OF

ISLINGTON.

BY THOMAS COULL,

AUTHOR OF THE "HISTORY AND TRADITIONS OF ST. PANCRAS," ETC.

[OLD ISLINGTON CHURCH.]

LONDON:

PUBLISHED BY T. MILES, UPPER STREET, ISLINGTON.

AND MAY BE HAD OF ALL NEWSVENDORS THROUGHOUT THE PARISH.

1861.

THE

History & Traditions

OF

ISLINGTON.

BY THOMAS COULL,

AUTHOR OF THE "HISTORY AND TRADITIONS OF ST. PANCRAS," ETC.

LONDON :

PUBLISHED BY T. MILES, UPPER STREET, ISLINGTON.

AND MAY BE HAD OF ALL NEWSVENDORS THROUGHOUT THE PARISH.

1861.

Preface.

THE many interesting reminiscences and pleasant traditions with which Islington abounds, together with the increased interest which has been evinced during the past few years in local associations by its inhabitants, induced the author of this little work to collect all obtainable information, and present such to the public in a new and cheap form. In this arduous labour, which has also been one of pleasure, the author acknowledges he has been largely indebted to his predecessors, Mr. John Nelson and Mr. S. Lewis, jun., to Mr. Nichol's "History of Canonbury," Lysson's "Environs of London," Dr. Cromwell's "Clerkenwell," and other writers, with whose valuable works he does not attempt to compete. At the same time much entirely new information has been added, and the principal edifices and other places lately erected, have been noticed, with accounts of their history and origin. The object sought has been, not so much to enter upon statistical details, as to place before the public a few readable sketches of the customs, traditions, and social progress of the parish from its earliest period, in a manner suited to those who have not too much attention to spare, and who may desire the pleasure of history without its toils.

In conclusion, the author begs to thank all those kind friends who, by their valuable information, and the papers they placed at his disposal, assisted him materially in his efforts.

Barnsbury, September, 1861.

Contents.

THE

Ristory & Traditions

OF

ISLINGTON.

[OLD ISLINGTON CHURCH.]

INTRODUCTION.—EARLY HISTORICAL EVENTS.

HISTORY, even if considered as a source of rational amusement, will be found to far exceed in interest the most extraordinary fiction. It is particularly engaging when the scenes with which we are daily associated,—the place where we have a "local habitation and a name,"—are the subjects of our inquiry. The history of the parish of Islington will not be found wanting in those particular events which give the study of such a branch of learning its peculiar charm; indeed, there is not a suburb of the great metropolis whose annals are so full of pleasant and entertaining reminiscences of an instructive character.

To trace the origin of the villages in the vicinity of London, it is necessary to refer to a very remote period of our metropolitan annals. Previous to the arrival of the Romans, the adjacent country to the north presented one vast forest, thickly covered with natural wood. This forest was called the " Forest of Middlesex," and Caen Wood or Ken Wood, Highgate, is the only part that now remains to us of this once extensive tract in its natural state. It was first penetrated by the Romans, for the purpose of forming their great high road or military way, and the northern military highway called the *Ermin*, or Herman-street, left London by Cripplegate, and proceeded, it is supposed, northward, through Islington, nearly in the line of the present High-street.

Fitzstephen, a local historian, who died A.D. 1191, in commenting upon the appearance of the country about the north of London, writes as follows :—

" On the north side are fields for pasture and open meadows, very pleasant, into which the river waters do flow, and mills are turned about with a delightful noise. The arable lands are no hungry pieces of gravel ground, but like the rich fields of Asia, which plentifully bring forth corn and fill the barn of the owner with a dainty crop of the fruit of Ceres. Beyond them an immense forest extends itself, beautified with woods and groves, and full of the lairs and coverts of wild beasts and game, stags, bucks, boars, and wild bulls."

The meadows and mills referred to were more in the neighbourhood of Clerkenwell, the latter no doubt turned by the Fleet Brook and the other running streams which fell into it ; and the country beyond was one vast tract of forest land. Even as recently as the reign of Henry VIII. the neighbourhood appears to have afforded cover for game in considerable quantities, as the following proclamation issued by that monarch for its preservation will show :—

" A PROCLAMATION yt noe person interrupt the King's game of partridge or pheasant.
" *Rex majori et vicecomitibus, London. Vobis mandamus, &c.*

" Forasmuch as the King's most Royale Majestie is much desirous of having the game of hare, partridge, pheasant, and heron, preserved in and about his honour at Westminster for his disport and pastime ; that is toe saye, from his said palace, toe our Ladye of the Oke at Islington, toe Highgate and Hamsted Heath, toe be preserved for his own pleasure and recreation ; his Royale Highnesse doth straightwaye charge and commandeth all and singular of his subjects, of what estate and condition soev' they be, not toe attempt to hunt or hawke or kill any of the said game within the precincts of Hamsted, as they tender his favour, and would

eschewe the imprisonment of their bodies and further punishment at his Majesty's will and pleature."
" *Teste meipso apud Westm. vij die Julij anno trecisimo septimo Henrici Octavi, 1546.*"

As far back as the time of the Saxon monarchy, Islington was celebrated for its dairy produce, and that it retained its name through succeeding ages for such, the following extract from Laneham's account of Queen Elizabeth's Entertainment at Kenilworth Castle, will illustrate. A person called the " Squire Minstrel of Middlesex " was introduced by Dudley, Earl of Leicester, who at that time had as a residence, an ancient mansion in Islington, called Ward's Place. The minstrel was one of those who, during the celebrated festivities at Kenilworth, presented themselves as representatives of various towns, and were arrayed with fantastical insignia, peculiar to the village or place they came from. Displaying a rich coat of arms before her Majesty, the Minstrel began by informing her that he had come from Islington, and with pompous terms declared,—

" How the worshipful village of Islington, well-known to be one of the most ancient and best touns in England, next to London at thiz day (as well as at Cookez feast* in Aldersgate - street yeerely upon Holyrood-day, as also at all solemn bridals in the citie of London, in well-serving them of milk for their flawnez not yet chalk'd ; of cream for their custardes not yet thickened with flour, and of butter for their pastiez and pye-paste not made of curds, nor gathered of whey in summer, nor mingled in winter with salt butter and wash'd) did obtain long ago these worshipful arms in colour and form as ye see, which are a field argent, as the field and ground wherein the milkwives of this worthy toun do trade for their living. Undergraven is there written a proper word, well-squaring with the rest, taken out of Salem's ' Chapter of Things that most Nourish the Body,'—*Lac caseus, infans* ; that iz, ' good milk and young cheez.' And thus much, may it please your Majestie, have I to say for the arms of our worshipful toun of Islington.' And the minstrel, after making a mannerly bow, held his peace."

It is evident, from the foregoing, that the use of chalk and the pump in the manufac-

* The cooks or pastrymen of London were incorporated by charter from Edward IV, 1480, and their hall was situated opposite Little Britain.

ture of milk, was not unknown in Islington, even in those days.

Queen Elizabeth's partiality for the village is well-known. She paid frequent visits to Sir Thomas Fowler, of Islington, and to Sir John Spencer of Canonbury House, and the frequency of such visits has occasioned her name to be associated with many of the ancient houses in the parish, which will, in future pages, be more especially referred to. In the reign of James and Charles, Islington appears to have been a very favourite spot with the Londoners, amongst other inducements being the great number of dairies at which they could conveniently regale themselves, as well as the many houses of entertainment opened for their reception.

Among other interesting but detached records connected with the early history of the parish, the following are collected from various sources:—

In the Mostyn collection of papers relative to the cause of the disturbance in Wales during the reign of Edward I., it is stated, "that the Snowdon barons, accompanied by Llewyllen their prince, came up to London to do homage. These Welsh barons, with their numerous retinue, were quartered at Islington, and well entertained there. They, however, could not drink the wine or the ale of London; the English bread they slighted, and the environs did not afford milk enough for their large party, although Islington was at that time famous for milk. Their pride, too, was disgusted with the continual staring of the Londoners, who followed them in crowds to look at their uncommon garbs. 'No!' chorused the indignant Welshmen, 'we never again will visit Islington except as conquerors.' And from that instant they resolved to take up arms."

In 1465, Henry VI., after his escape from the battle of Hexham, was arrested at Islington by the Earl of Warwick, who, after taking the gilt spurs off his feet on the road, and otherwise treating him with dishonour, sent him to the Tower.

Henry VII., on his return to London after his defeat of Lambert Gimel, was met in "Hornsey Parke by the Lord maior, aldermen and sheriffs, and principal commoners of the citie of London, all on horseback and liverie to attend upon him, when he dubbed Sir William Horne, maior of London, knight, and betwixt Iseldon and London he dubbed Sir John Percival knight."

Henry VIII. frequently visited Islington, and during his reign several of the principal nobility resided in the parish, amongst them being Dudley, Earl of Warwick, and Algernon, Earl of Northumberland. The name of a pathway leading from the corner of Newington Green to the Turnpike road at Ball's Pond, has long been known as "King Harry's Walk."

During the great fire of London in 1666, the fields around Islington afforded a welcome, though wretched asylum, to multitudes of the houseless and destitute citizens, who were driven to seek shelter under tents and hovels, and depended for food on the sympathy of their fellow-creatures. Towards the assistance of these sufferers a collection is recorded in the Vestry minutes of the parish, under the year 1666, to the following effect:—"The 10th day of October, collected in the parish church of St. Mary, Islington, the sum of £17 19s. 1d. for the relief of poore distressed citizens of London, whose distress came by fire." Of the general desolation caused by that event, Evelyn in his memoirs draws a melancholy picture:—"The poor inhabitants," he says, "were dispersed about as far as Highgate, several miles in a circle, some under miserable tents and hovels, many without a rag, a bed, board, or necessary utensils, who from delicateness, riches, and easy accommodation in well furnished houses, were now reduced to extremest misery and poverty.... I walked towards Islington and Highgate, where one might have seen 200,000 people, of all ranks and degrees, lying along by their heaps of what they could save from the fire, deploring their loss, and though ready to perish from hunger and destitution, yet not asking one penny for relief, which to me appeared a stranger sight than any I ever yet beheld."

Topography.—The Ancient Manors.

THE parish of Islington lies within the Finsbury division of the Ossulton Hundred of the County of Middlesex. It is bounded on the north by the parish of Hornsey; on the west by St. Pancras; on the east by Stoke Newington and Hackney; and on the south by the parishes of St. Luke, Shoreditch, and Clerkenwell. It is three miles two furlongs in length, two miles one furlong in breadth, and ten miles two furlongs in circumference; and contains an area of 3,032 acres. Exclusive of the village from which the whole parish is now named, it contains the hamlets of Holloway, Ball's-pond, Battle-bridge, and Newington-green. Its soil is principally a gravelly loam and clay; the whole of the arable land throughout the parish does not exceed thirty acres.

As regards the derivation of the name of this now populous suburb, few places have experienced more orthographic changes. In ancient records the word has been written Isendune, Isendon, Iseldon, and Yseldon. Isendune, which name occurs in the most ancient records belonging to the church of St. Paul's, as well as in the Domesday Book, signifies, in the Saxon language, the *Hill of Iron*, from the circumstance, that several springs of mineral water, impregnated with iron, were found rising in its vicinity. The present name, Islington, appears to have been generally adopted about the close of the 16th century.

Islington is divided into six great Manors, viz.,—The Prebend, Barnsbury, Highbury, Canonbury, St. John of Jerusalem, and Clerkenwell. In that ancient and valuable record called the "Domesday Book," which was prepared by order of the Conqueror, and which gives an account of the condition and value of landed property in England at the close of the eleventh century, we have the following statement of property at Islington:

"*The Canons of St. Paul's hold two hides at Isendune, the land is one caracute* and a half, on which there is only one plough, but another might be kept half employed. This estate, the present and former value of which*

---

* *A caracute* was as much land as could be cultivated by one plough.

is 40s. per annum, has been, time out of mind, parcel of the demesnes of the church.*

"*The same Canons hold two other hides of land at Isendune, which furnishes employment for two ploughs, and is all in culture. There are four villiens* who hold this land under the canons, four bordars,† and 13 cottars. This estate, which also belongs to the church, had been valued in King Edward's time at 40s., but when the survey was taken at 30s. only.*

"*Gilbert holds of Geoffrey of Mandeville, half a hide of land, which is cultivated to its full extent. There is one villien and one bordar. Valued in King Edward's time at 20s., now at 12s. It was formerly the property of Grim, a servant of King Edward, who could alien it at pleasure.*

"*Dernan holds half a hide of the king, which is valued at 10s; it was formerly the property of Ilgar, a servant of King Edward.*

"*Ranulf, brother of Ilgar, holds Tolentone of the king for two hides. The land is two caracutes, the villiens have two ploughs. There are five villiens who hold half a virgate‡ each, two bordars who hold nine acres, one cottage, and one slave, pasture for the cattle, acorns for 60 hogs, and 5s. rents. This manor was valued in King Edward's time at 40s. when it was granted to Ranulf at 60s.; now worth only 40s. It was formerly the property of Ilgar, a servant of King Edward, who had the power of alienating it at pleasure.*

For the sake of perspicuity a short account of the history of the several manors in which the parish has been divided since the Conquest, will be given separately, commencing with Canonbury.

---

* *Villiens* were commonly tillers of the soil, and were the absolute property of the proprietors of the land on which they laboured. They could hold no property of their own, and were sold with the estate just the same as the cattle, or were transferred from one estate to another like any other goods and chattels.

† A *bordar* or *cottar* was a little higher in the social scale than a villien. He generally rented a piece of land and a cottage, for which he undertook to supply the lord of the manor's table with a certain quantity of eggs, butter, poultry, &c.

‡ A *virgate* is the fourth part of a caracute.

The Manor of Canonbury.

IN the Domesday Survey the Church estates at Islington are described as being very large, and it is thought by Lyssons and other good authorities, that the greater portion of such estates, said to have once belonged to St. Paul's, came into possession of the Berners family about the year 1290. Canonbury, however, one of the most extensive of these estates, was not long retained in the hands of this family, as Ralph de Berners, who died in 1297, gave it to the Priory of St. Bartholomew, in West Smithfield, in whose possession it remained until the dissolution of the monasteries in the reign of Henry VIII. As regards the origin of the name it is most probable that this site being chosen on which to erect a mansion for the Priors of the Canons of Bartholomew, it received the name of " Canonbury," or "Canons' House." *Bury* is synonymous with bower, or burgh, and signifies generally a mansion or dwelling-place. For this purpose, as is observed by Malcolm, "Canonbury was certainly most convenient and pleasant ; we can easily imagine the beautiful views they must have had from thence, even to the gates of the Priory of St. Bartholomew, for the smoke of London was not then as dense as it is at present, and but very few buildings intervened."

Robert Fuller, Abbot of Waltham Holy Cross, 1522, was the last Prior of St. Bartholomew. He surrendered his estate to the King on the 25th of October, 1539, in the thirty-first year of Henry's reign. In 1540 the Manor of Canonbury, with the adjoining Manor of Highbury, was bestowed upon Thomas Lord Cromwell, Lord Privy Seal, Vicar-General, and Lord Great Chamberlain of England. This nobleman, however, shortly after having been raised to the Earldom of Essex, was attainted of high treason, and executed at the Tower, and his estates were seized by the Crown. Canonbury was next granted by Edward VI. to John Dudley, Duke of Northumberland, who was likewise attainted and beheaded under Queen Mary. This nobleman is spoken of as being the most powerful subject England possessed, but unjust, haughty, and of insatiable ambition. He appears, however, to have been as abject in adversity as he was haughty in prosperity, and while under sentence of death in the Tower, begged for life in the most servile terms. In a letter to the Earl of Arundel, written from the Tower, he exclaims, "Alas my good lord, is my crime so heinous that no redemption but my bloode can washe awaye the spottes thereof? An old proverb there is, and that most true, 'that a livinge dogge is better than a dead lyon.' Oh! that it would please her goode grace to give me life, yea, the life of a dogge, that I might live and kisse her feet !"

The manor then came into possession of Thomas Lord Wentworth, to whom it was granted by Queen Mary. In 1557, this nobleman alienated it to John Spencer, Bart., famous on account of his enormous wealth, being popularly known as *Rich Spencer*. Sir John Spencer was a citizen and clothmaker of London, and was elected Lord Mayor in the year 1594. Many are the interesting anecdotes with which his history abounds. It was said he was worth a million of money, (an extraordinary amount for a private individual to be possessed of in those days) and his fame was so great that a pirate of Dunkirk laid a plot to carry him away from his house in order to obtain a large ransom. In a pamphlet, published in 1651, entitled the "Vanity of the Lives and Passions of Men," occurs the following remarkable passage in relation to the above incident :—"In Queen Elizabeth's time, a pirate of Dunkirk laid a plot with twelve of his mates, to carry away Sir John Spencer, which, if he had done, fifty thousand pounds would not have ransomed him. He came over the seas in a shallop with twelve musketeers, and in the night anchored at Barking Creek, and leaving the shallop in the custody of six of his men, with the other six came as far as Islington, and there hid himself in a ditch near the path in which Sir John came along to his house at Canonbury ; but, by the providence of God, Sir John was forced by some extraordinary occasion to stay in town that night, otherwise they had taken him away ; and the pirates, fearing that they should be discovered, went back during the night time to their shallop, and so returned to Dunkirk."

Sir John had one daughter, named Elizabeth, sole heir to his immense riches, and who of course, was an object of ambition to many an ardent suitor. Lord Compton, then President of Wales, managed to gain the girl's affections, but the old man, her father, objecting to the match, she contrived to elope. Her escape is stated by Mr. Nichols to have been accomplished in a most singular manner. Lord Compton hired a baker to enter the knight's mansion, and engage to carry her off in his basket. That this circumstance is really a fact, is confirmed by a splendid picture still in the possession of the Compton family at their seat in Castle Ashby in Northamptonshire, representing the incident. By the marriage which followed this elopement in 1594, the estate of Canonbury was carried into the Compton family. The knight was at first so much enraged at the elopement of his daughter, that he totally discarded her, until at last a reconciliation took place by the kind interference of Queen Elizabeth. The way such reconciliation is said to have been brought about was as follows:—The Queen requested that Sir John would stand sponsor to the first offspring of a young couple discarded by their father. The good knight readily complied, and a babe being brought forward, her Majesty dictated his own surname for the Christian name of the child. The ceremony being performed, Sir John assured the Queen, that having discarded his own daughter, he would adopt the boy as his own son. "Right glad am I to hear you say so," said the Queen, "for it is your own grandson, the son of your discarded daughter, Elizabeth!" The surprise of the old knight can be well imagined, but with so powerful an intercessor, he could not refuse, and the child ultimately succeeded to the honours of his father, and the wealth of his grandfather.

For the truth of this story we have no definite authority, although from the intimacy between the knight and the Queen, together with the well-known eccentricity of the latter, it is likely to be a matter of fact. This pleasant tradition has afforded subject for many stories.

Sir John Spencer died March 30th, 1609, at an advanced age, and was buried in the church of St. Helen's, in Bishopsgate-street, his monument having the effigies of himself and his lady in recumbent postures as large as life, with their daughter kneeling at their feet. The town residence of Sir John was in Crosby-place, a large and sumptuous house in Bishopsgate-street, which had been built by Sir John Crosby. It was once the residence of the Duke of Gloucester, afterwards King Richard. "This house," says Stow, "Sir John Spencer lately purchased; he made great preparations, and kept his mayoralty there, and has since builded a large warehouse near thereunto." Here, in 1603, he splendidly entertained the Duke of Sully, the celebrated French minister, who arrived in England with a superb train soon after the accession of King James I.

Sir John Spencer possessed much loyalty and patriotism. From Nichol's "History of Canonbury," we learn, during the year of his mayoralty there was a great scarcity of food in the country, "and by this means the various city companies were ordered to purchase a quantity of foreign corn and lay it up in their granary in the Bridge-house to provide against a dearth in the city. Before this, however, could be effected, an obstacle presented itself which well-nigh frustrated the provident intention of the mayor. Sir John Hawkins, to whom the care of the Queen's fleet belonged, happened to require at this time the Bridge-house Granary for himself, for the bringing in and laying up there provisions for the navy, and the ovens for the making of ships' bread. In this strait Sir John sent a message to the treasurer Lord Burleigh, telling him that the city 'could not well conveniently spare the same,' and after pointing out the great necessity the citizens had 'for their granaries and ovens,' observed 'that he was informed her Majesty had garnets (granaries) about Tower-hill and Whitehall, and Westminster; and also, that if they would not serve, had in her hands Winchester House, wherein great quantities might be laid.' Upon this stout answer Burleigh told him that he should hear no more to his further dislike, and he bade him, that if he did not procure any letter for the same, he doubted not, but to answer him to their lordship's good acceptance. And that now having received letters for the same from some of the Counsel, he humbly prayed the Lord Treasurer's good favour, that the garnets, being the city's, might be employed for the use of the same, that there might be no want or outcry of the poor for bread, or else that if there fell out a greater want and dearth of grain than there yet was, and that the city was unprovided, his Lordship would be pleased to hold him excused, and so most humbly submitted himself to his lordship's good pleasure."

The worthy knight was buried with the greatest pomp, and the following curious letter relating to the funeral has been happily preserved, and serves to show his immense wealth. It is directed from a Londoner, Mr. John Beaulieu, to a friend residing in Brussels, a Mr. Trumbell :—

"London, April 10, 1609.

"MY DEAR FRIEND,—Upon Tuesday last the funeral of Sir John Spencer was made, at which some thousand men did assist in mourning cloaks or gowns, amongst which there were 320 poor men, who had every one of them a basket given them, stored with the following particular provisions, set down in this note enclosed—

"'A black gowne, four pounds of beef, two loaves of bread, a bottle of wine, a candlestick, a pound of candles, two saucers, a spoon, a black pudding, a pair of gloves, two red herrings, four white herrings, six sprats, and two eggs.'

"But to expound to you the meaning of such antique furniture I am not so skilful an Œdipus, except it doth design the horn of abundance, which my Lord Compton found in that succession. That poor Lord is not like (if God do not help him) to carry it away for nothing, or to grow very rich thereby, being in great danger to lose his wittes for the same; whereof, being at the very first newes, either through the vehement apprehension of joy for such a plentiful succession, or of carefulness how to take it up and dispose of it, became somewhat distracted, but afterwards reasonably well-restored; he is now of late fallen again (but more deeply) at the same frenzy, so that there seemeth to be little hope of his recovery. And what shall these thousands and millions avail him if he come to lose, if not his soul, at least his witts and reason? It is a fair and ample 'subject for a divine to course riches, and a notable example to the world not to woo or trust so much in them.'

"JOHN BEAULIEU."

In another letter upon the same subject, about the same date, Mr. Beaulieu wrote as follows :—

"Here is dead, within these two days, the old Lady Spencer, following the heels of her husband, who gave away amongst her kindred £13,000 of the £15,000 which she was to have of my Lord Compton, who is now altogether distracted and so franticke as that he is forced to be kept bound. The administration of his goods and lands is committed to the Lord Chamberlain, Privy Seal, and Worcester, who, coming the last week into the City, took an inventory (in the presence of the sheriffs) of the goods, amongst which (it is said) there were bonds found for £133 000."

Sir Thomas Edmondes, in a letter to Sir Ralph Winwood, dated April 17th, 1609, writes, "The Lord Compton hath been so transported with joy for the great fortune befallen him by the death of Sir John Spencer, his father-in-law, as the overworking of the same in his mind did hinder him from taking any rest, whereby he was grown half-distracted, but now he is reasonably well recovered again."

Lord Compton, after a short time, recovered from his temporary derangement of intellect, and soon after took possession of Sir John Spencer's wealth and his estates at Canonbury. Elizabeth Compton, his daughter and heiress, lived in great state. A quaint letter written by that lady to her husband soon after her father's decease, is still preserved to us in Nichol's "History of Canonbury," and as it gives a very interesting account of the ideas of a lady of quality in those days, will well bear quotation and repay perusal :—

"MY SWEET LIFE,—Now I have declared to you my mind for the settling of your estate, I suppose that it were best for me to bethink or consider with myself what allowance were meetest for me ; for considering what care I have of your estate, and how respectfully I dealt with those which, both by the laws of God and nature, and of civil polity, wit, religion, government, and honesty, you, my dear, are bound to, I pray and beseech you to grant me £1,600 per annum, quarterly to be paid.

"Also, I would (beside that allowance for my apparel) have £600 added yearly (quarterly to be paid) for the performance of charitable works ; and those things I would not, neither will be accountable for.

"Also, I will have three horses for my own saddle, that none shall dare to lend or borrow—none lend but I, none borrow but you.

"Also, I would have two gentlewomen, lest one should be sick, or have some other lett ; I also believe that it is an indecent thing for a gentlewoman to stand mumping alone, when God hath blessed their lord and lady with a good estate.

"Also, when I ride, a hunting or hawking, or travel from one house to another, I will have them attending me ; so for either of these said women, I must and will have for each of them a horse.

"Also, I will have six or eight gentlemen, and I will have my two coaches, one lined with velvet to myself, with four very fair horses, and a coach for my women, lined with sweet cloth, and laced with scarlet, with four very good Horses.

"Also, I will have two coachmen, one for my own coach, the other that of my women.

"Also, at any time when I travel, I will not only be allowed two coaches and spare horses for me and my women, but I will have such carriages as shall be fitting for all; orderly, not pestering my things with my women's, nor theirs with chambermaids, nor theirs with washmaids.

"Also, for laundresses when I travel, I will have them sent away before with the carriages, to see all safe; and the chambermaids I will have go before with the greens,* that the chamber may be ready, sweet and clean.

"Also, it being indecent to crowd myself up with my gentleman-usher in my coach, I will have him to have a convenient coach, to attend me either in city or country; and I must have two footmen. And my desire is that you defray all the charges for me.

"And for myself, besides my yearly allowance, I would have twenty gownes of apparel, six of them excellent good ones, eight of them for the country, and six of them *very* excellent good ones.

"Also, I would have to put in my purse, £2,000 and £200, and for you to pay my debts.

"Also, I would have me £6,000 to buy me jewels, and £4,000 to buy me a pearl chain.

"Now, seeing I am *so reasonable* unto you, I pray you to find my children apparel and their schooling, and also my servants (men and women) their wages.

"Also, I will have all my houses furnished, and all my lodging-chambers to be suited with all furniture as is fit, as beds, stools, chairs, suitable cushions, carpets, silver warming-pans, cupboards of plate, fair hangings, and such like; so for my draw-

* Referring to the custom of strewing the floors with green rushes.

ing chambers in all houses, I will have them delicately furnished, both with hangings, couch, canopy, glass, carpet, chair cushions, and all things thereunto belonging.

"Also, my desire is that you build Ashby House, and purchase lands; and lend no money (as you love God) to the Lord Chamberlain, who would have all, perhaps your life, from you. Remember his son, my Lord Warden, what entertainment he gave you when you were at the Tilt-yard. If you were dead, he said he would be a husband, a father, a brother, and he said he would marry me I protest I grieve to see the poor man have so little wit and honesty to use his friend so vilely. Also, he fed me with untruths concerning the Charter House, but that is the least. He wished me much harm. You know him. God keep you and me from such as he is.

"So, now, that I have declared to you what I would have, and what that is that I would not have, I pray that when you be an earl, to allow me £1,000 more than I now desire, and *double* attendance.

"Your loving wife,
"ELIZA COMPTON."

On the 2nd of August, 1618, Lord Compton was created Earl of Northampton. He had two daughters, and a son who succeeded him in his title and estates. The Earl died somewhat suddenly, and an old but authentic document records the event in the following terms. It is dated July 2, 1630 :— "Yesterday se'nnight the Earl of Northampton, Lord President of Wales (after he had waited on the king at supper and had also supped) went in a boat with others, to wash himself in the Thames, and so soon as his legs were in the water but to the knees, he had the cholic and cried out, ' *Have me into the boat again, or I am a dead man!*' and died a few hours after at his lodgings in the Savoy, within the suburbs of London, on June 24, 1630, and was buried at Compton with his ancestors."

The Manor of Canonbury still belongs to the same family. Charles, the ninth earl, was created Marquis of Northampton, and his issue is the present proprietor.

Manor of Highbury.

THE MANOR OF HIGHBURY occupies that portion of ground called by the name of *Tolentine* in the Domesday survey, Tollington Park and other places, being a corruption of the old original name. In the time of the Conqueror, as has been mentioned, it was held of the King by one Ranulf, the manorial rights being then valued at 40s. per annum. The manor is now divided into two distinct parts, intersected by the Canonbury and the Prebend Manors; the northern portion, which extends to Newington and Kingsland Greens being by far the largest. It contains about 987 acres. Tolentone or Tallington-lane, afterwards called Duval's, and now the Hornsey-road, separates this estate on the north-west side from that of the Manor of St. John of Jerusalem, to the knights of which order both once belonged.

The origin of the name "Highbury" is derived from the removal of the Manorhouse. In the fields on the east side of the Hornsey-road there stood the remains of a moated site, the ancient residence of the lords of the manor, and in old records denominated *Lower-place.* This house or mansion having fallen to decay, another residence for the proprietors of the soil was afterwards built on the high ground to the east, and from that circumstance was called "High-bury," or *Tigh-burgh*, to distinguish it from the old site in the *Lower-place.* Various opinions have been stated as to why this manor received the additional name of *Newington Barowe.* Some local antiquarians affirm that such a designation originated from the fact that the spot selected for the erection of the new house was the same as that formerly occupied by the Roman camp which is well known to have stood there. Others, however, contend that it originated from Alice de Barowe, who was in possession of this manor about the middle of the thirteenth century. This Lady Alicia or Alice de Barowe, gave the entire lordship of Highbury and Newington to the Priory of St. John of Jerusalem, Clerkenwell, on the condition that she and her heirs should for ever be mentioned in the masses of the convent.

The Manor-house of Highbury, after the bequest by Alice de Barowe, became a kind of country residence for the Lord Prior of the convent of St. John, and was frequently resorted to in summer-time by the head of that House. It continued to be used as such until it was destroyed by Jack Straw, at the time of the insurrection under Wat Tyler, in the year 1381. In referring to the outburst of popular fury which occurred at the time referred to, against the Lord Prior, Hollinshed writes as follows :—

"The haughtinesse and ambition of the Knights Hospitallers of St. John's, and the excessive riches they had accumulated, gave such offence to the common people, that in the insurrection under Wat Tyler, after consuming with fire their magnificent priory of St. John's, at Clerkenwell, 'causing it to burne for the space of seven days together, nor suffering any to quench it,' a detachment of the insurgents, headed by Jack Straw, proceeded with the same intention to the Prior's country house at Highbury."

The prior's house being built almost entirely of stone, the insurrectionists "found no small difficulty in demolishing it, and were obliged to pull down, by main force, the firmer parts of the house which the flames could not consume." Sir Robert Hales, the then Lord Prior, fled to the Tower for safety. That stronghold, however, proved no safe refuge to the prior, for it was besieged and taken by Wat Tyler, and Hales was brought out and beheaded on Tower Hill. After the insurrection had been quelled, Richard II. created the Earls Marshall and Pembroke, and knighted several others "upon the sandhill, towards Iseldonne."

The Manor of Highbury continued in the possession of the Knights of St. John of Jerusalem until the dissolution of the religious houses in the reign of Henry VIII., who, seizing all the lands belonging to the Priory, consisting as they did of an immense number of estates in almost every part of the kingdom, granted this manor to Thomas Lord Cromwell, but upon his attainder, it again reverted to the crown. The Manor of Highbury was then settled on the Lady Mary (afterwards Queen), and from the time of her accession continued in the possession of the crown till the reign of James I., who, upon creating his eldest son Henry Prince of Wales, bestowed this manor upon him. The survey taken upon this occasion is stated to be in the possession of the present lord. It is inscribed "The plot of the Manor of Newington Barowe, parcel of the possessions of the High and Mighty Prince Henry, Prince of Wales, Duke of Cornwall, and Earl of Chester, taken in July, 1611, by Rocke Churche." The premises are described as consisting of a yard where anciently was a castle or mansion house, called Highbury Castle, with two woods, called Highbury Wood and Little St. John's Wood. In the plan attached to the survey Highbury Barn is delineated as a high building within the castle yard.

At the death of Henry Prince of Wales, the King granted it to his son Charles, who afterwards, when he himself came into possession of the crown, granted it to Sir Allen Apsley, who sold it to Thomas Austen, Esq., who, in 1723, alienated it to James Colebrooke, Esq., from whom it descended to Sir George Colebrooke, Bart. It was then purchased by Jonathan Eade, Esq., of Stoke Newington, and is now in the possession of Samuel Pett, Esq., nephew of the above.

Little St. John's and Highbury Woods, covering an area of 42 acres, which was part of this manor, was *not* included in the grant of King Charles to Sir Allen Apsley, but continued in the crown till within the present century, from whom they were purchased some forty years ago by Mr. Felton.

Manor of Iseldon Berners,

COMMONLY CALLED BARNSBURY.

THIS Manor at the time of the survey, was also part of the large estates belonging to the church in this parish. In the year 1290, however, together with that of Canonbury, it came into the possession of the Berners family, for we find about the date of the above period Ralph de Berners was "seised of the Manor of Iseldon, held under the Bishop of London, as of his castle at Stortford, by a service of quit-rent and the service of warding the castle."

In the records of the time of Edward I., when the estate was in possession of Edward de Berners, son and heir of Ralph, who held it by military service, the value and extent of this manor is thus stated:—"A capital messuage, with the garden, &c., valued at 18s.; 180 acres of land valued at 2d. per acre; five of meadow at 1s. 6d.; rent of assize 26s. 3d.; a pair of gilt spurs, payable by Thomas Meuse, of East Smithfield, 6d.; customary rents, 71s.; 48 hens, 4s.; 144 days' work, due from 48 customary tenants 18s., being a 1½d. each day's work: the reaping of 48 acres of corn, 12s.; the carrying of hay, 2s.; weeding corn, 2s.—Edmund de Berners, 26 years of age, abroad in Gascony."

Barnsbury continued in the Berners family for some time. Sir John de Berners died 1396, "seised of the Manor of Berners, in Iseldon, valued at £24 per annum, his son and heir being then in the fourteenth year of his age." After passing through several descendants of the same family it came into the possession of Phillipa Lady Berners, whose daughter Margaret married Sir John Bouchier, into whose family it passed through intermarriage. This Sir John Bouchier was styled Lord Berners in right of his wife, and became Chancellor of the Exchequer. He is recorded among the noble authors, having published a translation of "Froissart's Chronicles." This was the last Lord Berners. He had an only daughter, who married Edward Knivett, Esq. In 1548 the manor became the property of Thomas Fowler, gent., in whose family it continued till 1656, when it passed to Sir John Fisher, who married Sarah, the daughter and heir of Sir Thomas Fowler. By the marriage of Ursula, daughter and heir of Sir Thomas Fisher, the estate came into the possession of Sir William Halton, Bart., and continued in the possession of that family till, in 1754, it was devised by Sir William

Halton, grandson of the above, to William Tuffnell, Joliff, Esq., who died in 1798, and is now in the possession of William Tuffnell, son of the above. According to a survey taken some years ago, this estate contains 212 acres.

Prebend Manor,

AND

THE MANOR OF ST. JOHN OF JERUSALEM.

IT appears that the Conqueror, in or about the year 1065, restored to the Canons of St. Paul's certain estates, of which they had been unjustly deprived, and amongst them were nine cassats of land in Islington. The only property, however, in the parish now belonging to the Church, is the Prebendal Manor, consisting of about one hundred acres, in the neighbourhood of the " Rosemary Branch " Inn. The prebendal stall in the Cathedral of St. Paul's, is the eleventh in the north side of the choir, and is inscribed "*Islington. In convertendo Dom capt.*" In the year 1649 this manor was sold to one Maurice Gethin, citizen of London, for the sum of £275. The gross annual income attached to the preferment of the prebendary of Islington, is about £79, and the duty of such prebendary is to preach in the Cathedral once in two years. Amongst the men who have held the office of prebend to this parish may be mentioned—

PHILLIP LOVELL.—From being steward to the Earl of Winchester he was called up to the service of Henry III., in the year 1251. He was, however, soon after accused by his enemies of privately taking some very valuable vessels from a wealthy Jew to ease him of the king's tax. By payment of 1,000 marks, accompanied by a great deal of intercession and degrading humility he managed to re-establish himself in the king's favour. In 1258, while holding the offices of king's clerk, special counsellor, and treasurer, upon information being given to the king of certain damages he had done to the Royal Forest, his Majesty was so incensed against him that he commanded him to be taken into custody. This disgrace so preyed upon his mind that he died through grief, on the festival of St. Thomas the Martyr, at Hamestable.

RICHARD FLETCHER, D.D., 1572. — He was made Dean of Peterborough in 1583 ; was present with Mary Queen of Scots, when she suffered death at Fotheringhay, in Northamptonshire, in February, 1586, and he endeavoured to persuade her much to the unfortunate Queen's annoyance, to renounce her religion. In 1594 he was made Bishop of London. He fell under the displeasure of Queen Elizabeth, by marrying a second wife, the handsome widow of Sir John Burke of Sissinghurst, and was forbad the Court a year and suspended from his spiritual functions six months. This disgrace is supposed to have shortened his life. He died while sitting in his chair smoking tobacco, on the 15th June, 1596, and was buried in St. Paul's Cathedral. He left nine children, of whom the eldest was John Fletcher, the dramatic poet.

EDWARD STILLINGFLEET, D,D., 1666. —This celebrated man was also Archdeacon of London and Bishop of Worcester. He was greatly distinguished for his numerous polemic writings, particularly " Origines Sacræ ; or a Rational Account of the Grounds of Natural or Revealed Religion ;" a work which for extensive and profound learning, solidity of judgment, strength of argument, and perspecuity of expression, has been justly esteemed one of the best defences of revealed religion that has ever been published in our own or any other language.

WILLIAM HALE HALE, M.A., 1829, succeeded Archdeacon Nare, who was instituted Prebend in 1798. He was examining chaplain to the late Bishop of London, and preacher at the Charter House. He has written several religious works.

THE MANOR OF ST. JOHN OF JERUSALEM.

THIS Manor is very extensive, consisting of a tract of land situated partly in this and partly in the adjoining parishes of Clerkenwell, Hornsey, and St. Luke's. As is generally well-known, it at one time belonged to the Knights of St. John of Jerusalem, who, indeed, prior to the dissolution of the monasteries, owned nearly the whole of the parish. These knights, who used to call themselves "*servants* to the poor servants of the Hospital at Jerusalem," were, according to Dugdale, in the year 1240, "in possession of 19,000 manors in various parts of Christendom, and the knights finding that such superabundance could find no vent in hospitality, turned their revenues from the source of benevolence into the channel of war and conquest, making the world resound with their prowess." How they came into pos-

session of this manor is uncertain. In the reign of Henry VI. it is stated that the priors of St. John held half a knight's fee in Islington, which formerly belonged to William de Vere. At the dissolution, along with Canonbury and Highbury Manors, it came into possession of the crown. In the year 1625 it was granted to Robert Nixon and William Whalley. It was afterwards divided into moieties, one of which came into the family of Short, and another into that of the Newton family, who held possession of it in 1643. The present owners are John Hassard Short and Thomas Jacob, Esqs. That part of the manor included in this parish lies south of Barnsbury, between the Liverpool-road on the east to Maiden-lane on the west, including the lower half of the Caledonian-road. The manor also formerly comprehended Pentonville and reached nearly as far as Smithfield.

Persecution of the Protestants,

BURNING OF THE REFORMERS IN THE FIELDS AT ISLINGTON.

DURING the reign of Mary, many were the contrivances which the Protestants were compelled to resort to in their efforts to assemble together in order that they might worship according to the dictates of their consciences. The severe persecution, however, in that Queen's reign did not extinguish the light of the Reformation, for though great numbers were driven into exile, and multitudes suffered in the flames, yet many who loved the Truth more than their lives were enabled to endure the storm. Congregations were formed in various parts of the kingdom, with whom, on account of their number and unanimity, the Bishops were for some time afraid to interfere. They constantly attended their private meetings and never went to the parish church, but at length an order was made requiring these people to receive the Popish sacrament, which, however, was unanimously refused compliance. At length Bishop Bonner issued his charge that every one was to go to church on the following Lord's Day, or, in case of non-compliance, to appear before the Commissary to give an account of their conduct. The most considerable of the London

congregations who came under this order, was that which met in and about Islington, and though about 200 in number, they remained for a considerable time undiscovered. Sometimes, to screen themselves from their persecutors, they met at night, and many instances are narrated of providential deliverances upon being discovered. In *Strype's Annals*, a number of these deliverances are related, from amongst which the following is selected :—

"On one of these nocturnal occasions, a congregation being assembled at a house situate by the side of the river in Thames-street, they were discovered, and the house was so guarded and surrounded, that their enemies were sure none could escape. Among the congregation, however, was a worthy mariner, who, seeing no other way of deliverance, got out at a back door, and swimming to a boat in the river, brought it to the house, and, having received all the good people into it, he made *oars of his shoes* and conveyed them all away in safety."

Upon various other occasions, however, they were not so fortunate. For instance, in the year 1557, a number of Protestants assembled themselves at Islington on the third Sunday in Advent, under the pretext of witnessing a performance that was to take place there, but in reality to join in divine service. In Fox's "Acts and Monuments," the event is recorded as follows.—"On the third Sunday in Advent, 1557, John Rough, with Cuthbert Sympson, and others, through the craftye and traitorous suggestion of a false hypocrite and dissembling brother, called Roger Sargeant, a tailor by trade, were apprehended by the vice-chamberlain of the Queen's house, at the 'Saracen's Head,' in Islington, where the congregation had then purposed to assemble themselves, to their godly and accustomed exercises of prayer and hearing the word of God; which pretence, for the safeguard of all the rest, they continued to be covered and excused by the hearing of a play that was then appointed to be at that place."

The charge brought against Rough by the infamous Bishop Bonner, was that he had assembled at the house above-mentioned to read the Communion-book according to the accustomed fashion as in the later days of King Edward VI.

Rough was one of the most distinguished of the Puritans, and was of that noble band which included Thomas Bentham, Edmund Scambler, John Pullain, and others, who ministered unto these staunch upholders of the Reformation. In the reign of Edward VI. Rough was celebrated as a preacher both in England and Scotland, and a sermon which he preached at the parish church of St. Andrew Edinburgh, was the means of inducing the celebrated John Knox to engage in the public ministry of the Reformation. Upon the apprehension of this excellent man at Islington, he was taken before the Council, and after several examinations, he was sent to Newgate, and his case committed to the management of the cruel Bonner. The character of this prelate, whose hands were so deeply stained with innocent blood, needs no colouring; history holds it up to the execration of mankind. Under his hands John Rough met with the most relentless cruelty. Not content with degrading him and delivering him over to the secular power, the furious prelate at one time flew at him and tore the beard from his face.

Mr. Cuthbert Sympson, who was apprehended along with Rough, was, it appears, the deacon of the church which assembled at the "Saracen's Head." He was a pious, faithful, and zealous man, labouring incessantly to preserve the flock from the errors of Popery and the danger of persecution. At the time of his apprehension the whole of the people composing the church to which he belonged were in the utmost danger. It was Mr. Sympson's office to keep a book containing the name of every individual belonging to the congregation, which book he always carried to their private assemblies. If this book had been found upon his person it would, of course, have implicated the whole body of the church, but it so happened that a few hours before his apprehension, he left it with Mrs. Rough, the minister's wife. In Fox's "Book of Martyrs" the following is related as having been dreamt by Mr. Rough a few nights before the apprehension of himself and Mr. Sympson.—

"A few nights before his apprehension Mr. Rough had a remarkable dream. He thought he saw Mr. Sympson taken by two of the guard, and with the book above mentioned. This giving him much trouble he awoke and related the dream to his wife. Afterwards, falling asleep, he again dreamt the same thing. Upon his awaking the second time he determined to go immediately to Mr. Sympson and put him on his guard, but lo, while he was getting ready to depart Mr. Sympson came to his house with the book, which he deposited with Mrs. Rough."

Two or three days after his apprehension Sympson was sent to the Tower. During his confinement, because he nobly refused to tell where the book was to be found, or to make known the names of the people, he was put to the torture three several times, by being placed upon the rack, and afterwards having an arrow tied between his two forefingers and drawn out so violently as to cause the blood to gush forth. Torture, however, proving of no avail, he was at length committed to the tender mercy of Bishop Bonner, who bore this testimony concerning him before a number of spectators: "You see what a personable man this is, and for his patience, if he were not a heretic, I should much commend him. He has been thrice racked in one day, and in my house he hath endured some sorrow, and yet I have never seen his patience once moved." A noble testimony to the fortitude of a Christian! The relentless prelate, nevertheless, condemned him, ordering him first into the stocks in his coal-hole, and from thence to Smithfield, where, with two others, Fox and Davenish, who were members of the same church at Islington, he ended his life in the flames. Poor Rough was also soon afterwards burnt at the stake at Smithfield. Four others, named Richard Roth, Ralph Allerton, James Austoo, and Margery Amtoo, were all burnt in one fire at Islington on the 15th of September, the same year.

In the following year, 1558, forty people, who might be called the first Covenanters, assembling in the fields at Islington, near to where the "Angel" now stands, for the purpose of worshipping God, were apprehended by the constable of Islington, and taken before Sir Roger Chomley, when thirteen were condemned to be burnt and twenty-two sent to Newgate. The following interesting account of this melancholy affair, taken from the book before quoted, will be found interesting:—

"June 27, 1558.—Secretly in a field by the town of Islington, were collected and assembled together a certain company of godly and innocent persons, to the number of forty men and women, who there sitting together at prayer, and virtuously occupied in the meditation of God's holy word, first cometh to them a certain man unknown, who looking over unto them, so stayed and saluted them, saying, 'that they looked like men who meant no harm.' Then one of the said company asked the man if he could tell whose field that was and whether they might be so bold there to sit. 'Yea,' said he, 'for that ye seem unto me such persons as intend no harm,' and so departed. Within a quarter of an hour after cometh the constable of Islington, a man named King, with six or seven others on the same business, one with a bow and another with a bill, and others with their weapons likewise. The which six or seven persons King left behind him in a close place, there to be ready if need should be, while he should go and view the party; and so doing, he asked what books they had, and bade them deliver them up. They, understanding that he was constable, refused not so to do, and then cometh forth the remainder of his followers, who bade them stand and not depart. They answered again they would be obedient, and ready to go whithersoever they would have them. And so they were first taken to a brewhouse a little way off, while some of the soldiers ran to the Justice nearest at hand, but he was not at home, so they were taken before Sir Roger Chomley.* In the mean-

time some of the women, being of the same number of the aforesaid forty persons, escaped away from them, some in the close, some before they came to the brewhouse; for so they were carried, ten with one man, eight with another, and with some more and with some less; in short, as it was not hard for them to escape that would. In fine, they that were carried to Sir Roger Chomley were twenty-seven; which Sir Roger Chomley and the Recorder, taking their names in a bill, and calling them one by one, so many as answered to their names they sent to Newgate; in the number of which of them that answered and that were sent to Newgate were twenty-two. These were seven weeks in Newgate before they were examined, and to whom word was sent by Alexander the keeper, that if they would hear a mass they should all be delivered. They nobly refused, and thirteen of them were burned, seven in Smithfield and six at Brentford."

Such are a few of the incidents in the annals of the parish in connection with the persecution of the Protestant Reformers during the reign of the bigoted Mary. The blood of those martyrs who were thus driven from their usual places of religious resort and compelled to assemble in the hedges and fields of Islington, in order that they might be enabled to worship their Saviour according to the dictates of conscience, was, however, like good seed, for every drop that was shed raised up a hundred staunch opponents to the errors of Popery. Nor should the expression of our gratitude for these early reformers be forgotten. Long before the Covenanters of Scotland had to fight the battle of faith, the little band who thus suffered themselves to be banished outcasts, and met in various parts of the outskirts of the city, under cover of hedge or copse, went through the terrible ordeal of persecution for the "Truth's sake." We are too apt to forget the humble Christian patriotism of the sufferers of the early age, in the stirring events and exciting deeds of heroism which have been so fully recorded of the latter in the pages of our greatest historians. Who can picture the venerable John Rough, and the other patriarchs of those early reformed Protestant churches, assembled under the blue canopy of heaven, with their little band of followers, partaking of the Sacrament, comforting and consoling each other, and finding their strength and their courage increase as they prayed and sang together, without feeling that they were heroes in the truest sense of the word, and without thank-

* This Sir Roger Chomley was the son of the knight who founded the Grammar School at Highgate, near the "Gate House" Inn.

fulness for the freedom and privileges which such men have won for us, their children. It is, perhaps, more the province of history to detail facts, than thus to assume the ideal, but it is deeply interesting to contemplate such events, and even to call in the aid of the imagination to realize them more fully, especially to those whose associations are bound up with the neighbourhood whose soil has been hallowed by such deeds.

Battle Bridge.

BATTLE-BRIDGE, situate at the south-western extremity of this extensive parish, was in the year 1750, a little out-of-the-way hamlet in the vicinity of London, but is now one of the great centres of traffic of this great metropolis. It is, however, one of the most classic spots which the suburbs can boast, it having been the scene of a remarkable event which happened in the early history of our country, and it is to be regretted that the authorities have thought fit to alter its name to the common-place appellation of "King's-cross."

It is said that Julius Cæsar, with Mark Antony and Cicero, encamped upon this spot for two succeeding years. This, however, is much to be doubted; but it is tolerably certain, that in the immediate neighbourhood of Battle-bridge there was fought that battle so fearful in its results, of which Bœdicea, Queen of the Iceni, was the heroine. The occasion of it was the following: The Queen had placed herself at the head of that portion of her countrymen who resolved to throw off the Roman bondage. She urged the exasperated Britons to put all the foreigners to death. Excited by the exhortations and complaints of this warlike Queen, the Britons fell upon the Romans throughout the various colonies they had founded, killing every one they came in contact with. Indeed, they carried their revenge to a shock-

ing extent, inventing tortures and punishments of the most barbarous description; wives were hung with children suckling at their bosoms; virgins had their breasts cut off and crammed into their mouths, and many were impaled to the ground alive, and left to die a lingering death. The British army had increased to 100,000 men, commanded by Bœdicea in person, when Paulinus, the Roman General, heard the news of the rebellion. On his arrival near London, he found Bœdicea and her army posted near or about the spot known as Battle-bridge, and there a terrible engagement ensued in which the British Queen was taken prisoner. Many relics have at various times been found in the neighbourhood, which support the testimony of historical tradition upon this point.

Besides this important battle, it is stated that an engagement took place between King Alfred and the Danes upon the same spot. The hamlet is also associated with other reminiscences. Cromwell had an observatory situated at King's Cross. The original Roman road to the north commenced here. A few years ago a dumpy miserable statue of George IV. stood upon the spot, in compliment to which the name of the locality was changed. In 1842, this statue, as well as the toll-gate, were taken down.

Maiden Lane.

MAIDEN-LANE forms the western boundary of the parish of Islington. It is one of the most ancient roads in the north of London. The historian Camden says, "it was opened to the public in the year 1300, and was then the principal road for all travellers proceeding to Highgate and the north." It was formerly called "Longwich-lane," and was generally kept in such a dirty, disreputable state as to be almost impassable in winter, and was so often complained of that the Bishop of London was induced to lay out a new road to Highgate-hill, so that a carrier might get to the north by avoiding Longwich-lane.

Norden, in his work called the "Speculum Britanniæ," says, "The old and ancient highwaye to High Barnet, from Gray's-inn and Clerkenwell, was through a lane to the east of Pancras Church, called Longwich-lane, from whence, leaving Highgate on the west, it passed through Tallingdon-lane and so on to Crouche Ende, thence through Hornsey Great Park to Muswell Hill, Coanie Hatch, Fryene Barnete, and so on to Whetstone. This anciente waye, by reason of the deepness and dirtieness of the passage in the winter season, was refused by wayfaring men, carriers, and travellers, in regard whereof it is agreed between the Bishop of London and the countrie, that a new waye shall be laide forthe through Bishop's-park, beginning at Highgate-hill, to leade directe to Whetstone, for which a certain tole should be paid to the Bishop, and for that purpose has a gate been erected on the hill, that through the same all travellers should pass, and be the more aptly staide for the tole." This new road,

however, was convenient only to those who passed to the north through Islington, and numerous accidents and inconveniences attendant on the continued bad state of Maiden-lane caused many complaints, and in the *Public Advertiser* of August 5, 1770, a letter recommended that a road, commencing from the "Bull," in Kentish-town, should be made to run eastward, avoiding the hill.

In 1778 a dispute arose between Islington and St. Pancras as to which parish should bear the expenses of the repairing of this road, which gave rise to legal proceedings. On the 11th of May, 1791, an indictment was laid against the parish of Islington by St. Pancras for the non-repair of the road. It appeared that a boundary-stone belonging to Islington had been incautiously removed from the east side of the lane to the west, thereby including the whole of the road within that parish; after which St. Pancras refused to bear any more expense. Islington contended that it was a party-road, and urged the fact that the plan of the Manor of St. John of Jerusalem extended only to the centre of the lane, which manor defined the boundary of Islington; evidence was also brought forward from the records of the Manor of Cantelows, and from the Chapter House of St. Paul's. Notwithstanding all this evidence, however, it was decided that Maiden-lane belonged to Islington, and though they appealed against such a decision, it was confirmed by the King's Bench, and has ever since been under their jurisdiction.

The Amusements of "Mercie Islington"

IN THE OLDEN TIME.

THE commanding situation of the parish, the many beautiful views to be obtained of the metropolis and the country around, and the well-known excellency of its dairy produce and famous village inns, rendered Islington, from a very remote period, a Ifavourite resort with London holiday folk This was more especially the case during the reigns of Elizabeth, James, and Charles, and also during the last century. In the reign of Henry II., Fitzstephen, who has been before quoted, speaking of the country in the immediate neighbourhood, says, " There are on the north part of London many fountains of water, sweet, wholesome, and clear, streaming forth among the glistening pebble-stones, in this number, Holywell, Clerkenwell, and St. Clement's well, are of most note, and frequented above the rest when scholars and the youth of the city take the air abroad on the summer evenings."

The amusements of the Londoners, as described by the ancient writers, were chiefly confined to the vicinity of the city, but it appears that at this period it was not unusual for wrestling matches, shooting with the bow, casting the stone, and other pastimes, between the citizens and the villagers, to be held at places farther distant from the metropolis than either of the situations above-named, for Stow tells us, " that on St. James's Day, the citizens of London kept games of defence and wrestling near the hospital of St. Matilda, St. Giles-in-the-fields, where they got the mastery of the men of the suburbs." The same author, in speaking of the fields in the northern environs of London, describes them as " commodious for the citizens to walke, shoote, and otherwise to recreate and refresh their dulled spirits in the sweete and wholesome ayre." He also mentions, " that it was customary of old times for the officers of the citie, namely, the sheriffs, the porters of the king's beam or weighhouse, and others of the citie, to be challengers of all men in the suburbs to wrestle, shoot the standard, broad arrow, and fight for games at Clerkenwell and Finsbury

Fields." Another historian of the same date informs us, " that in the afternoon the youth of the citie were accustomed to go into the fields, with their teachers, to play at ball, the scholars of every school having their particular balls ; while the ancient and wealthy citizen came out on horseback to see these youngsters contending at their sport. Exercises on horseback, to qualify them for military pursuits, were engaged in every afternoon in Lent, and on these occasions the citizens mustered in great numbers." He also adds, " that the citizens took great delight in birds, such as sparrow-hawks, gosshawks, and in dogs, for following the sports of the field."

Among the practices of ancient times, however, none appear to have been more attended to than the practice of using the long bow, and the fields, extending from the city walls to Islington, Hoxton, and Shoreditch, and known by the name of the Finsbury Fields, were kept in common for that purpose ; a right which appears to have been from time immemorial, enjoyed by the Londoners in the exercise of all their amusements. The encouragement of this pastime was a measure of the first political importance, of which the kings of England were fully cognizant, as is evidenced from the many statutes enacted for the regulation of the exercise. In 1365, Edward III. commanded the sheriffs of London to make proclamation " that every one in the said citie, strong in bodie, at leisure times, on holidays, should use in their recreations bows and arrows, or pellets, or bolts, and learn to exercise the art of shooting, forbidding all and singular, on our behalf, that they do not, after any manner, apply themselves to the throwing of stones, hand-ball, foot-ball, bandy-fall, lambuck, or cockfighting, nor such other like vain plays which have no profit in them." In 1392 an act was passed to compel the citizens to shoot with bows and arrows on holidays and Sundays ; and of such importance was excellence in this art considered, that Sir John Fortescue, an eminent lawyer of the reign of Henry VI., declared "that the might of the realme of England standyth upon archers."

During the reign of Henry VIII. several laws were passed for the protection of archery. In the 29th year of that monarch's reign he granted a patent to Sir Christopher Norris, Master of the Ordnance, and others, that they should be overseers of the science of artillery, "to wit, long bowes, cross bowes, and hand-gonnes; with liberty for them and their fraternity to exercise shooting at all manner of marks and butts, and at the game of the popinjay, and others, as at fowls, as well in the city and suburbs, as in all other places." In this patent there was one curious passage, "that in case any person was shot or slain in these sports by an arrow shot by any one of these archers, he was not to be sued or molested, if he had immediately, before he shot, used the word *fast*."

Every father was directed by the same king to provide a bow and two arrows for his son when he should be seven years old; also in the sixth year of the same reign, a law was passed obliging all persons, except the clergy and judges, to shoot at butts. There was, however, scarcely a need for these ordinances, for the people were passionately fond of archery; nor does the lapse of a few centuries appear to have lessened the inherent love of the population for martial exercises, as is evidenced by the patriotic spirit of the present age in the volunteer movement.

With reference to the origin of the titles of the "Marquis of Islington," "Duke of Shoreditch," and the "Earl of Pancras," which were enjoyed by the best shots of the several villages they represented at that time, it is stated to have originated upon the occasion of a splendid shooting match held before Henry VIII. and his court at Windsor. When the exercise was nearly over, his majesty observing one of his guards, named Barlow, preparing to shoot, exclaimed, "Beat thou all, and thou shall be Duke of Archers." Barlow drew his bow, executed the king's command, and was created Duke of Shoreditch, that being the place of his residence. Several others of the most expert marksmen at this *fête*, and who sustained the reputation of the Finsbury Archers, were in like manner honoured with titles, the "Marquis of Islington" and the "Earl of Pancras," being the best shots from the villages they represented.

In 1583, there was a splendid shooting-match at Smithfield under the direction of the Duke of Shoreditch, Captain of the London Archers, with his several officers, the Marquesses of Islington and Clerkenwell, and

the Earl of Pancras. This took place upon Tuesday, September 17, 1583, and we are told "that in remembrance of the shooting by the Duke of Shoreditch and the Marquis of Islington on that occasion, "the archers went to Shoreditch Church, and from thence turned down into Hogsden-fields, into a faire large green pasture-ground of goodly compass, where a tent was set up for the Duke and his chief citizens." These exercises lasted two days, and there were archers assembled to the number of 3,000, each having a sash, a long-bow, and four arrows. On the evening of the second day, the victors were led off the field, mounted on horses, and attended by 200 persons, each bearing a lighted torch in his hand.

Archery continued to be the favourite pastime of the citizens till the introduction of gunpower, when it began to decline, or at any rate, to lose that prestige formerly attached to it, for in the reign of Elizabeth the bowers, fletchers, stringers, and arrowhead makers, petitioned the Lord Treasurer concerning their decayed condition, "by reason of the discontinuance of the use of archery, and the toleration of unlawful games."

In the reign of James I. Stow laments that archery had fallen into disuse. He says, at that period, "it had almost become cleane left off and forsaken;" for he continues, "by means of the closing in of common grounds, our archers, for want of roome to shoote abroade, creepe into bowling alleys and ordinary diceing houses neerer home, where they have room enough to hazard their money at unlawful games." To remedy this state of things and to give encouragement to the exercise, King James, in 1605, directed letters patent to the Lord Mayor and others (including Sir Thomas Fowler, of Islington), alleging that certain persons, possessing lands, "had taken away from the archers the exercise of shooting in such fields and closes, as time out of mind had been allowed to be shot in, by making banks, hedges, and plucking up the old marks, and making ditches so broad without any bridges, &c., and directing these commissioners to survey the ground within two miles compass of the citie and suburbs as used to have marks and be used for shooting, and to reduce the same to proper order and condition as in King Henry VIII.'s time."

This patent, however, it appears, did not do much permanent good. Houses and villas soon rose upon the site of the demolished hedges and ditches, for Stow remarks, in alluding to the subject, "But soon afterwards we saw the thing in worse case than ever, by means of enclosures for gardens, wherein are builded many faire summer-houses, and, as in other places of the suburbs, some of them like midsummer pageants, with towers, turrets, and chimney-pots, not so much for use or profit, as for show and pleasure, and betraying the vanitie of men's mindes, much unlike to the disposition of the ancient citizens, who delighted in the building of hospitals and almshouses for the poore, and therein both employed their wit and spent their wealth, in preferment of the common commoditie of this our citie." The dwellings here referred to were, no doubt, somewhat after the style of many of the unsubstantial but showy little villas so plentifully abounding in Islington at the present day, and which then began to be extended along the roads leading to the villages in the vicinity of London.

During the time of the Commonwealth the practice of archery appears to have received no encouragement, but rather to have fallen into disrepute. Sir William D'Avenant, in a poem entitled "The Long Vacation in London," thus sarcastically describes the shooting-matches made between the attorneys and proctors :—

" Each with solemn oath agree
To meet in Fields of Finsburie,
With loynes in canvas, bow-case tyed,
Where arrowes stick with mickle pride ;
With hats primed up and bow in hand,
All day, most fiercely, there they stand,
Like ghosts of Adam Bell and Clymme :*
Sol sets for fear they'll shoot at him!"

The Society of London Archers at length became incorporated with the Honourable Artillery Company, and after the discontinuance of archery the fields were used for the practice of firing ball. In 1737 there were twenty-four of the ancient shooting-marks standing in the Finsbury Fields. Two old shooting butts remained in this parish, near the " Rosemary Branch," till 1780, and were occasionally used by the Toxopholite body of archers from the metropolis. A target butt, defended with iron plates, for the exercise of ball-firing, was erected near

* Adam Bell and Clym of the Cleugh were the names of two noted outlaws whose skill in archery rendered them famous in the three northern counties, the same as Robin Hood was in the midland. The "marks" in Finsbury Fields were sometimes named after these outlaws.

the same spot about the year 1810. In 1811, Nelson says, "an old inn yet remains, fronting the fields at Hoxton, which was formerly much resorted to by the Finsbury archers. It bears for its sign the ' Robin Hood,' and has, to this present day, written underneath the following inscription :—

" Ye archers bold and yeomen good,
Stop and drink with Robin Hood ;
If Robin Hood is not at home,
Stop and drink with Little John."

There were, however, other sources of attraction in Islington to the citizens, besides archery, namely, its pleasant fields, lanes, tea-houses, and inns, which, in the summerseason, rendered it a favourite retreat from the cribbed and confined streets of old London. In the poem before quoted, "The London Vacation in London," are the following doggrel lines :—

" Now damsel young, that dwells in Cheap,
For very joy begins to leap,
Her elbow small she oft doth rub,
Tickled with hope of syllabub,
For mother (who doth gold maintaine
On thumb, and keys in silver chaine)
In snow-white clout wrapt nook of pye,
Fat capon's wing and rabbit's thigh,
And said to hackney coachman, ' Go ;
Take shillings six,' say I, ' or no ?'
' Whither ?' says he. Quoth she, ' thy team
Shall drive to place where groweth cream.'

But husband gray now comes to stall ;
For prentic'd notch'd he straight doth call :
' Where's dame ?' quoth he. Quoth son of shop,
' She's gone her cake in milk to sop !'
' Ho! ho !—to Islington—enough !
Fetch Job, my son, and our dog Ruffe,
For there in poud, through mire and muck,
We'll cry, ' Aye, duck, there, Ruffe, aye duck !' "

It was common in former times for citizens to bring their dogs to the ponds in this neighbourhood, for the purpose of duck-hunting. Several of the ponds existed in Islington during the latter part of the last, and the beginning of the present century.

In 1681 there was acted at Newmarket a dramatic piece, called the "Merry Milkmaids of Islington," whose scene was laid at one of the public houses of Islington. Amongst the characters were, Tapster, an innkeeper, two town gallants, a gay woman, and a milkmaid, the heroine of the piece. An extract, showing that "mine host" of that day was as good an adept in making out a bill as he is at the present, will be found interesting :—

SCENE : *A Public-house at Islington.*

Lovechange, Sir Jeffrey Jolt, Artezhim (the Lady Jolt), and Tapster.

Lovechange: What is the reckoning, land-lord?

Tapster : Nine and elevenpence.

Sir Jeffrey: How's that? Let's have the particulars. Mr. Lovechange shall know how he parts with his money.

Tapster: Why, sir, cakes two shillings, ale as much, a quart of mortified claret, eighteenpence, stewed prunes, a shilling—

Lady Jeffrey : That's too dear.

Tapster: Truly, they cost a penny a pound of the one-handed costermonger out of his wife's fish-basket! A quart of cream, a crown—

Lady Jeffrey : That's excessive.

Tapster : Not if you consider how many car-rier's eggs miscarried in the making of it, and the charge of islinglass, and other ingredients, to make cream of the sour milk.

Lady Jeffrey : All this does not amount to what you demand.

Tapster : I can make more : Two threepenny papers of sugar, a shilling ; then you had bread, sir—

Sir Jeffrey : Yes, and drink too, sir ; my head takes notice of that.

Tapster : 'Tis granted, sir ; a pound of sau-sages, and forty other things ! Our bar never errs.

In another comedy, written by George Colman, and performed at Drury Lane Theatre in 1756, entitled the "Spleen, or Islington Spa," are some remarks respecting " the journey of a citizen and his wife in the coach-and-three from the end of Cheapside to Islington, and the packing up of neat's tongues and ham preparatory to the journey." In reference to the coach-and-three, it was necessary in those days to have that number of horses on account of the badness of the roads.

Entertainments of a not very commend-able character were extensively patronized by the lower orders. Duck-hunting bull-baiting, and prize-fighting, were the most common amusements. Prizefighting was an especial favourite with both the upper and lower orders, and evil women used to exhi-bit their skill in pugilism. The *Public*

Advertiser of the 22nd of June, 1768, in-forms us, " On Wednesday last two women fought for a new shift, valued at half-a-guinea, in the Spa Fields, near Islington. The battle was won by a woman called *Bruising Peg,* who beat her antagonist in a terrible manner."

Spa Fields was also famous for bull-bait-ing and duck-hunting, and various ponds in the village itself were also noted for this sport. Ball's Pond, and the Wheel Pond by White Conduit House afforded ample space for this amusement, and Goldsmith, in his " Citizen of the World," mentions another in the middle of the town, probably near the Green.

About this period there sprang up in the north of London a great number of houses of entertainment and tea-drinking gardens, such as "Sadler's Wells' Music House," the " Old Queen's Head," the " Three Hats," " Dobney's Jubilee Gardens," " Bagnigge Wells," the " Hugh Myddelton," " White Conduit House," "Merlin's Cave," and others, which were much frequented. There were also pleasant little breakfasting houses, other-wise " huts," as they were generally desig-nated, where, if the citizen took a walk in the outskirts on a summer's morning, he could, surrounded by rural scenery, in the midst of rustic gardens, enjoy "the cup which cheers but not inebriates." These were much patronized by the sober and early-rising inhabitants of the metropolis, and if the custom were still in vogue, it would not be a thing at all to be regretted, though, certainly, the " citizen" of the present day would have to journey some distance before he could anticipate taking his cup with the fields spread out before him, under the refreshing shade of the outspreading branches of some fine old tree. In the *Daily Adver-tiser* of May 6, 1745, there is an interesting advertisement relative to the attractions which one of these little breakfasting houses offered to the public :—

" This is to give notice to all ladies and gentlemen that at Spencer's original Break-fasting Hut, between Sir Hugh Myddelton's Head and St. John Street Road, fronting Sadler's Wells, may be had every morning (except Sundays) fine tea, sugar, bread, butter, and milk, at fourpence per head; coffee at three-halfpence per dish. And in the afternoon, tea, sugar, and milk at three-halfpence per head, with good attendance. Coaches may come up to the furthest gar-den door next the bridge. N.B.—Ladies are desired to take notice that there is anothe person set up in opposition to me next door, which is a brick house, and facing the little gate by the Sir Hugh Myddelton, but mine is the little boarded house by the river side, and my back door faces the same as usual, for,

"I am not dead, I am not gone,
    Nor liquors do I sell,
But as at first, I still go on,
    Ladies, to use you well;
No passage to my Hut I have,
    The river runs before,
Therefore your care I humbly crave:
    Pray don't mistake my door!
            "Yours to serve,
                    "S. SPENCER."

Goldsmith's partiality for Islington is well known; the breakfasts of hot-rolls and butter at White Conduit House are duly celebrated in his writings. It was occasionally his custom to enjoy what he termed a "shoemaker's holiday," which was a day of great festivity with the poet. Three or four of his friends met at his chambers in the Temple early in the morning. They first breakfasted, after which they set out, proceeding along by the City-road and through the fields to Highbury Barn to dinner; about six o'clock in the evening they adjourned to White Conduit House to drink tea, and concluded the evening by supping at the Grecian or Temple Exchange Coffee Houses, or at the Globe, in Fleet-street.

"Poor Robin," in his Almanac of 1796, says:—

"At Islington
    A fair they hold,
Where cake and ale
    Are to be sold;
At Highgate and
    At Holloway,
The like is kept
    There every day;
At Totnam Court
    And Kentish-town
And all those places
    Up and down."

At Upper Holloway, the "Half-Moon" and the "Mother Red Cap" were, more than a century ago, celebrated for their "cheesecakes," and one of the London cries of the past generation was "Holloway cheesecakes! Holloway cheese-cakes!" by a man who used to come down to town on horseback and vend them through the streets from off the back of the animal.

But not only did people resort to Islington for pleasure; it was held in high esteem by those seeking the restoration of health. In the beginning of the present century, from the great number of valetudinarians who resorted to it, the village obtained the name of the "London Hospital." Nelson says, "the number of deaths and interments that take place here, have been remarked by some as rather extraordinary, considering the general character of the place for healthfulness and salubrity of air. But the fact may easily be accounted for when it is considered that the bracing air of Islington is often had recourse to by persons in the last stage of disease; and frequently when all the powers of medicine have been of no effect; thus there can be little wonder that its piercing keenness, contrasted with the closeness of the city, from which they have been removed, may have a contrary effect to the one desired, that of hastening, rather than protracting an event which mankind in general are so anxious to avoid."

A publication called the *Monthly Mirror*, in commenting upon the great disproportion between the baptisms and deaths, in consequence of this resort on the part of invalids to Islington which occurred at the time mentioned, says—

"The late ingenious Dr. Hunter used to relate a story of a lady, who, in an advanced age and declining state of health, went, by the advice of her physician, to take lodgings at Islington. She agreed for a suite of rooms, and on coming down stairs observed that the bannisters of the house were much out of repair. 'These,' she said to the landlady, 'must be mended before I can think of coming to live here.'—'Madam,' replied the landlady to her visitor, 'it would answer no purpose the bannisters being mended, as the undertaker's men, in bringing down the coffins from up stairs, are continually breaking them." The old invalid lady, as may be imagined, was so shocked at this funeral intelligence, that, without further parley, she at once declined taking the apartments."

Islington, at the present period, is one of the healthiest suburbs in the vicinity of the metropolis. During the late fearful visit of the cholera, 1849, an immense number of people flocked into it from all parts, so that there was scarce a lodging to be had, the rate of mortality from that disease being very low in this parish compared with other districts.

Canonbury House.

CANONBURY HOUSE, whose old brick tower and quaint door, are always objects of interest to the beholder, was, as we have already mentioned, built as a mansion-house for the Priors of St. Bartholomew. It was originally of considerable extent, covering nearly the whole site of ground now called Canonbury-place, and having a park with spacious garden-grounds and domestic offices. Stow says, William Bolton, Prior of Bartholomew, 1520, "builded anew the manor-house of Canonbury at Islington, which belonged to the Canons of the house." Mr. Nelson, however, thinks it probable "that he only reinstated the decayed parts of the original mansion, at the same time making great improvements on the old foundation, and that the Prior's *new* building was confined to the premises with the brick tower just mentioned." The whole edifice was again thoroughly restored by Sir John Spencer, on his coming to reside there about the year 1599. Some interesting parts of the old mansion at Canonbury are yet remaining a little eastward of the tower building, which have for many years been divided into several houses. In these houses are some very handsome carved and stucco work belonging to the time of Queen Elizabeth. The ceilings are embellished with ornaments consisting of ship, flowers, foliage, &c., with medallions of Alexander the Great, Julius Cæsar, Titus Vespasian, &c., together with the arms of Queen Elizabeth. One of the chimney-pieces exhibits a very elaborate piece of workmanship in carved oak, containing figures of the Christian and Cardinal Virtues, with other devices, also the arms of the City of London, with those of Sir John Spencer and the Clothworkers' Company, of which he was a member. In another room the chimney-piece is devided into three compartments, containing a male and female figures, in long robes, with the arms of Sir John Spencer in the centre, surrounded by tritons, griffins, serpents, fruit, finely carved, and intersected by beautiful columns with Corinthian capitals. The whole is supported by two figures, bearing on their

heads baskets of fruit. The tower, which is yet remaining, is seven stories high. The staircase of this tower is of oak and of considerable width, and ascends through the tower to the several apartments, of which there are 23 in the building, with convenient closets on the landing-place attached to them. The two principal rooms, which are in the first and second stories, form each a square of about 20 feet, and in height 12 feet; they are very handsome in regard to internal decoration, having each a wainscot of oak from the floor to the ceiling. These apartments appear to have been fitted up for the use of Sir John Spencer during his residence at Canonbury. From the top of the tower a magnificent panoramic view of the City, Hampstead, Highgate, and the adjacent parishes, is to be obtained. There formerly stood a fish-pond of considerable depth in the north part of the building, which, in 1812, Mr. Nelson says, contained some very good carp and tench.

At one time a tradition prevailed that the monks of St. Bartholomew had a subterranean communication from Canonbury to their Priory in Smithfield. This story arose, no doubt, from the prejudice entertained against the Romish clergy at the time of the Reformation, and it gained strength from the discovery, at various times, of brick archways underground, of sufficient height to admit of persons standing upright. An excavation of this kind, partly choked up with earth, was some time since explored by Mr. Leroux, and found to extend under Canonbury-lane, from the park, in a southern direction. It had an open square entrance within a few yards of the roadside. From the fine sediment found at the bottom of this, which had evidently been deposited by water, there was no doubt that it was the remains of one of the old conduit heads, which was formed to receive that element from the springs situated in the higher grounds, and from whence it was conveyed in pipes to the wells and reservoirs in connection with the Priory at Smithfield.

Since the Reformation many distinguished

persons have resided at Canonbury House. The charter of incorporation granted to the Butcher's Company in 1665 is signed by Thomas Egerton, Baron of Ellesmere, then Lord Chancellor, and dated at Canonbury, when this peer was then on a visit to Sir John Spencer. The Compton family also appear to have resided here after the marriage of the second lord with the heiress of Sir John Spencer, for a daughter of Lord Compton was born here in 1602. From 1627 to 1635 Canonbury House was rented by the Lord Keeper Coventry. In the " Stratford Papers" is a letter from the Earl of Derby, dated January 29, 1635, from " Canbury Park, where he was staid from St. James's by the greatest fall of snow he ever saw in England." William Fielding, Earl of Denbigh, died at Canonbury House in 1685. Several literary characters have at various times had lodgings at this mansion, amongst others may be mentioned Samuel Humphreys and Ephraim Chambers, the latter the well-known author of the Cyclopædia which bears his name.

Oliver Goldsmith had apartments in the old turret building, where, under pressing pecuniary difficulties, it is stated he wrote that most admirable of fictions, " The Vicar of Wakefield." These pressing difficulties unfortunately occurred very often with the impulsive and generous Oliver, and another less agreeable memory of Canonbury House in connection with him is, that he frequently hid himself there for fear of arrest. The warm-hearted bookseller Newberry, for whom Goldsmith wrote so much, then rented the house. The beautiful views of Highgate and Hampstead, obtained from the windows, were no doubt often a temptation for him to throw aside his books and take a stroll into the surrounding country.

The Islington Volunteers

OF 1797—1803.

DURING the panic caused by the great French Revolution of the last century, and the contemplated Napoleon invasion, volunteer corps sprung up in all parts of the country. Islington then as now was not behind-hand in its loyalty, and in 1797 Alexander Aubert, Esq., the celebrated proprietor of Highbury House, originated a company of volunteers for this parish, and to which he was unanimously chosen commandant. It consisted of a regiment of infantry and one of cavalry, the latter being commanded by Captain Anderson, and the number, within a few months after forming, amounted to 300. The uniform consisted of a blue jacket with white facings, scarlet cuffs, collars, and epaulets, and trimmed with silver lace; white kerseymere pantaloons, short gaiters, helmet, and cross belts. Their arms and accoutrements were provided by government.

In consequence of an unfortunate dispute having arisen between some of the officers and the lieutenant-colonel after the corps had been established four years, a great number resigned, and the establishment was totally broken up in 1801. The members, upon this occasion, to testify the high sense they entertained of the loyalty, ability, and spirited conduct of the commandant, presented him with an immense silver vase of exquisite workmanship and design. The cover of the vessel contained a grand display of military insignia, among which were introduced the particular accoutrements of the corps, the standard of the cavalry, &c. In the centre was a figure of Fame, seated on a mortar, sounding a trumpet and supporting the colours of the Loyal Islington Volunteers, on the staff of which was the British Cap of Liberty. Vine-leaves, grapes, roses, &c., arranged in festoons of singular richness, surrounded the upper part of the body of the vase, and were collected together in a knot on the principal front by a Bacchanalian head, from which was suspended a shield with the following inscription :—

This Cup
Was presented by the late Corps of
ROYAL ISLINGTON VOLUNTEERS,
To Alexander Aubert, Esq.,
Their Lieutenant-Colonel Commandant,
In testimony of their respect and esteem for
Him ; in approbation of his firm and
Spirited behaviour
In support of the honour and independence
Of the Corps
Previous to its general resignation ;
And in grateful acknowledgment
Of his judicious and liberal conduct
Upon all occasions
As their Commander.

Embodied 4th March, 1797 ;
Unanimously resigned 20th Jan., 1801 ;
At that period consisting of 314 Members,
Cavalry and Infantry.

After a short interval of peace, in 1803 the old threat of invasion being repeated, a meeting of the inhabitants of Islington was held at " Canonbury Tavern," in the month of July that year, for the purpose of reforming the corps. It was soon re-established and ultimately attained to great perfection. The corps was commanded by Mr. Wheelwright, of Highbury-terrace, and consisted of about 300 members. The uniform was different to that of the original corps, being a scarlet jacket, turned-up with black, light blue or gray pantaloons, short gaiters, and beaver cap.

Upon the occasion of presenting their esteemed adjutant, Mr. Dickson, with a sword, the following verses, written by a member of the corps, were addressed to him :

" Honour, that guides our patriot band,
Presents with an impartial hand
A sword of merit, where 'tis due.
To zeal and science found in you;
Rude was our corps and form'd in haste,
Till, modelled by your just design,
They march, they wheel, they form in line,
Expert in onset, fierce to close,
Or pour a volley on their foes ;
Or, frequent by manœuvres skilled,
Seem bold for conquest in the field.

The corps continued their exercises till October, 1806, when, in consequence of their funds being exhausted, it was dissolved. The adjutant, Mr. Dickson, having procured an ensign's commission in the 82nd Regiment of Foot, proceeded with the British army, under Lord Cathcart, to the attack upon Copenhagen, where he was killed by a shot from a cannon.

The Old Conduits of Islington.

THE NEW RIVER AND SIR HUGH MYDDELTON.

IN ancient times the principal source from which the Londoners used to derive their supply of water was from the springs rising in the high grounds of the northern district of the metropolis. The water from these springs was conducted by pipes to various parts of the city, and from thence was taken in pails and other vessels, to the private houses. In the year 1500, water-carrying was a regular trade in the city, hundreds of poor people being constantly employed vending and carrying it from the conduit-heads. Stow tells us that William Lamb, the founder of the "Lamb's Conduit," which had its head at the bottom of Snow-hill, directed in his will, "that 120 pails should be given to poor women wherewith to carry and serve water." The more common vessel in which the liquid was carried was a kind of conical tankard, which held about three gallons, in the shape of a cone or sugar-loaf, and which being fitted at the small end with a cup, was easily portable on a man's shoulder.

Several of the most important of these conduits were situated in the parish of Islington. The "White Conduit," which supplied the Charterhouse, was one of the most famous of these. On a stone of this conduit was carved the date 1641, and the initials and arms of Thomas Sutton. Thomas Sutton was the Protestant founder of the Charterhouse, the Chartreuse of Roman Catholic times, but it is quite clear that the conduit was erected long before that date, and that it conveyed water to the Chartreuse monastery by means of leaden pipes. In digging for the foundations of the houses which now occupy the site of White Conduit Fields, near Warren-street, the old piping was frequently met with, and proved to be uniformly of lead, about three inches in diameter, exclusive of the thickness of the metal, which was at least half an inch. Another spring at Highbury supplied the Priory of St. Bartholomew, at Smithfield. At the time of digging for the foundation of Highbury House, in the year 1781, a great collection of pipes, made of red earth, baked, resembling those used for the conveyance of water about the time of Elizabeth, were dug up, and discoveries of leaden pipes have been made at different times in the fields between Canonbury and Highbury.

These conduits, and the springs from whence they derived their supply, were, as may be supposed, objects of great attention with the Corporation of the City of London, and some of its members bestowed considerable sums in establishing and keeping them in proper condition. It was also customary for the citizens, on certain occasions, to appoint "committees on view," who were sent out to inspect and report upon the condition of these conduits, and, as is the case in the present day with business of a like nature, it was made a time of rejoicing on the part of the committee, an allowance being made out of the City purse, for the provision of a good dinner. Strype, in his "Annals," noting one of these occasions, says "that on the 18th of September, 1562, the Lord Mayor, Aldermen, and many worshipful persons, rode to the conduit-heads, to see them, *according to the old custom*. Then they went and hunted a hare before dinner, and killed her, and thence went to dinner at the head of the conduit, where they were entertained by the Chamberlain. After dinner they went to hunt the fox. There was a great cry for a mile, and at length the hounds killed him at the end of St. Giles's, with great bellowing and blowing of horns at his death; and thence the Lord Mayor, with all his company, rode through London to his palace in Lombard-street."

Sir William Eastfield, who was Lord Mayor in 1438, was "a great benefactor" to the water-conduits; he caused "water to be conveyed from Highbury in pipes of lead to the parish of St. Giles's, Cripplegate," where it was collected in immense cisterns. In 1546, Stow says "water was conveyed in great abundance from divers springs lying between Hoxton and Iseldon, to a conduit at the west end of the parish church of St. Margaret, Lothbury."

In a report made upon a view of the Islington and Dalston springs, ordered by the Lord Mayor and Common Council of the City of London, we have a very interesting description of the ancient method of supplying the city with water by means of these conduits. After the report has stated the condition of the conduit-heads and their pipes, at Dalston, which then supplied the conduit-head at Aldgate, it says, "and we cannot be informed that the said pipes, or any other from the said springs, are employed to any other use than the service of the said conduit, except a *quill*, laid into a tenement in Bell-lane, belonging to one Shephard, to whom, as we are informed, the same was granted by the city about five years' since, in consideration of their laying their conduit pipe through and under the said tenement." From this we understand the privilege it must have been considered to be allowed a service pipe, even if in the shape of a "quill," of pure water; indeed, such a boon was only to be purchased by a concession such as that mentioned. The report then goes on to state the condition of the conduits near Islington, as follows:—

"And we have, also, in pursuance of the said order, viewed the springs and water belonging to the citie neare Islington, and find the same in two heads, one covered over with stone, in a field neare 'Jack Straw's Castle,' which is fed by sundry springs in an adjunct field, and is usually called the 'White Conduit,' the water whereof is conveyed from thence through Chamberry (Canonbury) Park to the other conduit in Chamberry Field, and from thence, the water of the said heads, so united, is conveyed in a pipe of lead across the New River in a caut, into the Green Man Fields, and entering from thence a garden into a field on the east side thereof; and from thence cross the north-east corner of a garden into Frogg-lane, into a field belonging to the Company of Clothworkers; and from thence through the field next to and west of the footway from Islington, unto the stile by the Pest-house, where it crosseth the said way, and so along the east side thereof, cross the road at Old-street, and under the bridge there into Bunhill Fields, and from thence on the east side of the said field, by the *Artillery Garden*, crossing Chiswell-street, into and down the middle of Grubb-street into Fore-street, and so on the south side thereof to the conduit at Cripplegate; and we cannot find the said waters are employed

to any other use than to the service of the said conduit.

"And we consider that the pipe from the furthest conduit-head to that in Chamberry Field, beyond Islington, is stopped, for that the cistern in the first is full of water, and the water joining to the latter is not above a quarter pipe, whereas it hath used to come a full pipe; also, that the plankes of one of the draines feeding the said furthest head is broke about six foot square, and two stones wanting in the covering; and also, the like quantity of planke is broke over the cesspool at the head in Chamberry Field. All of which we humbly certify, this 20th day of December, A.D. 1692.

"T. GLENTWORTH.
"J. NALTON.
"R. TARLTON."

As the population of London increased, these conduits became quite inadequate to supply London with its necessary want. Sometimes the pipes were stopped up, at other times frozen, and during the reigns of Elizabeth and James a number of schemes were projected for supplying the capital with water. In the third year of the reign of King James, an act was passed empowering the Lord Mayor and Aldermen "to bring a fresh stream of water to the north parts of the City of London from the springs at Chadwell and Amwell, and other springs in the county of Hertford, by means of a trench of the breadth of ten feet, upon condition of their maintaining and preserving the same, making satisfaction to the owners of the grounds through which the river should be made, and making and maintaining convenient bridges for the king's subjects over the said river."

The Lord Mayor and City Council, after calculating the cost and labour of such an undertaking, considered that the difficulties in the way of its accomplishment were so great, that they declined having anything to do with it, and pronounced it impracticable.

At this juncture a private citizen named Hugh Myddelton, a native of Denbigh, citizen and goldsmith of London, made an offer to the Common Council, March 28, 1609, to commence the work within two months, on condition of their transferring to him the powers with which they had been vested by the Act of Parliament. The offer was accepted by the Council, and Hugh Myddelton immediately set to work, he having proposed to complete it in the space of four years from its commencement.

The distance of the springs at Chadwell

and Amwell is about 20 miles from London, but it was found necessary, in order to avoid the eminences and valleys in the way, to make it run a course of thirty-eight miles, for, as Stow says, " the depth of the trench in some places descended full thirty feet, if not more, whereas at others, it required as sprightfull arte again to mounte it over a valley in a trough between a couple of hills, and the trough all the while borne up by wooden arches, some of them fixed in the ground very deep, and rising in height above twenty-three feet."

Like most benefactors, Myddelton experienced immense difficulties and obstructions, especially from owners of land, and landlords of various kinds. The industrious projector was so harassed by the opposition of some of the landed gentry, that he was obliged to ask the corporation to give him a prolongation of time, which they did. Having adjusted all controversies, and brought the water as far as the neighbourhood of Enfield, he found himself so impoverished by the expense of the undertaking, that he was obliged to apply to the City of London to help him in it. But they refused to have anything to do with so hazardous a work. He then asked the king, and with more success, for he agreed to pay half the expenses of the whole work past and to come, and to allow the river to pass through all royal manors and lands, if a moiety were made over to him. To this Hugh Myddelton joyfully acceded, provided the interest was retained in a subject and not in his Majesty, and the work went on without interruption until it was finished on the 29th of September, 1613, and the water flowed into the New River Head, Clerkenwell.

Stow gives the following pleasing account of its opening:—

" Being brought to the intended cisterne, but not as yet the water admitted entrance thereto, on Michaelmas day, 1613, being the day when Sir Thomas Myddelton, (brother to the said Sir Hugh Myddelton) was elected Lord Mayor of London for the year ensuing, in the afternoone of the same day, Sir John Swinnerton, Knight, Lord Mayor, accompanied by the said Sir Thomas, and many of the worthy aldermen, rode to see the cisterne and the first issuing of water thereinto, which was performed in this manner: A troupe of labourers to the number of 60 or more, well apparalleled, and wearing green Monmouth caps, all alike, carrying spades, shovels, pickaxes, and such like instruments of laborious employment, marching after

drummes, twice or thrice about the cisterne, presented themselves before the mount, where the Lord Mayor and a worthy company beside, stood to behold them. One man, on behalf of the rest, delivered the following speech in verse:—

Long have we laboured, long desired and pray'd
For this great work's perfection, and by the aid
Of Heaven and good men's wishes, 'tis at length
Happily conquered by cost, art, and strength.
And after five years' dear expense, in dayes
Travail and paine, besides the infinite wayes
Of Malice, Envy, false suggestions,
Able to daunt the spirit of mighty ones
In wealth and courage, this, a work so rare,
Only by one man's industry, cost, and care,
Is brought to blest effect; so much withstood,
His only ayme the citie's generalle goode;
And where (before) many unjust complaints
Enviously seated, caused oft restraints,
Stops, and great crosses, to our master's charge,
And the work's hindrance, Favour, now at large,
Spreads herself open to him, and commends
To admiration, both his paines and endes—
The King's most gracious love. Perfection draws
Favours from princes, and from all applause.
Then, worthy magistrates, to whose content,
Next to the state, all this great care was bent,
And for the public good, (which grace requires,)
Your love and furtherance chiefly he desires,
To cherish these proceedings, which may give
Courage to some that may hereafter live,
To practice deeds of goodness and of fame,
And gladly light their actions by his name.
Clerk of the Work, reach me the book, to show
How many arts from such a labour flow.
First, here; the *Overseer*, that tried man,
An ancient soldier, and an artizan;
The Clerk, next him Mathematician,
The Master of the Timber Work takes place,
Next after these, the *Measurer* in like case,
Bricklayer and *Engineer*; and after those
The *Borer* and the *Pariour*. Then it showes
The *Labourer* next; keeper of Amwell Head,
The *Walker's* last; so all their names are read
Yet they're but parcels of six hundred more,
That (at one time have been employed before)
Yet they're in sight, and all the rest will say

For all the work they had their royal pay.
Now, for the fruits then ; flow forth precious
        spring,
So long and dearly sought for, and now bring
Comfort to all that love thee ; loudly sing,
And with thy crystal murmurs strook to-
        gether
Bid all thy true well-wishers welcome
        hither !"

At which words the gates flew open, the
streame ranne gallantly into the cisterne,
drummes and trumpets sounding in a trium-
phant manner, and a brave peal of chambers
gave full issue to the intended entertainment."

The cost of the formation of the river was
£500,000 an amount which in those days represented a much larger sum than it does
now, and to which King James only contributed the sum of £6,500. Its course from
the fountain head at Chadwell is by Hoddes-
don (near Rye House), Cheshunt, Enfield,
Hornsey, and Stoke Newington, into Islington, and to the River Head. About the
place where the river enters this parish it
was formerly conducted over the valley by
means of an enormous wooden trough, 462
feet in length, supported on strong timbers,
standing on piers of brick, and was at that
period nicknamed the "Boarded River." In
1776 this trough was removed in consequence
of its being continually out of repair, and the
present clay banks were thrown up in its
place. It has 154 bridges over it, and forty
sluices in its course. At the period the
river was formed, it was not foreseen that in
summer-time there might be a scarcity of
water from drought and the consequent in-
efficiency of the springs, but when this was
learnt from experience the company had to
borrow from the overplus of the mill-stream
of the river Lea, for which privilege they
pay an annuity. An anecdote is recorded of
the bargain made upon this occasion by the
engineer of the Company. Having agreed
with the proprietors of the lands on the
River Lea for a cut of two feet of water from
that river at a certain rate, he offered them
double the amount if they would allow him
to make a four foot cut or canal, to which
the proprietors, ignorant of the principles of
mathematics, consented, not considering that
by such a concession, the company, instead
of *double*, would receive at least, *four* times
the supply or water afforded by a two feet
cut.

Soon after the commencement of the undertaking by Sir Hugh Myddelton, he found
that the scheme had so impoverished himself

and his family, that in order to gain sufficient
support to complete it, he was obliged to
divide the property into shares, and it was
accordingly divided into seventy-two. Thirty-
six of these shares, or one half, were vested
in Sir Hugh Myddelton, and twenty-eight
persons took up the other thirty-six amongst
them, and which were called Adventurer's
Shares. A Company was then formed and a
charter of incorporation granted which is
dated June 21, 1619, forming the twenty-
nine shareholders into a body under the title
of "The Governor and Company of the New
River, brought from Chadwell and Amwell to
London." Sir Hugh Myddelton was appointed Governor of the Company.

The moiety of the concern which had been
vested in the crown, was, on account of the
unpromising aspect of the affairs of the
company for a long time after its completion,
re-granted to Myddelton, his heirs and as-
signs for ever, on condition that £500 per
annum should be paid into the royal exchequer. Towards the payment of this amount
Myddelton set apart a number of shares; and
these shares, besides being liable to pay
the £500 annually out of their profits, have
no voice or management in the concern, as
Myddelton, to prevent the undue influence of
courtiers, precluded James from having any
such control, and merely allowed a represen-
tative of the king to be present at the Company's meetings to guard the royal interest.
This yearly sum of £500 is still paid.

Some considerable time elapsed after the
opening of the New River, before its waters
came into general use in the metropolis, the
difficulties connected with the supply of each
house being very great. The value of shares
at first, were therefore very small, and for
nineteen years the annual profit of each
scarcely amounted to twelve shillings As
its value and importance, however, came to
be better understood, their worth rose considerably, and at the present day there is no
description of property that is more sought
after than a proprietorship in the New River
Company. The following statement of the
dividends that have been paid at various in-
tervals since its formation will give an idea of
its progressive improvement :—

		£	s.	d.
Dividend for	1633	3	4	2
do	1640	33	2	8
do	1700	201	16	6
do	1770	255	13	11
do	1804	396	19	6
do	1840	706	11	11

In 1727 a single share was valued at

5,000 guineas; and they have since fetched £17,000. The direction is vested in 29 holders of Adventurer's Shares, and when a vacancy happens in their number, the remaining 28 elect another to fill up his place from amongst those who hold moieties or parts of shares. The chief officers belonging to the corporation are a Governor, Deputy-Governor, Treasurer, and Secretary. The capital expended from the commencement of the company has amounted to nearly one million five hundred thousand, including the recent improvements and engine-house at Stoke Newington, which raises the water to the several reservoirs. Before the application of steam-power, a windmill on the top of the high-ground where the reservoir in Claremont-square, Pentonville, now is, used to raise the water into that receptacle. From that reservoir the one at the corner of Charles street, Hampstead-road, near the baths and washhouses, was formerly supplied. A recent act compelled the company to cover all their reservoirs within a certain distance of the metropolis, and also to provide filter beds for their reservoirs at Stoke Newington.

SIR HUGH MYDDELTON.

THIS distinguished man, as has been already mentioned, was a native of Denbigh in Wales, and owner of some mines in Cardiganshire, by which he became considerably enriched. He was also a citizen and goldsmith of London. Unfortunately very litttle is known of his biography. It was at his suggestion that the Lord Mayor and Council first applied to have an act passed for the construction of a river to supply the metropolis with water. He did not labour for gain, but to benefit his fellow-men, and, to leave some monument behind him, which,

"Like footprints on the sand of time"

should show to succeeding generations what energy and genius can accomplish under difficulties; for it is acknowledged, that to accomplish anything great, there must not only be the possession of calm and enlightened judgment and the advantages of education, but also a resolute energy and perseverance combined, to support and carry through that which judgment and education pronounce honourable and useful. It is, however, satisfactory to know that what ever may have been Myddelton's misfortunes with respect to pecuniary means arising out of his great undertaking, he was not in a state of positive want at the time of his death, though equally far from being wealthy. The historian Pennant (himself a Welsh-man) speaks upon the enterprising character of his countryman with much pride. "He was," he says, "a person whose useful life would give lustre to the greatest family. This gentleman, afterwards Sir Hugh, displayed very early his great talents, and began, as we are told by himself, by searching for coal within half a mile of his native place. His attempts did not meet with success; his genius was destined to act on a greater stage. This metropolis offered him ample space for his vast attempts; few readers need be told that he planned and brought to perfection the great design of supplying the city with water. This plan was meditated in the reign of Elizabeth, but no one was found bold enough to attempt it. In 1608 the dauntless *Welshman* stept forth and 'smote the rock.' He sacrificed private fortune to the public good." In another place with a spirit equally natural, the writer says, "No one ought to be ignorant that this unspeakable benefit is owing to a *Welshman*."

In his later days he had recourse to the profession of a civil engineer for his subsistence, and in that capacity still rendered service to his country by his schemes for mining and draining. The time of his death and the place of his interment are unfortunately unknown. Some historians say that he died in 1631. In the *Gentleman's Magazine* of September, 1809, it is stated that there had been a traditional report that the celebrated Sir Hugh Myddelton, in the latter period of his life, retired to Kemberton near Shiffnall, Shropshire, where he resided for some time under the assumed name of Raymond, and was buried in the chancel at the end of the church, on the 10th March, 1702. The two dates are greatly at variance, and it is to be feared the true time and place of his death, will now never be known.

He left one son, William, who married, and had several children. William's eldest daughter married John Grene, a secretary of the company. Grene's son Hugh was the last male heir, but he left daughters, one of whom was resident in Nottingham, as appears from the following incription, which is affixed to the north wall under the tower of the old church of St. James's, Nottingham:—

"Near this place lies interred ye body of
MRS. ELIZABETH MYDDELTON,
Of Nottingham,
Eldest daughter of Sir Hugh Myddelton,
Bart. and Knt.,
Who departed this life Jan. 6, 1725,
In the 43rd year of her age."

In Goldsmith's Hall is an original portrait of Sir Hugh, in good preservation, and in the engineer's house, at the New River Head, is his coat-of-arms. To the Goldsmith's Company he bequeathed a few shares, to be applied to charitable purposes, and upon certain occasions his descendants have received pensions from the company. Lady Myddelton, the wife of one of the descendants and mother of the last baronet, received a pension of £20 per annum from the Goldsmith's Company, which, at the solicitation of a gentleman, was continued to her son Hugh, the last baronet. The *Gentleman's Magazine*, vol. 64, says, in alluding to this last baronet, "He afforded a melancholy proof of the fact, the truth of which we have too frequent evidence, namely, that a man may convey his blood, but not his brain, to his posterity. All his employment and all his amusement consisted in drinking ale in any company he could pick up. Mr. Harvey, of Chigwell, Essex, took care of him, and put him to board at the house of a sober farmer, near Chigwell, on whom he could depend, and there he lived and died, a striking and unhappy contrast to his great ancestor."

At Amwell, an urn has been erected to the memory of Sir Hugh Myddelton, by Robert Mylne, Esq., late engineer to the New River Company. It stands on a monumental pedestal of Portland stone, with an inscription on each side. On the south side are the following words :—

"Sacred to the Memory of
SIR HUGH MYDDELTON, Baronet,
Whose successful care,
Assisted by the patronage of his King,
Conveyed this stream to London :
An immortal work,
Since man cannot more nearly
Imitate the Deity
Than in bestowing health.

———

Robert Mylne, Architect, Engineer, &c.,
MDCCC."

It is to be hoped that the contemplated monument to this great man will soon be placed upon its appropriate site at Islington Green, as nothing could be more becoming than that some tribute should mark his memory near the spot where he ended his labours. It will be an honour to Islington, though late in the day, to thus recognise his merits; and it will freshen the memories and encourage the aspirations of those who, under like circumstances, may now be endeavouring to benefit their fellow creatures.

Highbury House.

IT is the opinion of antiquarians that the Roman garrison of London had a summer camp on the hill at Highbury, and from the commanding situation of the place, and other circumstances, this seems highly probable: nor is it unlikely that the moated site of the Prior's house and the present mansion, was that of the prætorium of such an encampment. When Sir George Colebrook was in possession of the mansion he sold the site of the old moat, called "Jack Straw's Castle," to John Dawes, an eminent stockbroker, who, at an expense of £10,000, erected, in 1781, an elegant mansion on the spot where the Prior's house formerly stood. In digging for the foundation of this house a number of ancient tiles were discovered, but whether of Roman or Norman manufacture, could not be ascertained. After the death of Mr. Dawes it came into the possession of Alexander Aubert, Esq., F.R.S., who purchased it for £6,000. This gentleman made considerable alterations and improvements in the estate, adding much to its attractions. Among other things he erected near the house a large and spacious observatory, which he furnished with a very complete collection of instruments, particularly a fine reflecting telescope by Short. The largest and most important instruments, in order to prevent the effect of vibration, were insulated from the floors, being placed upon piers of solid stone carried up from the earth and rising through the centre of the building. In its construction he was assisted by Smeaton, the celebrated engineer. Highbury Observatory was long well-known by the scientific world, and was constantly visited by the first astronomers in Europe, and a person in the employ of the government went regularly at stated times, to take astronomical observations. Upon the death of Mr. Aubert in 1805 his unrivalled collection of astronomical instruments were put up for sale, and eagerly purchased by men of science. The house was also sold by auction.

Mr. Aubert was a gentleman highly esteemed, and particularly endeared to the inhabitants of Islington for his kindness and unbounded generosity, as well as for the great interest he ever displayed in local affairs. There are still living many old inhabitants who bear his memory in grateful remembrance.

The Hornsey Road.

CONDITION OF THE VILLAGE IN 1660—1712.

THE thoroughfare now known as the "Hornsey-road" was one of the bridle-ways of ancient times. It was formerly called Tallington-lane, and was much used by packmen and foot-travellers in journeying to the north. In the reign of Charles II. and also in later times, it was often frequented by highwaymen, and a tradition is handed down to us that the celebrated Claude du Val made it a favourite place of retreat, and the scene of some of his most daring exploits. There is nothing improbable in this tradition, as the road was well-suited for his predatory habits; it is moreover supported by the fact that for a long period the road was known by the name of "Du Val's Lane," and an old inhabitant who resided in Holloway, used to relate that it was changed in consequence of being frequented by that famous robber. In a survey of the neighbourhood, taken in 1611, an old house in the Hornsey-road is marked as "Devil's House in Devil's Lane,"—so, with one circumstance and another, it appears not to have enjoyed a very good reputation, and was no doubt a bye-word of terror to the inhabitants in what are called "the good old times." In reference to Claude du Val using this road, Butler, the author of "Hudibras" describes his depredations and exploits in a manner that would be in keeping with the locality. In a poem he says:—

"He, like a lord of the manor, seized upon
Whatever happened in his way
A lawful weft and stray;
And after, by the custom, kept as his own.
He would have starved the mighty town,
And brought its haughty spirit down;
Have cut off all relief,
And, like a wise and valiant chief,
Made many a fierce assault
Upon all ammunition carts,
And those who bring up cheese or malt,
Or bacon from remoter parts.
No convoy, e'er so strong, with food
Durst venture on the dangerous road.
He made the undaunted waggoner obey,
And the fierce higgler, contribution pay;
The savage butcher, and the stout drover,
Durst not to him their feeble troops discover."

This "hero of the road" was executed at Tyburn, in the reign of Charles II. Jan. 21, 1669, in his 27th year. In a memoir of this notable character, written in 1670, it appears that certain of the fair sex, by whom it is said, he was much admired (he, by common report, never molesting ladies) procured him a decent funeral after his execution. The memoir, in referring to the event, says:—

" After *lying in state* at the "Tangier" Tavern in St. Giles', he was buried in the middle aisle of Covent Garden church, and his funeral was attended with many flambeaux and a numerous train of mourners, whereof most where of the beautiful sex."

The outskirts of the metropolis, particularly the northern roads were the constant scenes of systemised robbery. Sometimes malefactors were hung in chains as a warning to these depredators. It is recorded that in the year 1712 two criminals were hung in chains at Holloway, " viz., William Johnson for shooting the turnkey at Newgate in the open court at the Old Bailey, when the judge was sitting, and John Price, otherwise Jack Ketch, (who had been public executioner) for murdering Elizabeth White, a poor woman who sold gingerbread in Moorfields, in March, 1798."

Nothwithstanding these terrible warnings, during the early part of the last century the roads and footpaths in this parish, and those leading from the city, were so infested with footpads and highwaymen, that at a Vestry meeting held in Dec. 1739, a resolution was passed, empowering the churchwardens to pay a reward of £10 to any person that should apprehend a robber. It was also customary with persons walking from the city to Islington, after dark, to wait at the end of John-street until a sufficient number had assembled together, when they were escorted by an armed patrol appointed for that purpose. The robbery of the passengers by the Islington stage coach appears to have been a very common occurrence, for a journal of 1742 states, " that scarcely a night passes without some one being robbed, either on foot or in coach between the ' Turk's Head' and the road leading to Goswell-street."

Indeed, such was the insecure state of the village in this respect, that at another Vestry meeting it was resolved to recommend the inhabitants of the parish to furnish themselves " with firelocks and other arms sufficient for the equipment of one man." In the year 1771 the inhabitants subscribed a sum of money for rewarding any persons apprehending burglars, in consequence of many dwellings and out-houses being broken open, and soon after an Act of Parliament was obtained to enable the Vestry to better light and watch the town. The papers about that period were full of accounts of the depredations committed on the outskirts. In the *Public Advertiser* of September 3, 1780, there is a song on the "Islington Protection Association," bearing the following title:—

" Four great and Horrible Murders, or *Bloody News from Islington*, being a full and true relation how a woman's brains were knocked out with her own pattern, robbed, and her throat cut, on Tuesday, the 5th instant ; a man beaten to death the 8th of the same month, and a woman drowned in a pond at Islington."

White Conduit House.

THIS noted house of entertainment was celebrated for its beautiful prospect over the fields towards Hampstead and Highgate, and the glimpses that are even now to be obtained of the distant country from some of the side streets in the Barnsbury-road, enable us to form an idea of the charming view which must have presented itself ere bricks and mortar took the place of the green fields. The exact date of the origin of "White Conduit-house" is not known with any certainty, but from notices in the public journals of the last century, it appears to have first risen into notoriety about the year 1740.

The original "Conduit-house," however, which gave the name to the famous tea-gardens, was of a far more ancient date. From a "Set of Views of Noted Places near London," drawn and engraved by C. Lempriere, in 1731, we observe a single brick-built cottage of one storey high, standing completely by itself away in the country. Hedgerows run along the front and on either side of it, and out upon the distant horizon is Highgate and Hornsey Woods, the intervening space being filled up with fields of corn and meadow-land. An old stone conduit is depicted in the engraving as standing near the house, which bore on a carved stone in front the date 1641, and the initials and arms of Thomas Sutton. The pipes leading from this conduit, and a smaller one at the back of White Conduit Gardens, contiguous to the spot now occupied by Warren-street, were frequently found in digging for the foundation of the new streets in Pentonville. The last general inspection of the pipes was made in 1654, by order of the governors of the Charterhouse, and the supply of water was then found so scanty and the probable expense of restoring it, so great, that they directed the adoption of the New River water in its stead.

So late, however, as the commencement of the present century, a neighbouring residence, called Herme's Hill, was supplied with water by a communication from the ancient conduit. The Conduit-house itself appears to have derived its supply from a spring issuing from the ground at the distance of forty-three perches north of it, from whence the water was conducted by a brick channel; in the conduit was a massive leaden cistern, with an aperture at the bottom for carrying off the waste water through a pipe of the same metal. Until about 1811 the building remained in a tolerably perfect state, but at that time, in consequence of the preacher William Huntingdon, known as the "coalheaver" (who lived at Herme's Hill) attempting to clear the spring for the use of the inhabitants, some low people in the neighbourhood, who had taken a dislike to him, wantonly injured it, and during the night threw loads of soil on the spring that supplied it, thereby rendering the water impure. At length the progress of buildings and the parish officers effected, in 1831, what time had failed to effect, the destruction of the little old Conduit-house, and it was pulled down, the materials of which it was composed being carted off to repair the New-road.

At the time the gardens were most noted, they were laid out in a neat and tasteful manner, having in their centre a circular basin of water, with boxes around it, decorated with paintings, in which the company sat and took refreshments. This basin, however, was in later years filled up and its site planted upon; the paintings were removed, and a new dancing and tea-room, called "the Apollo Room," erected at the north-west angle; an orchestra and a small theatre were also set up in the grounds, and a set of noble apartments for balls, concerts, dinners, &c., overlooked the fields. The following poem, published in the *Gentleman's Magazine* for May, 1760, contains a lively picture of the place and the kind of company that frequented it at that date :—

"WHITE CONDUIT HOUSE.

" And to White Conduit House
    We will go, will go, will go."
            Grub Street Register.

"Wish'd Sunday's come; mirth brightens every face,

And paints the rose upon the housemaid's
cheek—
Harriet or Moll—more ruddy.   Now the
heart
Of prentice, resident in Ample-street,
Or Alley-kennel wash'd—Cheapside, Corn-
hill,
With joy distends: his meridian meal o'er,
With switch in hand, he to the White Con-
duit-house
Hies merry hearted.   Human beings there.
In couples multitudinous assemble,
Forming the drollest groups that ever trod
Fair Islingtonian's plains.   Male after male,
Dog after dog succeeding.   Husbands, wives,
Fathers and mothers, brothers, sisters, friends,
And pretty little boys and girls.   Around,
Across the garden's shady maze
They walk, they sit, they stand.   What
crowds press on,
Eager to mount the stairs, eager to catch
First vacant bench or chair in Long Room
placed.
Here with prig holds conference polite,
And indiscriminate the gaudy beaux
And sloven minx do mix.   The red-arm'd
belle
Here shows her tasty gown, proud to be
thought
The butterfly of fashion ; and forsooth
Her haughty mistress deigns for once to
tread
The same unhallow'd floor.   'Tis hurry all,
And rattling cups and saucers.   Waiter here,
And waiter there, and waiter here and there,
And everywhere ;
At once is called Joe! Joe! Joe! Joe! Joe!
Joe on the right, and Joe upon the left,
For every vocal pipe re-echoes Joe.
Alas! poor Joe, like Francis in the play,
He stands confounded, anxious how to please
The many-headed throng.   I say but little
more,
Suffice it for my prophetic muse to sing,
As fashion rides upon the wings of Time,
While tea, and cream, and buttered rolls can
please,
While rival beaux and jealous belles exist,
So long, White Conduit-house, shall be thy
fame!"

Goldsmith, in his " Citizen of the World,"
celebrates the hot rolls and butter of White
Conduit-house.   " After having surveyed the
fair and beautiful town of Islington," he says,
" I proceeded forward, leaving a fair stone
building, called White Conduit-house, on my
right.   Here the inhabitants of London often
assemble to celebrate a feast of hot rolls and
butter.   Seeing such numbers, each with

their little tables before them, employed on
the occasion, must no doubt be a very curious
sight to the looker on, but still more so to
those who perform in that solemnity." Goldsmith himself, as noticed previously, was a
frequent visitor at White Conduit-house.

In the year 1754 White Conduit-house
was rented by a man named Robert Bartholomew, originally a farmer of fortune.   During his proprietorship the house became more
famous than ever, not only as the resort of
the working-class of people, but by tradespeople and their families as a tea-garden,
and he spent great sums in improving and
decorating the place in order to render it as
attractive as possible.   In the *Daily Advertiser*, of August 10th, 1754, he informed the
public of the accommodation which was to
be had at White Conduit-house in the following advertisement :—

" This is to acquaint the public, that at
the White Conduit-house, the proprietor, for
the better accommodation of gentlemen and
ladies, has completed a long walk, with a
handsome circular fish-pond, a number of
shady pleasant arbours, enclosed with a fence
seven feet high, to prevent being the least
incommoded from people in the fields outside.
Hot loaves and butter every day ; milk
directly from the cows ; coffee and tea, and
all manner of liquors in the greatest perfection ; also a Long Room from whence is the
most copious prospect and airy situation of
any now in vogue.   I humbly hope for the
continuation of my friends' favours, as I
make it my chief study to have the best accommodation, and I am, Gentlemen and
Ladies, your obliged humble servant, *Robert
Bartholomew.*—Note : My cows eat no grains,
neither any adulteration in the milk or cream.
Bats and balls for cricket, and a convenient
field to play in."

The history of the landlord of White Conduit-house in its palmy days, affords a lesson
fraught with a significant moral, and is well
worth perusal.   Nelson in his " History of
Islington," gives the following account of his
life :—

" Robert Bartholomew was a person who
inherited a good fortune from his parents, and
he brought much trade to the place by the
taste he displayed, and the excellent manner
he conducted the business of the house.   Unfortunately, with every prospect of success,
and even eminence in life, he fell a victim to
the unconquerable itch for gambling in the
lottery.   At one time, not only White Conduit-house and tea-gardens were his freehold,

but also the 'Angel Inn;' he also rented land to the amount of £2,000 a year in the neighbourhood of Islington and Holloway, and was remarkable for having the greatest quantity of haystacks of any grower near London. At that time it is believed he was worth £50,000, kept his carriage and servants in livery, and upon one occasion, having been unusually fortunate in winning at the lottery, gave a public breakfast to more than 100 of his friends to commemorate, as was expressed upon the tickets of admission, 'the Smiles of Fortune.'

" At times he had some very fortunate hits in the lottery, and which no doubt tended to increase the mania which hurried him to his ruin. He had been known to spend upwards of £2,000 in a day for lottery insurance, to raise which, stack after stack of his immense hay-crop was cut down and hurried off to market as the readiest way of obtaining the supplies necessary for these extraordinary outgoings. Having at last been obliged to part with his house from an accumulation of difficulties and embarrassments, he passed the last thirteen years of his life in great poverty, subsisting by the charity of those who knew him in his latter days.

" Still his propensity to be engaged in this ruinous pursuit never forsook him, and meeting one day in the year 1807 an old acquaintance, he related to him a strong presentiment he entertained that if he could but purchase a particular number in the ensuing lottery (which he was not then in a position to accomplish) it would prove successful. His friend, after remonstrating with him on the impropriety of continuing a practice which had already been attended with such evil consequences, was at length persuaded to go halves with him in a sixteenth part of the favourite number, which, being procured, was drawn a prize of £20,000. With the money issuing from this extraordinary turn of fortune, he was prevailed upon by his friend to purchase an annuity of £60 per annum; yet he was so fatally addicted to this habit, he disposed of it and lost it all.

"He was known frequently to apply to those persons who had been served by him when in prosperity for an old coat or a left-off article of apparel, and not many days before he died he solicited a few shillings from a friend to buy himself necessaries. He died in the back room of a second floor in Angel-court, Windmill-street, Haymarket, in March, 1809, aged 68, without a friend to console his dying moments and in circumstances of the deepest poverty. Let the fate of Robert Bartholomew, the wealthy proprietor of White Conduit-house, be a warning to all who are addicted to the vice of gambling."

Long after the house had passed out of the hands of Bartholomew, it kept up its reputation as a place of entertainment, and even within the last twenty years was frequented by large numbers of people. Like many other places of the same character, however, it at length succumbed to bricks and mortar; it was pulled down a few years ago and streets were erected upon the site of the gardens. There is a public-house, which still bears its name.

The fields in the vicinity of White Conduit-house were much frequented by cricketers, and from an association of noblemen and gentlemen who used to assemble there to play matches, the present well-known Marylebone Club was first formed. Among other reminiscences of White Conduit Fields may be mentioned, that in July, 1799, George III. met the Islington Volunteers there, and proceeded with them from thence to Hyde Park. The neighbourhood about eighty or ninety years ago, was often the scene of Rowland Hill's preaching on the Sunday afternoons, when, as the pleasure-seekers crowded the paths to White Conduit-house, they were attracted in large congregations to hear his powerful denunciations of profligacy and vice.

Sir Richard Whittington.

THE ALMSHOUSES.

THE history of this celebrated man has been so frequently written both in prose and poetry, and is so associated with our earliest study of biography, that it appears a kind of profanity to depict a Sir Richard Whittington without a cat or a cook, a ship load of gold, and all the other little etceteras which have such a charm for the juvenile mind. However, the truth must be told, and though his real life was very different from that which we have been accustomed to read of in story books, it is not divested of those incidents which excite our admiration, but commemorated by far nobler incidents than are related in improbable stories and romantic traditions.

Richard Whittington was the son of Sir William Whittington, knight, a merchant of London, but said to have been born in Shropshire. The Rev. W. Roberts, rector of Whittington, in Shropshire, in writing a history of the place, mentions a tradition retained in that village, which no doubt gave birth to the tale of "Whittington and his Cat." In a life of Whittington, written by the author of the "Memoirs of George Barnwell," it is stated that "he was born near Ellesmere, in the year 1354, and that he was 'patronized' in London by a person of the name of Fitzwaringe, or Fitzwarner. This was the name of the family residing at that time at Whittington Castle, and part of Ellesmere parish is only a mile from the village of Whittington. One of the family of Fitzwarner might have been in London, and his residence known to young Whittington, who, in his friendless situation, might have called as a relation on the lord of his native village, and, by stating whence he came, obtained the patronage he sought."

If such an event as the foregoing did occur it could not have happened to the Whittington who was three times Lord Mayor, but might possibly have been the case with one of his ancestors, for Sir Richard himself, being the son of opulent parents, was put to the trade of a mercer. He was a man en-dowed with great intelligence and business habits, and soon acquired the esteem of his fellow citizens as well as a princely fortune. He served the office of Mayor three times, viz., in the reign of Richard II., 1397; Henry IV., 1406; and Henry V., 1419; he was also sheriff in 1393. He founded several public edifices and charitable institutions, and in his day was esteemed the richest and most munificent subject in the kingdom. Some conception of the wealth he possessed may be gathered from the following, as related by Entick: "To have a true idea of this gentleman's wealth and the little regard he paid to money, which, to those who adore it, is 'the root of all evil,' we must recite the entertainment he gave King Henry V. and his Queen at Guildhall, after his conquest of France. On this occasion Sir Richard caused a fire to be made of wood mixed with cinnamon and other aromitics, with which the King was much pleased. The knight said he would endeavour to make it still more agreeable to his Majesty, and immediately tore and burnt in that fire the King's bond of 10,000 marks due to the Company of Mercers, another of 1,500 marks, due to the Chamber of London; another of 2,000 marks, due to the Grocers' Company; and others of 3,000 marks, due to other companies, and divers others to the amount of sixty thousand pounds sterling, borrowed by the King to pay his army in France, and then told his Majesty that he had taken in and discharged all those debts and made his Majesty a present of the whole."

For these and other services the King conferred upon him the honour of knighthood. Whittington, with pious generosity, rebuilt his parish church of St. Michael; he also built a splendid library for Christchurch, in Newgate-street, and gave four-fifths of the books to fill it. Honoured and beloved by his fellow citizens he died about the year 1425, and was buried in St. Michael's church, where his body remained till the Great Fire of London destroyed its resting-place; subsequent to this, however, his tomb was twice sacriligiously broken into and the body rifled, the thieves being enticed to the deed by the rumours of the wealth which the tomb contained.

By his will, dated September 5, 1421, Whittington gave his house in College-hill, and all his other estates in London, to his executors in trust, to convert the house into a college for a master, four fellows, clerks, &c., and an almshouse, or hospital, for thirteen poor women. The remainder of his property he directed to be laid out in various acts of charity, among which was the building of the first gaol of Newgate, "as an asylum for those unhappy persons who on account of their offences are compelled to be confined in prison, but who before were shut up in dungeons, and were turned out from thence, at the expiration of their imprisonment, declaring open war upon society." He also requested that a great part of Guildhall should be rebuilt at his expense, and left a large amount of property for the support of St. Bartholomew's Hospital.

In a scarce print of Whittington, by Elstrack, he is represented with his hand upon a cat, with his mayoralty robes, and at the bottom is the following quaint summary of his good deeds :—

"The true portraiture of Richard Whittington, thrice Lord Mayor of London; a virtuous and godly man, full of good works (and those famous) ; he builded the gate of London, called Newgate, which was before a miserable dungeon. He builded Whittington College, and made it an almshouse for poor people. Also, he builded a great part of ye hospital of St. Bartholomew's, in West Smithfield, in London. He also builded the beautiful library at Grey Friar's, in London, called Christ's Hospital. Also, he builded the Guildhall Chapel, and increased a great part of the east end of the said hall, beside many other good works."

The present Whittington stone, upon Highgate-hill, has only lately been put up. On one side is engraven his name, and the dates when he served his mayoralty. This stone is not on the site of the one which previously stood on the hill, and which marked the site of one still more ancient, and traditionally said to have been that upon which he sat down to think upon his hard fortune, after having been compelled to run away from his master's house on account of the ill-treatment he experienced at the hands of his fellow-servant, the cook. While still sitting there, pondering what he should do, he faintly heard the sound of Bow Bells pealing forth their merry sound, and they appeared to say—

"Turn again Whittington,
Thrice Lord Mayor of London !"

Which he obeyed, and for which obedience he was well rewarded afterwards. Another tradition concerning the stone is, that Whittington himself placed the stone on the hill, after he had risen to eminence and wealth in the City, for the convenience of mounting or dismounting from his horse at the foot of the hill, as he was accustomed to take his rides in the neighbourhood, and from that incident his name became attached to it. However these legends may have originated it is certain that his name has been associated with Highgate-hill for several centuries.

THE WHITTINGTON ALMSHOUSES.

THESE Almshouses, which are situated at the foot of the Archway-road, in the parish of Islington, were erected by the Mercers' Company, of which Whittington, as has been stated, was a member. In his will, and on his death-bed, he strictly charged his executors to ordain a house of alms for poor people, which they did. The almshouses, which are managed by the Company of Mercers, originally joined the church of St. Michael's Paternoster, but the charity being possessed of considerable property and reserved additions from benefactions, they fixed upon the present appropriate site, and the building was erected in 1824, at a cost of £20,000. The college (which is its proper designation) is a very handsome edifice in the later English style, and it encloses a well-kept pleasure-ground. In the centre is a neatly-designed chapel, and at either end is a residence for the chaplain and matron of the establishment. In the centre of the pleasure-grounds is a stone statue of the founder, represented as a lad in listening attitude, as if catching the sound of "Bow Bells." The almshouses are twenty-eight in number, and occupants must be widows of not less than fifty-five years of age, and not possess property of greater value than £30 per annum, in addition to what they receive from the charity, which is £30 a year, besides several minor gifts. In connection with the institution is a chaplain, who receives £125 per annum, also a matron, two nurses, and a gardener, or messenger.

Richard Cloudesley.

THE STONEFIELD ESTATE.

THE Stonefield estate, bequeathed to the church at Islington by Sir Richard Cloudesley, upon the condition that a number of prayers should be regularly said for the repose of his soul, is situated in the district parish of Holy Trinity, Cloudesley-square, and comprises about sixteen acres of freehold land in that neighbourhood. Though it was thus left by the above knight to be appropriated to superstitious uses, it escaped being seized upon by Henry VIII. at the dissolution of the chauntries, like other religious property. This result was probably effected in consequence of a certain portion of the produce from the estate being regularly given to the poor, and also from motives of respect to the testators, who were persons of great respectability and possessed some interest at Court, particularly Sir Thomas Lovel, who was connected with this parish.

Sir Richard Cloudesley appears to have possessed a mind deeply imbued with religious influences, but which were evidently perverted by the superstitious observances of the age. He belonged to a monkish establishment called the Brotherhood of Jesus, which was in connection with the parish church of Islington, and the will in which he bequeaths the Stonefield estate to this fraternity is preserved to us entire. As a specimen of the superstitious notions of the age, and the influence brought to bear upon weak minds by the priestcraft antecedent to the Reformation, it is unique. It is as follows :—

"In the name of God, Amen. In the name of the Father, Son, and Holy Trinity, Amen. The 13th day of the month of January, the year of our Lord 1517, and the 9th year of the reign of King Henry VIII., I, Richard, otherwise called Richard Cloudesley, clere of mind and in my good memory, being loved by Almighty God, make and ordain my testament or my last will in this manner, as followeth,—

"First, I bequeath and recommend my soul unto Almighty God, my Creator and Saviour, and his most blessed moder Saint Mary the Virgin, and to all the holy company of Heaven. My body, after I am past this present and transitory life, to be buried within the church-yard of the parish church of Islington, near unto the grave of my father and moder, on whose souls Jesus have mercy. Also, I bequeath to the high altar of the same church for tithes and oblations peradventure by me forgotten or withholden, in discharging of my conscience, 20s. Also, I bequeath to the said church of Islington, eight torches, price 6s. the piece ; four of them after my month's mind is holden and kept to remain to the Brotherhood of Jesus within the said church ; and the other four torches to burn at the saying of the high mass within the walls of the said church as long as they will last.

"Item, I give to four poor men of the parish of Islington, two gowns with the name of ' Jesu ' upon then, every gown, 6s. 8d. ; also, to two other poor men, two gowns, to have 'Marie' upon them, in honour of our Blessed Lady. I will that such gowns be given to those who will honestly wear them, and not to sell or put them in pledge.

"Item, I give and bequeath to the high altar of St. James's, Clerkenwell, 3s 4d ; to the churches of St. Pancras, Hornsey, Finchley, and Hampstead, each two torches, and to two poor men in each of the said parishes, two gowns, price 6s. 8d.

"Item, also to every parish priest of the said churches I give 20d., to the intent that they pray for me openly by name in their churches every Sunday, and to pray their parishioners to pray for me, and forgive me, as I forgive them and all the world.

"Item, I give and bequeath to the prisoners of Newgate in money, 3s. 4d. ; item, a load of straw, 4s. To the prisoners of the King's Bench, 3s. 4d. ; item, a load of straw. Item, to the prisoners of the Marchelsea, 3s. 4d., and a load of straw. Item, to the poor men or prisoners of Bedlam, 3s. 4d. and a load of straw. Item, I will that there be a load of straw laid me in my grave, the price five marks.

"Item, I give and bequeath to the repairing and mending of the causeway between my house that I now dwell in and Islington church, 40s. Item, I will that there be after my decease, as hastily as may be, a thousand masses said for my soul, and that every priest have for his labour, 4s. Item, I will that there be bestowed upon the amending of the highway between Highgate-hill and the stony bounds beyond King-cross, £20; and if the said £20 will not make it sufficient, I will that there be bestowed thereon another £20.

"Item, I give to the poor Lazars of Highgate to pray for me by name in their beadrole, 6s. 8d. Also, I beseech the Friars of Greenwich to sing a solemn dirge and mass by note for me, 40s. Also, I will a priest to sing for me at Scala Celi, at the Savoy, by the space of one year after my decease, and he to have for his salary, £6 16s. 8d. Also, I will every month after my decease, that there be an obit (funeral obsequies) kept for me in Islington church, and each priest and clerk have for their paines as they used to have afore this time. And I will that there be distributed at every obit to poor people, to pray for my soul, 6s. 8d.

"I will, that all that now be seised to my use, and to the performance of my will, or hereafter shall be seised to the same, of and in a parcel of ground called the *Stony-field*, otherwise called the Fourteen Acres, shall suffer the rents and profits of the same from henceforth to be counted to this use ensuing; that is to say, I will that yearly, after my decease, the parishioners of the parish of Islington, or the more part of them, once in a year, at the parish church aforesaid, shall elect and choose six honest and discreet men of the said parish of Islington, such as they think most meet to have the order and distribution of the rent and profit aforesaid, which rent I will shall by the said six persons be bestowed in manner and form following; that is to say, I will that there be yearly for ever, a solemn obit to be kept for me within the said church of Islington, and that there be spent at the obit, 10s. And also that there be dealt to poor people of the said parish at every obit, to pray for my soul, my wife's soul, and all Christian souls, 6s. 8d. And further, I will the said six persons shall yearly pay or cause to be paid to the Wardens of the Brotherhood of Jesus the sum of £1 6s. 8d. towards the maintaining of the mass of Jesus within the said church aforesaid; upon this condition, that the said wardens shall yearly for ever cause thirty masses to be said for my soul in the said church; and further, I will that the aforesaid six persons shall have among them for their labour, to see to the true performance of the same yearly, at every obit, 10s.

* * * * *

"Item, I will and ordain executors of this, my present testament, Thomas Dowsey, Lord of St. John of Jerusalem in England, Sir Thomas Lovell, John Fyneux, Knt., Bartholomew Westby, John Moore, Richard Hawkes, &c."

Poor Sir Richard Cloudesley appears to have been determined to get to heaven if other men's prayers could accomplish that desired object. He was buried in Islington churchyard, according to his wish, where a tomb was erected to his memory on which was inscribed the words,

"Here lyes ye body of
RICHARD CLOUDYSLY,
A good benefactor to this Parish, who died
9th Henry VIII. Anno Dominie, 1517."

The tomb has been at various times repaired, and in 1818 was newly-built and enclosed with iron rails, on which occasion his remains were found and deposited in a leaden coffin.

According to an ancient writer, Sir Cloudesley's soul did nor rest in that state of repose for which he left such strict injunctions prayers should be offered up; the monkish strains of the carefully-appointed masses failed to lull his spirit to sleep. The author mentioned, who appears to have been as superstitious as Sir Richard himself, after speaking of earthquakes and tremblings of the earth, says :—

"It is said, in like manner, in a certain fielde near unto the parish church of Islington, did take place a wondrous commotion in various parts, the earth swelling and turning up on every side towards ye midst of ye said fielde, and by tradition of this, it is observed, that one Richard de Cloudesley lay buried in or near ye place, and yet his bodie being restless on ye score of some sinne by him peradventure committed, did seem to signify that religious service should then take place to quiet his departed spirit; whereupon certain exorcists, if we may so term them, did at dead of night, nothing loth, using divers divine exercises at torch light, set at rest the unruly spirit of ye said Cloudesley, and ye earth did return anew to its pristine shape, nevermore commotion proceeding therefrom to this day, and this I know of a very certaintie."—*Purlet de Mir, Nat.* x, *c.* 4.

Such gross superstition as the above only shows how much needed the Reformation was to sweep away the trash by which the Catholic clergy endeavoured to obtain an ascendancy over the minds of the weak and ignorant.

At the time of Sir Richard Cloudesley's death the Stonefield estate only yielded £4 per annum, but such has been the great increase in the value of property since that date that it now yields £930. Most of this advance, however, it is only fair to state, has taken place within the present century, for in 1808 it was rented by a Mr. Samuel Rhodes for £84. In the year 1809 upon an application being made by the corporation of London to purchase the ground for a new cattle market, the fee simple of the land was then valued at £22,893. The rents and profits are divided among the churchwardens of four of the district churches, viz., St. Mary's, the parish church, Holy Trinity, St. John's, Holloway, and St. Paul's, Ball's Pond.

In Trinity Church, Cloudesley-square, which is built upon the estate, there is a handsome window of painted glass which commemorates Sir Richard Cloudesley. In the central compartment of the window is the portrait of a gentleman in the costume of the sixteenth century, kneeling, and beneath is the following inscription:—

"RICHARD CLOUDYSLY,
A parishioner of Islington, of pious memory, gave to this parish, by will dated the 13th of January, 1517, a certain parcel of ground called Stony-Field, comprising about 16 acres, upon part of which this church is built by the assistance of his Majesty's Commissioners for building churches, and dedicated to the service of Almighty God on the 19th day of March, in the year of our Lord 1829.
"To perpetuate the memory of so great a benefactor to the parish, the feoffees of the said estate have caused this window to be thus embellished."

Trinity Church was designed by Charles Barry, and is a very imposing and commodious Gothic structure. It was erected at a cost of £11,535, and contains 2,000 sittings, of which 800 are free. The present incumbent is the Rev. Mr. Vincent, who has established a great number of useful societies in connexion with the district. In addition to the National and Infant School completed in March, 1840, there is a Sunday School, and a Youth's Institute has lately been established by the Rev. Arthur Sweatman, M.A., the curate, which has been very successful, and holds its meetings at St. George's Hall, Barnsbury.

Cromwell House.

MOST pedestrians who have ascended Highgate-hill, have no doubt observed, near the turnpike-gate, half way up, a red-brick edifice called " Cromwell House." It was built by the Protector, about the year 1630, as a residence for General Ireton, one of the commanders in his army, and who married his daughter. It is said that Cromwell himself resided there, but it is not certain. Tradition also states that there was a subterranean passage between it and the Mansion-house at Highgate. Cromwell House was evidently built in accordance with the taste of its military occupant. The staircase, which is of handsome proportions, is richly decorated with carved oak figures supposed to be of persons in the general's army, in their costumes. The ceiling of the drawing-room is ornamented with the arms of Ireton, and carved devices, emblematical of warfare, abound in all parts of the building.

The Old Church.

THERE is no record of the first foundation of the church at Islington, but it can with tolerable certainty be said to have been in existence at the time of the Conquest, for we find that the Abbots of Walthamstow had a chapelry at Islington at a very early date.

A curious old image of the Virgin Mary, called "Our Ladie of Iseldon," and to whom the church was dedicated, was kept in the church, and held in high veneration by the inhabitants. This image was burnt at the time of the Reformation. The old edifice stood exactly upon the site of the present church. It was a spacious but low-built structure in the old English style of architecture, composed of a rough kind of masonry called boulder, or an intermixture of flint, pebbles, and chalk strongly cemented together. The roof was covered with tiles. It had a square tower built of the same rough material, with battlements along the summit. A little belfry supported by pillars surmounted the whole. In the tower there were six bells, also a sun dial on the south side near the top, bearing the date 1708, and the motto *Dum spectas fugit, Hora.* A clock was also on the west front facing the high road. The south-west end of the church was almost obscured from view by the old school-house, in front of which, in a kind of niche, stood the effigies of a boy and a girl. A low brick wall ran along the road, enclosing the church-yard to the west, while the south side, facing Shepherdess Fields, was enclosed by wooden palings. The dimensions of the old church were as follows :—

Length	92 feet.
Breadth . . .	54 „
Height	28 „
Altitude of tower .	74 „

Hatton, an eminent surveyor, who wrote a "New View of London," in the year 1700, on making an actual survey of old Islington Church, remarks, "that as near as could be guessed, from the order of the materials and other circumstances, it appeared to have been erected about 200 years ago. As to ornament, there was nothing very grand, though what there was, was good."

On taking down the old structure, however, in 1751, a date as early as 1483, written on the wall behind a wooden gallery which had been put up after the church was built, was discovered, and it is judged that about that period the church then standing was erected.

The old church contained three aisles, and was paved throughout with bricks and stones intermixed; the floor, to which there was a descent of several steps from the entrance, was raised higher in the neighbourhood of the altar than in other parts. The roof was divided into panels, and that part immediately over the altar painted with clouds in fresco. The pews were of oak, and the walls wainscotted in most parts seven feet high. That round the communion-table was somewhat higher than in other places, and painted of an olive-colour with gilt mouldings. The east end was adorned with a cornice of carved oak, having a glory in the centre, and between the two tables of the Decalogue, which was painted in black letters on a white wall, there was a spacious window, containing some remains of fine stained glass. The gallery was built in 1663 and the altar in 1671.

Old Islington Church contained many interesting monuments of departed worthies. Among the most noted may be mentioned one on a wall near the end of the south aisle, of white and veined marble, adorned with two columns and the entablature of the Corinthian order. There was also a group of pyramidical figures consisting of a lady lying on her left side under the arch, reading, and eleven children and grand-children in a kneeling posture. In front of the tomb were enrichments of cherubim, fruits, and leaves, partly gilt, the whole enclosed by an iron railing, with the following inscription :—

"Under the hope of the resurrection,
Here lyeth ye body of
ALICE OWEN
Widower, ye daughter of Thomas Wilks. This matron, having advanced and enriched all her children, kept great hospitalitie ; she

also in her lifetime furthered ye public weal of the state, as her charitable deeds to ye citie of London, both universities, Oxford and Cambridge, can testify; a monument of her piety to future ages being extant in the south end of this town, more worthi ie and largely expressing her pietie than these golden letters as much as deeds are above words. She having lived religiously to God, *sufficiently for nature, but not for her children and friends,* her just soul is in the han's of ye Almightie where her bodie departed 26th Oct. 1613.

"Was first married to Henry Robinson, by whom she had six sonnes, John, William, Henry, John. Thomas, and Henry, which said Henry the younger, was married unto Mary, ye daughter of Sir William Glover, Knight, Alderman of London; and five daughters; Margaret, married to Sir John Bret of Edmonton in ye county of Middlesex, knight; Susan; Ann, ye younger, married to Robert Rich of Horndon on ye Hill, in the county of Essex ; and Alice, married to John Washborne of Whichinforde, in ye county of Worcester, Esq.

" The second husband was William Elkin, Esq., Alderman of ye City of London, by whom she had issue only Ursula Elkin, married to Sir Roger Owen of Condover, in ye county of Salop, knight.

" The third husband was Thomas Owen, one of the judges of ye Court of Common Pleas to Queen Elizabeth."*

One of the earliest inscriptions in the old church was the following :—

"Here lyeth THOMAS WALKER, citizen and grocer of London, and Cicela his wife. Thomas deceased ye 25th day of ye month of July, ye year of our Lord, a thousand CCCCLXXXXVI. On whose souls Jesu have mercy."

Upon a plated stone in church text was engraven the following, which appeared to have been laid down in the life-time of the deceased. It was very old, but the date was not entirely filled up :—

" I pray the Christian man, that as ye do see this,
To pray for the souls of them that here buried is,
And remember that in Christ we be bre-threne,
The which hath commanded every man to pray for the other.

---

* There is a monument to the memory of Judge Owen in the south aisle of Westminster Abbey.

This saith Robert Midleton and Joan his wife, Here wrapped in claye. Abiding the mercy of Almighty God till Doomsdaye.
Which was su'tyme sunt to Sir George Hasting, Knt.*
Erl of Huntingdon passed this transitory life,
In the year of our Lord, MCCCCC,
And the   day of the moneth of
On whose soul Jesu have mercy."

There were a great many monuments to the Fowler family in the old church, which family was connected with the parish for many years.   One of the oldest was the following :—

" Here lyeth ALIS FOWLER, ye wife of Robert Fowler, Esq., who died 1540.

" Behold and see, thus as I am so sal ye be,
When he be dead and laid in ye grave,
As ye have done, so sal ye have."

Among other interesting inscriptions was the following on the south aisle :—

"Here lyeth ye body of JOHN MARKHAM, Esq., one of ye Sergeant-at-Arms to our most gracious Sovereign Lord King James, who died August 26th, 1610.

" He was gentilke born and gentilke bred,
And ere he died was well marryed
Unto a vertuous and loving wife,
Who, losing him, loathed her own life ;
Whose love hath built this for eternity,
That he may still be had in memory."

On the north side of the aisle of the old church was a very large marble monument, containing the effigies of Sir Nicholas Kempe between two of his wives in a kneeling posture, and enrichments of cherubim, gilding, and carved work, with the inscription :—

" Here lyeth the body of Sir NICHOLAS KEMPE, Knt., one of his Majesty's Justices of the Peace, and an honourable member of the High Commission Court, who had to his first wife Cecilia, with whom he lived in blessed amity near forty years together; with Sarah his second wife, six years, and having passed with much prosperity, love, and credit, the reverend years of 72, he changed this terrestrial condition for an everlasting state of blessedness, the third September, 1624.

" Wise, loving, liberal, religious, just,
This body fills the grave of him whose dust

---

* Sir George Hastings was afterwards made Earl of Huntingdon, and the probable interpretation is, that the monument was erected previous to the death of the Earl, who was most likely some friend of the deceased.

Lies here entombed. All that praise can
bring forth,
There are not words enough to express his
worth,
For his good works. This stone cannot com-
prise
Half the particulars of his pieties;
What goodness ever was, is, and to come,
In mortal man, that makes up his just sum."

The churchyard also contained, and many
are yet in a state of good preservation, a
great number of interesting monuments with
quaint inscriptions. One of the most ancient
is that of Sir Richard Clondesley's, before-
mentioned. It would take, however, a very
large portion of our space, to notice one-
fourth of them, and probably it would be uninteresting to the majority of our readers to
do so.

The Parish Church.

IN the year 1751 the old church was in
such a dilapidated condition that it was
resolved to pull it down. Before its final
demolition was determined upon, however,
it was examined by three surveyors appointed
for the purpose, and they were of opinion
that " it had gone so much to decay as to en-
danger the lives of the inhabitants assembled
therein ; that it could only be repaired at a
very great expense, and besides would not
accommodate the parishioners." Application
was then made to Parliament by the Vestry
to enable them to pull it down, and build
another. An act was accordingly passed
which enabled the trustees to borrow the
money by way of annuities on lives chargeable to a rate being put upon landlords and
householders, the landlords paying two-thirds
and the householders of the parish the remainder. Prior to the commencement of its
demolition notice was issued that all friends
who wished to preserve any special relic
would be permitted to do so upon proper application.

The contractor into whose hands the erection of the new church was given, undertook
to pull the old one down within a month. On
doing so, the tower was found to be so
strongly cemented together that it set the
efforts of the workmen to destroy it at de-
fiance. Gunpowder was used, but sparingly,
for fear of accident, but it did not have the
desired effect; whereupon the surveyor had
recourse to undermine the foundation, first
shoring up the superstructure with strong
timber. This being consumed by a large
fire kindled for the purpose, the tower fell to

the ground with a tremendous crash From
the great strength and solidity it displayed it
was considered that it might have stood at
least another hundred years without being at
all unsafe.

The present structure was built by Mr.
Steenman under the direction of Mr. Dow-
biggin, who furnished the design and superintended the work till it was completed.
The foundation-stone was laid on the 28th
of August, 1751, by James Colebrook, Esq.,
and in which was deposited a copper-plate
with the inscription :—

" This church was built at the expense of
the parish, and the first stone thereof was
laid by James Colebrook, Esq., the 28th day
of August, in the year of our Lord 1751."

It took two years and nine months in
building, and was opened for divine service on
the 26th May, 1774, the total expense including the fitting up of the interior, was
£7,340. Though perhaps not built in architectural rule it is allowed to be a handsome
edifice. It is constructed of brick, strengthened with stone groins, cornices, &c., in plain
rustic. The spire is said to be " a combina-
tion formed by the ingenious architect of the
various beauties of what he esteemed the
three handsomest churches in London, viz.,
St. Brides, Bow, and Shoreditch."

The altitude of the tower from the ground to
the vane is . . . . 164 feet
Length of the church . . 108 „
Width . . . . . 60 „

In the tower is an agreeable set of bells,

eight in number, six being recast from those in the old tower, and two smaller ones added by subscription to make up the octave. The tenor weighs 16 cwt., and was recast in 1808 to improve the tone. Around each bell is an inscription, of which the following is a copy :

1st bell. Although I am but slight and small,
    I will be heard above you all.

2nd bell At proper times our voice we'll raise,
    In sounding to our Benefactor's praise.

3rd bell. If you have a judicious ear,
    You'll own our voices sweet and clear.

4th bell. To honour both our God and King,
    Our voices shall in concert ring.

5th bell. Whilst thus we join in cheerful
    sound,
    May love and loyalty abound.

6th bell. In wedlock's bands all ye who join,
    With hand your heart unite,
    So shall our tuneful voice combine
    To laud the nuptial rite.

7th bell. Ye ringers all, that prize your
    health and happiness,
    Be sober, merry, wise, and the same
    will you possess.

8th bell. Cast 1808. Present, Edward Flower, churchwarden, Thomas Whitemore, John Blount, Edward Marston.

Thomas Meares and Son, London, *fecit.*

The contract entered into with the builder was as follows :—

For the church and the tower	£5,622	0	0
The spire, vane, &c.	.	.	577	0	0
Stone balustrades	.	.	23	0	0
Stone portico in front	.	.	97	0	0
		£6,319	0	0
A brass chandelier to hold 36 lights	.	.	50	0	0
The clock	.	.	73	0	0
Dials to ditto	.	.	13	14	11
Mr. Dowbiggin, surveyor	.	105	0	0
do. for extra trouble	.	18	18	0
Churchyard walls	.	.	93	10	0
Byfield and Green for Organ	400	0	0
Bells and frames	.	.	210	0	0
Extra charges	.	.	56	17	4
Total	£7,340	0	3

The interior fittings of the church are *plain* and neat. The pulpit and reading-desk are of mahogany ; the Decalogue is painted in gold letters upon a black ground, and above the pediment is a chaste painting representing the Annunciation, having on either side emblems of the law in *chiara scuro.* The church throughout exhibits an elegant plainness.

In 1787 the church underwent a thorough repair, and an electrical rod or conductor was affixed from the top of the spire to the ground to preserve the building from the effects of lightning. The means employed to effect this object were very ingenious. Thomas Birch, a basket-maker, resident in Islington, undertook for the sum of £20 to erect a scaffold of wicker-work around the spire, which he formed entirely of willows, hazel, and other sticks. It had a flight of circular stairs, reaching from the balustrade at the bottom of the spire, by which the ascent was as easy and as safe as the stairs of a dwelling-house. The spire, as may be imagined, presented a very curious spectacle on the occasion, being entirely enveloped, as it were in a huge basket, within which the workmen were performing the necessary repairs with safety. The emoluments received by the basket-maker on this occasion were very considerable, from the donations, not only of the inhabitants, but of others whose curiosity led them from London to view this piece of workmanship. The exhibition was advertised in the newspapers, and the following notice in the *Morning Post* of June 13, 1787, invited the public to view the scaffold in the following terms :—

"To the Curious.—Those ladies and gentlemen who have not had an opportunity of viewing the ingenious basketwork constructed round the spire of Islington Church for the purpose of repairing the vane, are desired to take notice that this most ingenious yet simple and secure invention will be exhibited for the satisfaction of the curious from ten to twelve in the morning, and from three to seven in the afternoon. And as it can only be shown within the afore-mentioned hours, and the term of performing the contract expires in a few days, when the whole apparatus will be taken down, the proprietor, Thomas Birch, hopes the public in general will take an early opportunity of seeing this very uncommon performance. Admission, 6d."

There are a few old inhabitants in Islington still living who vividly remember the above ; the writer being kindly offered some valuable information by a lady who has lived in the heart of the parish from her childhood, and recollects the occasion well.

There are many interesting monuments in the new church, some of which are preserved from the old. The earliest date of any register kept in the parish is 1557, and with the exception of the period during the civil wars in Cromwell's time, it was very fairly kept and written. The following is the average of baptisms, burials, and marriages:—

	Baptisms.	Burials.	Marriages.
1580	38	47	—
1630	67	127	—
1780	156	221	—
1820	389	400	307
1830	906	547	371
1840	994	653	364

In 1665, there were 696 burials, of which 593 were persons who died of the plague. From August 29 to Sept. 5 of the same year, 94 died in the one week in the parish. The following extract from the *City Remembrancer* of the period, showing how the plague was introduced into Islington, will be found interesting:—

"A citizen broke out of his house in Aldersgate-street, and attempted to escape into the country. On travelling as far as Islington, he tried to get lodgings at the 'Angel' or the 'White Horse' taverns, but was refused. At the 'Pyed Bull' he pretended he was going into Lincolnshire, that he was entirely free from infection, and required lodgings only for one night. They had but one garret-bed empty, and that but for one night, expecting drovers with cattle next day. A servant showed him the room, which he gladly accepted; he was well dressed, and, with a sigh, said he had seldom lain in such a lodging, but would make shift, as it was but for one night, and in a dreadful time. He sat down on the bed desiring a pint of warm ale, which was forgot. Next morning one asked, 'what has become of the gentleman?' The maid, starting, said she had never thought more of him, he bespoke warm ale, but she forgot it. A person on going up stairs, found him dead across the bed, his clothes were pulled off, his jaw fallen, his eyes open in a most frightful posture, and the rug of his bed clasped in one hand. The alarm was great, Islington having been free from the distemper, which spread immediately to the houses round about. Fourteen died of the plague that week in the parish."

The following are also interesting entries in the parish register:—

"*Sir George Wharton*, buried Nov. 10, 1609. *James Stewarte*, godson to King James, buried Nov. 10th, 1609."—These two persons were both servants to King James I. Some angry words having passed between them while at Court, they fought a duel near Islington with swords, and killed each other in the combat. It is recorded that when the King heard of the melancholy intelligence, he displayed great grief and ordered them both to be interred in one common grave at Islington. This event excited much public attention at the time, and in the year 1610, was published "A Lamentable Ballad of a Combat lately fought neare London between Sir James Stewarte and Sir George Wharton, Knights, who were both slaine at one time." In it were the copies of the letters which passed between the duellists previous to the fatal event. When they met upon the field they deliberately and calmly searched each others breasts to see if either had placed secret armour underneath his clothes; they then shook hands, and after a severe struggle mortally wounded one another. The letters are preserved, and giving as they do, the sentiment which prevailed amongst a portion of the fashionable world at that time, will be found interesting:—

"*Sir George Wharton's challenge to Sir James Stewarte, before they fought:*—

"SIR,—Your misunderstanding of my message gives me cause to think you're extreme vainglorious, a humour which ye valiant detest. And whereas you unjustly saide I durst not meet you in ye fielde to fight with you, you shall find you are much mistaken, for I will fight you with what weapon ye shall appoint, and meet you where you will, being contented to give you this advantage, not valuing ye what ye can doe.
"GEORGE WHARTON."

"*Sir James Stewarte's answer:*—

"SIR,—Your message either being ill-delivered or else not accepted, you have since, though ill-advised, retracted and repented it, for your messenger willed me from you that either of us should make choice of a friend to debate ye matter; to which I confess I did but lightly hearken, since I knew oddes which no breath could make even. And now you have to acknowledge no other speaker than you charged me with, which is, that I saide you durste not meet me in ye fielde to fight. True it is, your barbarous and uncivil insolency in such a place and before such a company (for whose respect I am only sorry for what I then did or saide) made me do and say which I now will make good. Wherein since you find yourself behind, I am ready to do you all ye right you can expect, and to that ende have I sent you ye length of my rapier which I will use with a dagger, and so meet you at ye further ende of Islington (as I understande nearer you than me) at three o'clock in ye afternoone, which things I scorn to take as advantages, but as my due, and which I have made indifferent. And in respect I cannot send any of my friends without hazard of discovery, I have sent my servant herewith, who is only acquainted with this business.

"JAMES STEWARTE."

The ballad alluded to, commemorating the event, is somewhat lengthy and commences thus :—

"It grieves my heart to tell the woe
That did near London late befall,
On Martlemas eve. O, woe is me !
I grieve the chance, and ever shall,
Of two right gallant gentlemen,
Who very rashly fell at words
But to their quarrel could not fall,
Till they fell both by their keen swords;
The one Sir George Wharton call'd,
The good Sir Wharton's son and heir,
The other Sir James, a Scottish knight,
A man that a valiant heart did bear."

"*Elizabeth Emma Thomas*, buried 29th Oct. 1808.—The following extraordinary circumstance took place on the interment of this person:—On Saturday, the 29th October, the corpse was brought from a house in Charterhouse-square, and buried in the churchyard of this parish. On the following Monday, a headstone was secretly brought and placed over her grave, with the inscription :—

"In Memory of
MRS. ELIZABETH THOMAS,
Who died 28th Oct., 1808, aged 27 years.
"She had no fault save what travellers give the moon,
The light was lovely, but she died too soon."

This mysterious transaction caused a great deal of local gossip and conjecture, which resulted in a letter being sent to the coroner, intimating that there had likely been some foul play with regard to the deceased, having died, been buried, and a stone erected with an inscription, all in three days. Application was made to the parish officers to have the grave opened, which was done, and on examining the corpse, a large wire pin was found sticking in the heart of the deceased,

having been thrust through the left side of the body. It appeared, however, in the evidence, that it was at her own request the pin was inserted by a relative to prevent the possibility of her being buried alive, and the jury returned a verdict, "Died by the visitation of God." The relation mentioned applied to have the body removed, and accordingly it was removed to the burying-ground of Whitfield's Chapel in Tottenham Court-road, and buried a second time, where the stone bearing the same inscription still remains.

The following is a list of the Vicars :—

1327. Walter Gerkin, the earliest vicar whose name is preserved, died in 1327.
1327. Egediac de Felsted.
1332. William de Southwerk.
1336. John Seman.
1336. Thomas Gunge.
1337. Henry Le Clerke.
1384. Laurence Sport.
1393. John Cooke.
1395. William Hardy.
1397. John Dames (Vicar of Ealing.)
—— William Chapel (resigned)
—— William Canon (resigned)
1427. Richard Dalby.
1434. John Crossley (afterwards Vicar of South Minns.)
1438. William Lake.
1443. John Farley.
1444. Robert Smith.
1454. John Wardall.
1472. Thomas Gore.
1487. Edward Vaughan, LL.D. (was afterwards Bishop of St. David's.)
1509. Thomas Warren.
1521. John Cocks, (Oxford College.)
1545. John Robinson.
1550. C. Williams, (had been rector of Allhallows, City.)
1583. Meredith Hanmer. In 1567 was Vicar of St. Leonard, Shoreditch, when, according to the inhabitants, he converted the brass of several ancient monuments to his own use. In Strypes "Annals" of 1584, in relating the scandal that the Earl of Shrewsbury had had a child by Queen Elizabeth, it is stated that among the witnesses examined before a jury in reference to the case was "one Meredith Hanmer, a Doctor of Divinitie and Vicar of Islington, who dealt as lewdly towards my lord in speeches, as did the other Walmesley. This doctor regardeth not an oath; surely he is a very bad man." He wrote several ecclesiastical and civil histories.

1592. Samuel Proctor.

1639. William Hunt.

1662. William Cave. A learned divine of great repute and chaplain to Charles II. In the year 1684 was installed Canon of Windsor. Was buried at Islington.

1691. Robert Gery, M.A.

1720. Cornelius Yeates, M.A., Archdeacon of Wilts.

1720. George Cary. It is recorded of this vicar that on a wet hay-making time in 1725 he went through the parish from house to house and begged money for the poor distressed haymakers, and collected for them a handsome sum which he afterwards distributed at the church.

1733. Richard Street.

1738. George Stonehouse.

1767. Sir Gilbert Williams.

1768. Richard Smith, M.A.

1772. George Strahan, D.D., Prebendary of Rochester, 1805. This gentleman was a great friend of Dr. Samuel Johnson, who frequently visited him at Islington; the vicar was with him a few days before his last illness. He left Dr. Strahan a great part of his valuable library. Dr. Strahan was much beloved by his parishioners, and at a Vestry meeting held April 26, a sum of money was voted towards erecting a tablet to his memory.

1824. Daniel Wilson, M.A., afterwards Bishop of Calcutta. He was educated at Oxford where he highly distinguished himself. Before leaving the parish to labour in the East, he was presented with a handsome testimonial by the parishioners, at a public breakfast given June 13th, 1832. Mr. Woodward was churchwarden at the time. By his resignation of the vicarage the various district churches were legally formed into separate ecclesiastical parishes, he giving up his right of supervision. A commodious hall has been erected to his memory.

1832. Daniel Wilson, M.A, son of the above.

As regards the population of the parish, it has immensely increased during the last ten years. The general healthiness and elevation of its site, and the great demand for suburban places of residence in consequence of the space required for warehousing merchandise in the city, in addition to the natural increase of the population, have been the chief cause of such result. Subjoined is a valuable statement made by the district registrar of the census lately taken, together with the number of houses in the parish.

Houses and Population in the Parish of Islington, according to the Census taken on the 8th April, 1861.

HOUSES.

Houses inhabited (1861) . .	.	20,676
„ uninhabited . .	.	888
„ building . .	.	501

Registrars' Districts.

Houses inhabited in the East District		11,175
„ uninhabited „ „		450
„ building „ „		380
Houses inhabited in the West Dist.		9,501
„ uninhabited „ „		438
„ building „ „		121

Ecclesiastical Divisions.

	Houses Inhab.	Uninhab.	Blg.
St. Mary's Parish Church including the Chapel of Ease .	2547	102	36
St. Andrew's District	1965	81	7
All Saints' „	1689	38	1
St. Peter's „	1679	33	4
Holy Trinity „	1882	35	—
St. Paul's „	1646	85	9
St. James' „	1420	74	28
St. Philip's „	1195	38	43
St. Stephen's „	977	25	1
St. John's „	1193	114	51
St. Mark's „	1114	102	129
St. Matthew's „	963	26	—
St. Luke's „	949	91	94
St. Jude's „	1010	24	52
Christ Church „	447	20	46

POPULATION.

Males	.	69,755
Females . .	.	85,536
Total Persons . .	.	155,291

Registrars' Districts.

Males in the East District .	.	35,105
Females „ „ .	.	44,753
Total . . .	.	79,858
Males in the West District .	.	34,650
Females „ „ .	.	40,783
Total Persons . .	.	75,433

Ecclesiastical Divisions.

	Males.	Females.	Total.
St. Mary's Parish Church, including the Chapel of Ease	7881 -	10328 -	18209
St. Andrew's District	8711 -	9376 -	18087
All Saints' ,,	. 7685 -	8016 -	15701
St. Peter's ,,	. 6262 -	7262 -	13524
Holy Trinity ,,	. 5741 -	7742 -	13483
St. Paul's . ,,	. 4831 -	6955 -	11786
St. James' ,,	. 4997 -	5630 -	10627
St. Philip's ,,	. 4229 -	4769 -	8998
St. Stephen's ,,	. 3293 -	4029 -	7322
St. John's ,,	. 3059 -	4140 -·	7199
St. Mark's ,,	. 2919 -	3944 -	6863
St. Matthew's ,,	. 2985 -	3807 -	6792
St. Luke's ,,	. 2982 -	3881 -	6863
St. Jude's . ,,	. 2920 -	3687 -	6607
Christ Church ,,	. 1260 -	1970 -	3230

Population of the Parish in every Census yet taken.

Year 1801	10212
,, 1811	15065
Increase in the ten years	4853
Year 1821	22417
,, 1831	37316
Increase . . .	14899

Year 1841	55690
,, 1851	95329
Increase . . .	39639
Year 1861	155291
Increase in the last ten years	59962

Mr. Wyatt, the Superintendent Registrar, remarks upon the above :—

"It will be seen that the increase during the last ten years is greater than the entire population was in 1841; and, it is believed, will contribute more to the general population of the present census than any other single parish in England. The increase alone (59962) is equal to some of our principal cities, and more than equal to the cities of Oxford and Cambridge combined.

"It will also be seen that the division of the parish for registration purposes is very equally divided as regards population, the divisional line taking the main thoroughfare from the "Angel" along the Upper-street to Highgate-hill; the area of the East District, however, is considerably larger than that of the West District, it being 1899 statute acres to 1228.

"The comparative statement, shewing the continued and rapid increase, must be viewed with great interest by most of the old inhabitants, seeing that their parish has grown from a little over 10,000 persons in the year 1801 (less than some of the ecclesiastical districts at present), to a population exceeding 155,000 souls."

Thomas Topham,

THE "STRONG MAN OF ISLINGTON."

THOMAS TOPHAM, commonly known as the "Strong Man of Islington," kept the "Duke's Head," which formerly stood at the south-east corner of Gadd's-row, (now St. Alban's-place,) near Islington-green. This remarkable man lived in the middle of the last century, and his "exhibitions of strength" as they were called, were generally attended by large crowds of people both in London and the provinces. The father of Topham was a carpenter, who brought up his son to the same trade. On attaining his full growth his stature was about five feet ten. He left his trade of carpenter at the age of 24, and being fond of those particular enjoyments peculiar to low "sporting men," opened a public-house called the "Red Lion," near St. Luke's Hospital. Here he failed, owing to the low company with which he became associated, that part of Finsbury then being the great resort of prizefighters, wrestlers, back-sword players, boxers, and such like fraternity. After that he removed to the "Duke's Head," which he kept for some years, and it was while living there that he performed many of those feats of strength which made him so famous, and which, were they not attested by credible witnesses, scarcely seem to be possible. Dr. John Desaguliers, a gentleman well-known in Islington at the time, and who wrote a very interesting account of his performances, saw most of his performances. Amongst the curiosities contained in the British Museum before the present one was erected, was a good-sized pewter dish marked near the edge with the following inscription :—" April 3, 1737, Thomas Topham of Islington, carpenter, rolled up this dish made of the hardest pewter, by the strength of his hands in the presence of Dr. John Desaguliers." His first feat of strength was that of pulling against a horse, by placing his legs round a post, and having a band round his body fastened to the harness of the animal. He took an iron poker about a yard long and three inches round and struck it upon his bare left arm till he bent the poker to nearly a right angle. With such another poker, holding the ends of it in his hands, and placing the middle of it against the back of his neck, he brought both ends together before him, and then pulled it almost straight again. He lifted a stone of 800 lbs. weight with his hands only. Perhaps his greatest exploit, however, was the lifting of three hogsheads of water in Bath-street, Cold Bath Fields, on May the 28th, 1741. This feat was performed in the presence of thousands of spectators in commemoration of the taking of Portobello by Admiral Vernon, and was witnessed by the Admiral himself and many of the aristocracy. The weight of the water was 11,831 lbs. ; the casks which contained it were so placed on a strong timber frame, that he, standing above them, was enabled by means of a strap over his shoulders fastened to a strong cord which bound and intersected the hogsheads, to lift the cumbrous load several inches from its deposit amidst great cheering from the multitude. At the time he thus exhibited himself, he probably resided at the "Duke's Head." Among many wonderful stories related by Dr. Desaguliers of the freaks Topham sometimes indulged in, the following will be found both interesting and amusing :—

" On his way home to Islington one night from the city, finding a watchman fast asleep in his box, near Barbican, he took both on his shoulders, and carrying the load with the greatest ease, carefully dropped the guardian of the night, together with his wooden tenement, over the wall of Bunhill-fields burying-ground, where the poor fellow, between sleeping and waking, on recovering from his fright, seemed to be doubtful whether he was in the land of the living, and appeared to be only waiting for the graves around to open and swallow him up. Another time, sitting at the window of a low public house, whilst a butcher from the slaughter-house was passing by with nearly half an ox

No. 7.

upon his back, Topham relieved him of it with such ease and dexterity, that the butcher, almost petrified with astonishment, swore that nothing but the devil could have flown away with his load. Upon another occasion, thinking to enjoy a little sport with some bricklayers, by removing part of a scaffold just before they intended to strike it from a small building, his grasp was so rude that a part of the front wall, following the timber, the bricklayers conceived it to be the effect of an earthquake, and immediately ran off into an adjoining field. Here, however, Topham was nearly paying very dear for his prank, for one of the poles struck him a severe blow on the side, which caused him considerable pain for some time after.

"Being one day persuaded by an acquaintance to accompany him on board a vessel that had just come home from the West Indies loaded with cocoa-nuts, a sailor presented one to him, which he had no sooner got into his hands, than he threw the Jack-tars into the utmost astonishment by cracking it close to the donor's ear as if it had been an egg-shell.

"Another time, upon the occasion of a race being run in the Hackney-road, a man with a horse and cart would persist in keeping close to the contending parties much to the displeasure of the crowd. Topham, who was a spectator, stepped into the road, seized the tail of the cart, and in spite of all the man's exertions in whipping his horse to get forward, he drew them both backwards with the greatest ease, much to the pleasure and gratification of the beholders and the chagrin of the driver, who only refrained from using his whip from fear.

"Having one day in his tap-room two guests extremely quarrelsome, he bore with their noise and insolence a long time, but at length they proceeded so far that nothing could satisfy them but fighting the landlord. As they would be appeased no other way, Topham seized them both by the nape of their necks with the same facility as if they had been children, and bumped their heads together till they became perfectly sensible of their error, and were as abject in asking forgiveness as they had before been insolent in giving offence."

The following particulars are related by Mr. Hutton, of Birmingham, in his " History of Derby :—" We learn from private accounts, well attested, that Thomas Topham, a man who keeps a public-house at Islington, performed surprising feats of strength, such as throwing his horse over a turnpike-gate, lifting three hogsheads of water, &c. ; but, how-

ever Belief might stagger she soon recovered herself when this second Sampson appeared at Derby as a performer in public, the charge being 1s. admission. Upon application to Alderman Cooper for leave to exhibit, the magistrate was surprised at the feats he proposed, and as his appearance was like that of other men, he requested him to strip that he might examine whether he·was made like them ; but he was found to be extremely muscular. What were hollows under the armpits and legs of others, were filled up with ligaments in him. He appeared to be above five feet ten in height, turned thirty years of age, well-made, and nothing singular about his person. He generally walked with a limping gait, caused by a foolish feat that he offered to perform. The feat was this: he laid a wager that three horses could not drag him from a certain post which he would clasp or hold by his feet only. The proper harness was arranged, and attached to Topham's body, and the utmost efforts of the horses in a straightforward pull, could not cause him to loosen his ho'd, but the driver giving them a sudden lash, turned them aside, and the unexpected jerk broke his thigh.

" The ordinary performances of this man, in which were united the strength of twelve, were such as rolling up pewter dishes of seven pounds weight as a man rolls up a sheet of paper ; holding a pewter quart at arms length and squeezing the sides together like an egg-shell, and lifting two hundred weight with his little finger. He raised a solid oak table, six feet long, with his teeth, and broke a rope which sustained three tons. He took Mr. Chambers, vicar of All Saints, who weighed twenty-seven stone, and raised him with one hand. One day four people, fourteen stone each, sat upon his body, while his head lay on one chair and his feet on another, and in such a situation he heaved them at pleasure. He struck a round bar of iron, one inch in diameter, against his naked arm, and at one stroke bent it like a bow. Weakness and feeling alike seemed fled together.

" Being a master of music he often sung the song of *Mad Tom* in a voice perfectly terrific. I heard him once sing a solo to the organ at St. Warburgh's Church, then the only one in Derby, and the voice seemed scarcely human. Though of a pacific temper he was liable to the insults of the rude. One day the ostler at the 'Virgin's Inn,' where he was staying, having given him disgust, he took one of the kitchen spits from the mantel-piece and bent it round the man's neck like a handkerchief ; but as he did not choose to tuck the ends in the ostler's bosom, the ornament excited the laughter of the company, until he condescended to untie his iron cravat."

William Hutton's authority may well be relied on, being a man whose probity and industry had gained for him the esteem of all men, and his own biography affords one of the best examples of successful perseverance that could be placed into the hands of any youth. After leaving Islington, Topham took another public-house in Hog-lane, Shoreditch, where he committed suicide on the 10th of August, 1749. This melancholy end of Topham was brought about through the infidelity of his wife, for, like Sampson, he was not without his Delilah ; and it had such a maddening effect on him, that unable to bear the reflections it excited in his mind, in a fit of frenzy, after beating her most severely, and stabbing her in the breast, he inflicted fatal wounds with the same weapon on his own person, and lingered for a few days in great suffering. His wife recovered.

The following notices of the event are taken from the papers of the period, and it is interesting to observe the effects of local gossip in those days. A rumour getting afloat that Topham had broken open his coffin though he was buried eight feet deep, the magistrates so far thought there might be some foundation for the report as to examine alleged witnesses upon the subject. The first is from the *Daily Advertiser* of August 11, 1749 :—

" Yesterday died Thomas Topham, known by the name of the Strong Man, master of a public-house in Hog-lane, Shoreditch, occasioned by several wounds he gave himself on Tuesday last, after having stabbed his wife in the breast, but who is likely to recover."

In the same journal of August 16th, 1749, there is a paragraph relating to the rumours mentioned :—

" For these few days past there has been a great commotion in Shoreditch parish, an apprehension that a resurrection had began it, and several witnesses have been examined by the magistrates in relation thereto. Yesterday it was said that Topham, the Strong Man, had, the night before, with the assistance of some surgeons, got the better of his grave, though some eight feet of earth had been laid on him."

In a collection of notes printed by Mr. J. H. Burns in reference to Topham, we learn the manner the public in those days appreciated exhibitions of the kind. They inform us that " A Concert of Vocal and Instrumental Music was performed at Stationers' Hall, on July 10, 1734, for the benefit of Mr. Topham, the Strong Man of Islington." A hand-bill of the time states, " that the great bills would express particulars of the concert, after which, at the desire of several gentlemen and ladies, Mr. Topham is to entertain the audience with his surprising ' Performances of Strength.' Tickets of admission, 5s. each." This bill is in the Burney collection at the British Museum, and has a large woodcut of Topham, extended between two chairs, his head resting on the seat of one, his heels on the other. In his right hand he holds a glass of wine, and on his stomach and thighs stand five men.

In the same collection there is the following bill containing a public challenge from Topham :—

" THOMAS TOPHAM,
Commonly called the Strong Man, and keeps the sign of ' King Astyages's Arms,' vulgularly called the ' Bell and Dragon,' in Hog-lane, near Norton Folgate, in the parish of St. Leonard, Shoreditch,
Where he intends to perform two actions of strength for the reward of five shillings, when there is to be no more than five spectators; all above that number are to pay a shilling each. A crown is the least he will take for showing the two feats ; and further, to invite the curious, the man who is able to do either of the two, shall have the then present reward which the above-mentioned Topham is to have for exhibiting the same, and the more to add to his honour, if required, he will at his own cost, publish the same in an advertisement, to let the world know there is a *man* as great a progidy as himself. He will also consent to be erased out of the memoirs of the Royal Society,[*] and the person who can perform the like recorded in his room. It is the same Topham who was applauded and most generously caressed in that honourable part of Great Britain, called Scotland. He also performed in the Kingdom of Ireland with good success

---

[*] So frequent at this period were the references to the patronage of the Royal Society, that at a meeting of that body in March, 1753, it was declared inconsistent with the honour of the Society to further admit or show 'rare monsters,' as the ridiculous exhibitors made use of their countenance, as well as that of the royal family, and persons of quality, as puffs to the public.

and great applause ; and in most parts of South Britain, where he was handsomely received and courteously entertained, particularly by the Hon. Corporation of Macclesfield in Cheshire, where he received a handsome purse of gold ; and that was not the period of their generosity, for they also made him a free burgess and presented him with a silver box to keep his copy in. For the favours he publicly received during the time of his travels, he returns his most humble and hearty thanks.

" As the Fate's will has preserved him through many a hard brunt, especially by sea, and protected him on the day that the bloody and scandalous engagement happened off Cape Toulon, in the Mediterranean, on Saturday, the 10th of February, 1734, he is in hopes Providence will stand by him his friend, and support him in his endeavours.

" *Vivere non potest, qui more non audet.*"
" July 1, 1745."

In another public notification we have the following :—

" THOMAS TOPHAM, commonly called the Strong Man, continues to perform his two actions at the sign of the " Bell and Dragon," in Hog-lane, near Norton Folgate, in the parish of St. Leonard, Shoreditch, and no where else ; his reward as usual (less than) five spectators to give one crown ; more than that number 12d. each. There have been no visitors yet, giants or dwarfs, to act in either of the two feats, which cause the curiosity to be greater.

" Although he dwells in mud and mire,
The beer he draws is good entire,

It warms the blood, nourishes the nerves,
Both meat and drink mankind it serves.
Finis Coronat Opus.
" July 25, 1745."

The above commendation of the qualities of " entire," would now-a-days meet with a strong denial on the part of the total-abstainer ; it is gratifying to know that the enlightened progress of the age is successful in its attempts to reduce the more gross species of intemperance. A century ago " to be as drunk as a lord" was looked upon with complacency by all classes of society, and the last man under the table was the hero of the party he made merry with.

The following notification of a treat to be given by Mr. Topham is amongst the collection referred to :—

" To the Worthy Beneficial Society of Wool-
combers."
" Thomas Topham, commonly called the Strong Man, in gratitude bound for a favour he received from them the 9th instant, will entertain them with a dish of beans and bacon at the " Three Coneys" in Clapton, on the 2nd July next, where he intends to conclude with a dessert of Alderman Parson's entire, and for their known zeal and affection to our Sovereign Lord King George and the present constitution, will conduct them by beat of drum and colours displayed by his own hands. Gentlemen,—I beg you will excuse this, my public invitation, and be so good as to give me a meeting at Shoreditch Church by 12 o'clock the above-mentioned day. Your sincere and affectionate friend,
" THOMAS TOPHAM, Fortitude.
" June 11, 1746."

Newington Green.

" MILDMAY HOUSE" AND HENRY VIII.—THE NONCONFORMISTS.

THREE sides of the square of Newington-green are in the parish of Islington, and perhaps there is no single spot in the district where there are so many quaint, but commodious, old-fashioned red-brick mansions as those situated round the enclosure mentioned. Previous to the year 1745 the Green was covered with large elm trees. On the south side are the remains of an old house, now divided into two—one of which was formerly called " Mildmay House Boarding School"—once the residence of Henry VIII. In the survey taken in the year 1611, William Halliday, Alderman and Mercer of London, held these premises, with an orchard and a pasture-ground behind, called the " Park," which consisted of forty-four acres, and extended south almost as far as Ball's-pond. Sir Henry Mildmay, to whom Parliament granted the woods at Highbury, and who was one of the judges on the trial of King Charles I., afterwards became possessed of this estate by marrying the daughter and heiress of Alderman Halliday. At the Restoration Sir Henry's estates were forfeited to the Crown in consequence of the part he took against the King, but Newington-green having been settled on his wife, as being her own inheritance, it continued in the family, and is now the property of Lady Mildmay. It is a singular circumstance that while the Sir Henry Mildmay above-mentioned sat in judgment against King Charles, his brother, Anthony Mildmay, was so devoted to the unfortunate monarch, that he attended his execution as a confidential servant, and was one of those who superintended the interment of his remains at Windsor; and, perhaps, it was to the influence exercised by Anthony, on behalf of his brother, that the Newington estate, though belonging to his wife, was not forfeited.

In the interior of the old houses alluded to, there is some very handsome carving. In one of the rooms is a carved chimney-piece of oak, having in the centre a shield bearing three esquires' helmets, the arms of Alderman Halliday; the ceiling, which is wrought in stucco, contains the arms of England, with "J. R.," the initials of King James, and medallions of Hector, Alexander, &c.

Another large old house was, at the beginning of the present century, standing at the north-west corner of the Green; the site is now covered with modern dwellings. It was a square building, composed of wood and plaster, having a court-yard in the centre and communication to the various apartments all round, by means of small doors opening from one room to another. For a number of years this house was divided into small tenements for poor people, and was called "Bishop's-place." On its being taken down some parts of the old wainscotting were found to be very richly gilt and adorned with paintings, proving that at one time it had been a mansion of some considerable note. A very general tradition affirms that both this and Mildmay House were once in the occupation of Henry VIII., and that the latter was held by him for the purpose of keeping a number of his concubines, whom he used to very frequently visit.

There is every reason to believe that this tradition is not without a good foundation, inasmuch as this spot appears to have been a favourite retreat of many of the nobility at that time. A branch of the Dudley family, the Earl of Warwick, possessed the adjoining manor of Stoke Newington, and the following letter of Henry Algernon Percy, Earl of Northumberland, dated at "Newington Greene," was very probably written at one of the ancient houses above described. This letter was indited to Lord Cromwell, the then Secretary of State, for the purpose of exculpating the writer from the pretended suspicions of Henry in regard to a matrimonial contract supposed to have been made between the Earl and Ann Boleyn previous to her marriage with the King:—

"MASTER SECRETARIE,—

"This shall be to signify unto you that I perceive by Sir Reynold Carnaby, that there is supposed a pre-contract to be between the king and me. Whereupon I was not only heretofore examined upon mine oath before the Archbishops of Canterbury and Yorke, but also received the blessed Sacrament upon the same, before the Duke of Norfolk and other the king's highness council learned in the spiritual law; assuring you, Mr. Secretarie, by the saide oath and blessed bodie, which after I received and hereafter intend to receive, that the same may be *my damnation* if ever there were any contract of marriage between her and me.

"At Newington Greene, the 28th day of May, in the 28th year of the reigne of our sovereign lorde King Henry VIII.

"Your assured,

"NORTHUMBERLAND."

The Earl of Northumberland, who, according to a letter dated at Hackney, died the year following, is said to have prodigally given away a great part of his lands and inheritance to the king and others; which, indeed, is evident from numerous letters in his own handwriting still in existence. It is not unlikely, therefore, that in this manner one or both of the houses mentioned came into the king's possession; they might have been given by the earl to avert suspicion, for it was no joke for a courtier in those days to fall under the suspicions of such a jealous and licentious monarch.

The tradition of Henry's resorting to this place is still further strengthened by the circumstance that a path or roadway leading from the south-east corner of the Green to the turnpike at Ball's-pond, is still known by the name of "*King Harry's Walk*," and has been called by that name for generations past. In January, 1819, a man digging in a field behind Mildmay House, and adjoining this walk, found, at about two feet and a half from the surface, a curious old Roman ring of the purest gold, and not much corroded or damaged; the scroll-work on the sides was of good workmanship, and was apparently embellished with Roman enamel; three remaining stones (one being lost) were inferior diamonds, unequal in size and rudely set. Through a lens the whole had a very handsome appearance; the bunch of diamonds and its setting resembled a basket of fruit, supported by the scroll-work up the sides. From the size of the ring it appeared to have been worn by a lady, probably by one of the favourites of Henry VIII., and might have been lost while taking a stroll in the ground. This ring fell into the possession of Thomas Windus, Esq., of Stoke Newington-road.

Newington-green has had, however, other inhabitants, though, perhaps, not so great in political station, yet far more honourable and useful to society than Henry VIII. Towards the close of the seventeenth century many of the ejected and silenced Nonconformist ministers were living at Newington-green. The "Nonconformist Memorial" mentions, amongst others, Luke Milbourn, M.A., whose wife kept a school here by which she supported herself and her husband, he not being permitted to teach on account of his nonconformity. Charles Morton, M.A., was another ejected minister of that period, who took up his residence here; he kept an academy and educated scores of young ministers. The Rev. M. Starkey, of St. John's College, Cambridge, and Mr. Jonathan Screw, of the same University, also took shelter here after being turned out of their livings. At the academy of Charles Morton, Daniel Defoe, the author of that book of our boyhood, "Robinson Crusoe," was educated. His father had sent him to this school when twelve years old, intending that he should be brought up to the ministry, but it does not appear that he ever took upon himself that office. In Defoe's own account of his being intended for the ministry, he writes in a periodical paper of the time, called the *Review* : "It is not often I trouble you with any of my divinity; the pulpit is none of my office. It was my disaster first, to be set apart *for* and then be set apart *from* the honour of that sacred employ." All the education Defoe received was at Newington-green, where he remained at school four years. He was afterwards, for a considerable time, an inhabitant of the place.

Another distinguished resident of Stoke Newington was Samuel Wright, D.D., who died at his residence here, April 3, 1746. He was the son of a Nonconformist minister of Bedford, Notts. He was the author of many religious works, among which was a treatise on the "New Birth," which is said to have gone through fifteen editions; and he also wrote the hymn, "Happy hours, all hours excelling." In the preface to one of his works he says, "I had rather be the author of the small book that shall be instrumental in saving a soul from sin and death, than of the finest piece of science and literature in the world that leads only to accomplishments for the present state of being." In the pulpit he was so remarkably eloquent, especially in prayer, that Dr. Herring, Archbishop of Canterbury, is said to have attended the meeting-house where he used to minister, with a view to obtain hints for his own improvement in elocution. Mr. Wright, at the time of his death, gave nearly £20,000 to charitable uses. In his will, among other items, are the following:—

"*Item:* To six Nonconformist ministers of good life and conversation, and not worth £200 each in the world, each £100.

"*Item:* To six honest sober clergymen of temper and moderate principles to their dissenting brethren, and not worth £200 a year each, or provided with a living of upwards of £40 a year, each £100.

"*Item:* To forty poor decayed families that have come to poverty by losses and misfortunes unavoidable, each £100.

"*Item:* To forty poor widows of upwards of fifty years of age, and not worth £50 any one of them, each £50.

"*Item:* To forty poor maidens, whose parents formerly lived well, and now come to decay, and have not £100 each to their portion, each £100."

Large sums were also bequeathed to hospitals and institutions, £13,000, besides landed property, to his relations and friends, and the residue to the widows of Nonconformist ministers.

The Presbyterian Chapel, as it is called, on the north side of Newington-green, must not pass unnoticed in connection with this spot, a congregation having been established here soon after the Reformation. Lewis states, "it is certain, from the operation of the Act of Uniformity, passed in the reign of Charles II., Newington-green became one of the strongholds of dissent, several of the ejected clergy making it their place of abode, and though for a time prohibited from teaching or preaching, eventually succeeded in the establishment of a succession of academies, one alone of which it is said 'educated some scores of Nonconformist ministers as well as many other good scholars.' It was not, however, till the year 1708, in the reign of Anne, that the congregation who worshipped at a meeting-house were enabled to buy the ground and build the present chapel." It is a substantial brick- building of nearly square form, with the high tiled projecting roof common at the time of its erection ; it is fitted up in a plain but comfortable manner. Though holding its ancient name of "Presbyterian," the doctrine we believe now preached there is known by the name of "Unitarian," a change which was gradually brought about by some of its ministers, and which is greatly at variance with that taught by the Puritans and the early Nonconformists who established the Church, denying as it does the foundation-stone of the Church — the God-head of the Saviour. Among the monumental inscriptions in the interior of the chapel is a tablet to the memory of Mrs. Barbauld, the well-known authoress, whose husband was minister there. It is as follows :—

" In Memory of
ANNA LETITIA BARBAULD,
Daughter of John Aikin, D.D.,
And wife of the Rev. Rochemont Barbauld,
Formerly the respected
Minister of this Congregation.
She was born at Kibworth, in Leicester,
March 9th, 1825.

Endowed by the Giver of all Good,
With wit, genius, poetic talent, and a vigorous understanding, she employed those high gifts in promoting the cause of humanity, peace, and justice, of civil and religious liberty, of pure, ardent, and affectionate devotion."

The well-known Samuel Rogers, author of the "Pleasures of Memory," and other poems, and who lately died at his residence in St. James's, was born in that part of Stoke Newington situated in the parish of Islington, July 30th, 1763. His benevolence towards deserving members of the literary profession, and the kind encouragement he always gave to struggling talent, has caused his name to to be held in affectionate remembrance by many who are now famous and influential through such well-timed assistance.

Ball's Pond.

GEORGE MORLAND.—THE "BARLEY MOW."

BALL'S-POND was formerly a spot famous for the exercise of bull-baiting and other brutal sports ; it was much resorted to by the lower order of people from all parts of the metropolis, and in fine weather, on the Sunday afternoons, was frequently the scene of drunkenness and fighting. It derived its name from John Ball, the proprietor of a well-known house of entertainment called the "Salutation," about the middle of the seventeenth century. A large pond adjoined this house, frequented by duck-hunters, which by degrees became associated with the name of its proprietor, and hence "Ball's-Pond." This pond was filled up about the beginning of the present century. A copper token, which coin it was common for tradespeople to use at that period owing to the scarcity of a copper circulating medium, and which were generally stamped with something striking in connection with the neighbourhood in which they were circulated, was issued by John Ball, and is still preserved with the following inscription upon it:— "John Ball, at the 'Boarded House' near Newington-greene." On the one side are the words "His penny;" on the other, two figures saluting each other.

The "Rosemary Branch," erected in 1783, and situated at the meeting of the parishes of Shoreditch and Islington, also had a large pond of about an acre, chiefly supplied by the waste water of the New River, which was frequented by somewhat the same description of company as the above. Some years ago, on the west side of a lane called "Frog-lane," which ran at the back of the Clothworkers' Almshouses, at the bottom of Britannia-row, in the Lower-street, stood a place called the "Barley Mow," made notorious by being at one time the residence of that dissipated character, but great natural genius, George Morland, whose exquisite paintings of rural scenery are now so highly prized by connoisseurs, and which are always looked upon with pleasure by the visitors to our picture galleries. This eccentric but foolish man, having casually become a visitor at this house, in his stroll round the suburbs in the search of subjects, took such a liking to the establishment, that he remained there several months, and during that time he painted a few of his best pictures. His attention, however, was for the most part devoted to the degrading vice of getting drunk in the company of low and vulgar-bred associates. In fact he may be said to have painted only for drink, and generally his most delightful "bits" came into the possession of his lawyer, to whom he was continually indebted for extricating him from the difficulties daily arising from his many indiscretions; others fell into the hands of mercenary and ill principled acquaintances, who, taking advantage of his drunken moments, were pressing in their applications for specimens of his art, and which it is to be regretted, he would often in such moods, transfer to those who would join in the pleasures of the bottle for a very trifling consideration. Whilst at the "Barley Mow" he would frequently apply at a farm-yard opposite for portions of old cart-harness, saddles, collars, &c., which he copied into his sketch-book, and if he observed any rustic-looking character to whom he took a fancy, pass

down the road, he would send after him and obtain a sitting, generally remunerating the individual with something to drink and a shilling.

He would sometimes, in a sober and serious mood, determine to begin and finish a picture in his best style, one that when finished, should procure him a good sum; and for this purpose (according to the nature of the subject fixed upon), he would send to Billingsgate for fine and handsome fish to copy in his work, or explore the farm-yard for animals and objects suited to his purpose; but the same fatuity which attended him through life seldom permitted him to accomplish any work of this kind which he happened to take in hand. The fish would remain in his apartment till it was unfit for the table or his picture; and the work was accordingly scamped, the picture sent to market, and the supply of cash which it produced, though comparatively small, was sufficient to answer the exigencies of the moment, which was all that appeared to give any concern to this compound of genius and vice.

An anecdote is related of Morland while staying at the "Barley Mow" characteristic of his skill and versatility of talent. Observing a portrait of the landlord in one of the rooms which had been painted at a time when the said individual had worn his hair powdered and tied in a *queue*, but which he had subsequently been induced to exchange for a flowing peruke, Morland remarked that the picture was not like the original by reason of this difference in the head-dress, and offered to supply his host's likeness with a handsome brown wig, such as then adorned his head, adding, "that if he did not like it when done, he would replace his old head of hair on the picture for him." This alteration was agreed to, and a most striking resemblance of the landlord was shortly produced.

Copenhagen House and Fields.

THERE are but few residents in the north of London, who do not remember Copenhagen House, with its tea-gardens, cricket-matches, foot-racing, boxing, wrestling, skittling, pigeon-shooting, games at fives and racquet, cock-fighting, and bull-baiting—the head-quarters of what is generally known among the sporting fraternity as the "fancy," with fustian-jackets, "Newgate-knockers," and surly bull-dogs—every vestige of which is now swept away and numbered with the things of the past,—its site being covered by the New Cattle Market.

In looking over an old print in "Camden's Brittanica," published in 1695, and which, in the map of London, he describes as "Coopenhagen House," we observe a handsome country residence, surrounded by wooden palings and embowered in trees. On the eastern side of the house is a kind of detached room, to which an entrance is gained by a flight of wooden stairs. A country stile is in close connection with its western side, and before the house is a large pond in which ducks and other fowl are swimming. The country is completely open to the east, west, and north, and the whole neighbourhood has a secluded air of rusticity. Such is a description of Copenhagen House more than a century-and-a-half ago. It is traditionally said to have derived its name from the circumstance of a Danish prince or ambassador having resided there during the great plague of London, in King Charles's time. Another account, however, states, that on some political occasion, about the year 1620, when a great number of Danes resorted to the English capital, the house was opened by a person of that nation, and was much frequented by his countrymen resident in the metropolis. This latter tradition refers to the reign of James I., whose wife it will be recollected was a Danish princess (Anne of Denmark), and whose brother, the King of Denmark, paid a visit to London, accompanied by a host of his subjects.

Copenhagen House, or rather the oldest portion of it (which did not include the long-room), was about 250 years old. It is certain that upwards of a century ago, the house was licensed for the sale of beer, wines, and spirits, and for refreshments as a tea-house. There were gardens and grounds for skittles and Dutch pins. Before the country north of King's-cross was covered with houses, the views of the western district of the metropolis were very fine. Indeed, on a fine clear summer's day, even now, from that part of Maiden-lane between the "City of London Tavern" and New Copenhagen House, the glittering towers of the Crystal Palace, St. Paul's, Westminster Abbey, the New Houses of Parliament, and in consequence of the Thames taking a peculiar bend, the shining waters of the river, through the arches of Westminster-bridge, can be seen.

About the year 1770 Copenhagen House was kept by a person named Harrington, at whose decease the business was continued by his widow, wherein she was assisted several years by a young woman from Shropshire. Mr. Hone, the editor of the "Every Day Book," says, "that this female assistant afterwards married a person named Tomes, who kept a lodging-house at Islington, and from her he received the information that at the time of the London riots in the year 1780, a body of the rioters passed Copenhagen House on their way to attack the seat of Lord Mansfield at Caen Wood, but happily they did not attack the place. This so alarmed Mrs. Harrington and her maid that at their request Justice Hyde sent a party of soldiers to protect the establishment until the riots were quelled. During the time of the riots she remembered seeing from Copenhagen House in one night nine large fires burning in different parts of the metropolis."

Mr. Hone was also informed by the same person of a burglary which took place at Copenhagen House while she was in service there, and which at the time made a great noise not only in Islington but throughout the metropolis. Its details, and the Dick Turpin style in which it was committed, forcibly illustrate the lawlessness of the times. It was narrated as follows:—

"On the New Year's Day previous to the

above (the riots just mentioned) the house was broken into by burglars after the family had retired to rest. They first forced the kitchen-window, and mistaking the salt-box in the chimney-corner for a man's-head, fired a ball through it. They then hastily rushed up-stairs with a dark lantern, tied the man and maid-servant to the bed, and gagged them. They then burst open the lower panel of Mrs. Harrington's bed-room door, during which, knowing they were burglars, she contrived to secrete fifty sovereigns between the mattrass of her bed. On gaining an entrance three of them rushed to her bedside, armed with cutlass, crow-bar and pistol, while a fourth remained to watch outside. They then demanded Mrs. Harrington to deliver up her money, and upon her denying the possession of any, they wrenched her drawers open with the crow-bar, refusing to use the keys which she offered to them. In these they found about ten pounds belonging to her daughter, a little child whom they threatened to murder if she did not cease crying. After packing up all the plate, linen, and clothes which they could collect in readiness to carry off, they proceeded to the cellar, set all the barrels running, smashed the wine bottles, spilt the liquors, and slashed a large round of beef with their cutlasses. From this wanton destruction, they reserved sufficient to carouse with in the kitchen, where they ate, drank, and sang till late in the morning. Ere they finished their carousal they resolved to *pinch* the 'old woman' the landlady, who lay in terror listening to their brutal orgie. Upon this resolve they accordingly rushed up stairs in an excited state, and by the most horrible threats and violence soon obtained from her a disclosure of the hidden fifty pounds. This rather appeared to enrage than pacify them, and they proposed cutting her throat for the deception she had practised towards them in concealing the money. That crime, however, was not perpetrated, and they departed with their plunder." .

Rewards were offered by the Government and by the parish of Islington for the apprehension of these burglars, but nothing was discovered until the following May, when one of them named Clarkson was taken, and hopes of mercy tendered to him if he would turn King's evidence, and reveal the names of his accomplices, which he did. This man was a watchmaker in Clerkenwell, and the other three were also tradesmen. The information given led to the discovery of the robbers, and they were tried and executed. Clarkson the watchmaker, was pardoned, though he afterwards was hung for the rob-

bery of a box of plate from the "White Horse Inn," Fetter-lane. The above striking account reveals the unprotected state of property in the vicinity of London at that period. That a party of burglars should be able without any molestation to remain and boisterously carouse in a public dwelling-house for several hours, and then to decamp laden with booty with as great a leisure as if they were moving off some private property of their own, can scarcely be realised by the well-protected inhabitants of Islington of the present day.

The robbery at Copenhagen House was so far mitigated to Mrs. Harrington, that she obtained a subscription considerably more in amount than the value of the money and the property she had lost. Her landlord remitted her a year's rent of the premises, which at that time was £30. The notice of the robbery increased the visitors to the house, and new rooms were built to accommodate the influx. The house, too, became soon afterwards celebrated for fives playing. The circumstance which led to this is related by Mr. Hone as follows:—"I made the first fives balls," said Mrs. Tomes to me, "that was ever thrown up at Copenhagen House. One Hickman, a butcher at Highgate, a countryman of mine, used the house, and *seeing me country* we talked about our country sports, and amongst the rest I told him we would have a game some day. I laid down the stone in the ground myself, and against he came again made a ball. I struck the ball the first blow and he gave it the second, and so we played, and as there was company they liked the sport and it got talked of. This was the beginning of the fives play, which has since become so famous at Copenhagen House."

The game of fives was the "hand tennis" of times past. Hand-ball was played in the days of Homer, for he introduces the Princess Corayra, daughter of Alcinous, King of Phæcia, amusing herself with her maidens at hand-ball:—

"O'er the green mead the sporting virgins play,
   Their shining veils, unbound along the skies;
Tost and retost, the ball incessant flies."

It is related of St. Cuthbert, who lived in the seventh century, "that when he was eight years old, as he played at the ball with other children, suddenly their stood amongst them a 'fayre young chylde,' who admonished Cuthbert against 'vayne playes,' and seeing him take no heed, he fell down, wept, rose, and wrung his hands; then Cuthbert and the other children left their play and comforted him. Suddenly he vanished away, then he knew verily that it was an angel, and fro and forth on he left all such vain playes and never used them more."

Fives play at Copenhagen House was made celebrated by a man named Cavanagh, who frequently sported there. A memoir of this most famous of fives players, by Mr. Hazlitt, first appeared in the *Examiner* of February 17, 1819; amongst the remarks it contained the following is extracted:—

"It is not likely that any one will now see the game of fives played in its perfection for many years to come, for Cavanagh is dead and has not left his equal behind him. He could always tell the degree of force necessary to be given to a ball, and the precise direction in which it should be sent. He did his work with the greatest of ease; never took more pains than was necessary, and whilst others were fagging themselves to death, was as cool and collected as if he had just entered the court. Cavanagh was an Irishman by birth, and a house-painter by profession. One day he laid aside his working dress and walked up, in his best clothes, to the 'Rosemary Branch,' to have an afternoon's pleasure. A person accosted him and asked him if he would have a game, so they agreed to play for half-a-crown a game and a bottle of cider. The first game began; it was seven, eight, ten, thirteen, fourteen, all. Cavanagh won it. The next was the same. They played on, and each game was hardly contested. 'There,' said the unconscious fives-player, 'there was a stroke which *Cavanagh* could not take. I never played better in my life, and I cannot win a game. I do not know how it is!' However, they played on, Cavanagh winning every game, and the bye-standers drinking their cider and laughing all the while. In the twelfth game, when Cavanagh was only four and the stranger thirteen, a friend came in, who, recognising the Irishman, said, 'What, are you here, Cavanagh!' The words were no sooner pronounced than the astonished player let the ball drop from his hand, saying, 'What! have I been breaking my heart all this time to beat Cavanagh!' and refused to make another effort. 'And yet, I give you my word,' said Cavanagh, telling the story with triumph, 'I played all the while with my clenched fist.'

"Cavanagh would play for wagers and dinners against the wall of Copenhagen House

which supported the kitchen chimney, and it is authentically stated that the cooks on hearing a louder knock against the wall than usual, used to exclaim, ' Ah, that's the Irishman's ball !' and the joints that were cooking round the fire would tremble on the spits."

During the end of the last century and the commencement of the present, fives play was one of the chief diversions at Copenhagen House. On a Sunday morning, during the same period, the fives ground was generally filled with bull-dogs and ruffians, who lounged and drank to intoxication. As many as fifty to sixty bull-dogs have been seen tied up to the benches at once, while their masters drank, swore, and made match after match, then went out and set the dogs to fight before the house amid the uproar of idlers attracted by its bad name. This scene lasted throughout every Sunday forenoon, when the mob dispersed, the vicinity being terribly annoyed by the yells of the dogs, and the quarrelling of their masters on their return home. There was also a common field to the east of the house where bulls were baited, hence is was called "the bullfield." Here the excesses caused so much scandal in the neighbourhood that the magistrates, after repeatedly warning Tooth, the landlord, took away his license, and it was granted to another man, named Bath, who made it a rule to draw no beer, nor afford refreshment to any one who had a bull-dog at his heels. At the time of its destruction it was kept by a Mr. Garratt, of whom the Corporation of the City purchased the few years' lease it had to run.

In 1812 it was proposed by a company of projectors to bring sea water through iron pipes from the coast of Essex to Copenhagen Fields, and construct baths, which, according to the proposal, would yield twelve and-a-half per cent on a capital of £200,000, but the subscription list was not filled up, though the names of several eminent physicians sanctioned the undertaking.

In the year 1827 a London publication remarks: "This year, the Spanish and Italian refugees have resorted to this house in great numbers, and played many famous matches. Nothing, we are sure, can be more retired than the garden formed into bowers for visitors, and if the building mania should not recover, age will give the young plantations beauty, pleasure, and effect. Two new roads are made near Copenhagen House; the one leading from Kentish-town to Holloway; the other, from Holloway to Pentonville." The roads referred to are the Camden-road and the Caledonian-road, or " Chalk-road " as it was formerly called, both of which were constructed about the above date

Mr. Hone, to whose interesting book, published in 1827, we are largely indebted for this description of Copenhagen House, and of whom, on many occasions, Sir Walter Scott writes in terms of the highest praise, says,— "From very early impressions he could well recollect the meadows on the Highgate side of Copenhagen House. I have often rambled in them in summer time when I was a boy, to frolic on the new-mown hay, or explore the wonders of the hedges and listen to the songs of the birds. Certain indistinct apprehensions of danger arose in me from the rude noise of the visitors at Copenhagen House, and I scarcely ventured near enough to observe more than that it had drinking benches outside and boisterous company within. No house of the kind commands so extensive and uninterrupted a view of the metropolis and the immense western suburb, with the heights of Hampstead and Highgate, and the rich intervening meadows. Those nearest to London are now rapidly being destroyed for their brick earth, and being covered with houses, though from Copenhagen-street, which is built on the green lane from White Conduit House, there is a way to the footpath leading to Copenhagen House, from the row of handsome cottages called 'Barnsbury-park.' The latter buildings are in the manor of Berners, or Bernersbury, otherwise Barnsbury, the name being derived from the Berners family, of whom the most distinguished individual was John Bouchier, the last Lord Berners, and 'the fifth writer in order of time, among the nobility.' He was the author of a comedy actually acted in the great church of Calais, after vespers, of which town he held the appointment, by command of King Henry VIII.; he also translated several works, and particularly 'Froissart's Chronicles,' out of French into our maternal English tongue.

"West of Barnsbury-park, and close to the footpath from thence to Copenhagen House, are the supposed remains of a Roman encampment. It is a square of about one and twenty-feet, surrounded by a ditch, with a high embankment or breast-work to the west. This is presumed to have been a position oc-

cupied by Paulinus, the Roman general, when he destroyed eighty thousand of the Britons under Boedicea, in a memorable engagement supposed to have been fought from this place, in the fields of Pentonville, and in the plain at Battle-bridge. From Battle-bridge up Maiden-lane, and from Barnsbury-park, there are still footways to Copenhagen House, which, from standing alone on an eminence, is visible from every open spot for miles around."

In the early part of the French Revolution, the fields in the neighbourhood of Copenhagen House, became celebrated as a place for public meetings, convened by the "London Corresponding Society," and which created much alarm. The most remarkable of these was one held on October 26th, 1795, when not less than 40,000 people collected, and were harangued by different Chartist speakers, who threw out treasonable hints to the mob to attend to the circumstance of the King's going to the House of Parliament on the 29th. Accordingly, on that day an immense crowd assembled in the park, with the most desperate designs of mischief; but the king, although he was shot at, and otherwise incurred great risk, fortunately escaped unhurt.

On the 21st of April, 1834, an immense number of persons connected with the trades' unions assembled in Copenhagen Fields, prior to forming part of a procession of 40,000 men to Whitehall, for the purpose of presenting a petition to his Majesty, signed by 260,000 unionists, on behalf of their fellows, convicted at Dorchester for administering illegal oaths. Among the principal leaders of the unionists was the late celebrated Robert Owen, also the Rev. Dr. Wade, who appeared in his full, canonicals, and wore his robe of black silk with crimson collar round his neck. Still later than the foregoing and fresh in the memory of most residents in Islington, are the political meetings of 1848, and the Kossuth demonstration a short time afterwards.

A few years hence, and the New Cattle Market itself, which occupies the site of Copenhagen Fields, will be far away from the green fields, and in the midst of a busy and densely populated neighbourhood.

Islington Green.

THE OLD "QUEEN'S HEAD."

ISLINGTON GREEN was granted to the parish by the Lord of the Manor, and its "bit" of verdure imparts a cheerful appearance to the main thoroughfare of Islington. It is now decently railed in and seats provided, but in former times it used to be a depository for a great part of the filth, and dust, and dirt of the town; when, however, it came into the possession of the local authorities the nuisances were ordered to be removed under the direction of the trustees appointed in 1777. The watch-house, together with the cage, engine-house, and a pair of stocks, stood about the centre of the Green, until the watch-house was rebuilt at its southern extremity; the engine-house behind was erected in 1808. Since the passing of the Reform Act Islington Green has been made the place for the principal polling booth for the Borough of Finsbury.

At the north-west corner of the Green stood the old "Fox" public-house, rebuilt some years ago. It was a very ancient wooden structure, and a large chestnut tree used to stand in front of it, surrounded by wooden benches, and it thus became a favourite resort in the summer time for those who indulged in a glass and a pipe. It was kept by a landlord named Prince, who received a classical education, and was famed for his home-brewed ales and for capping Latin verses.

Another old and particularly famous place of entertainment in the Lower-road, was the "Queen's Head," said to have been built by Sir Walter Raleigh, and named in compliment to his royal mistress, Elizabeth. If, however, he did not erect it, as some assert, it is probable he made use of it as one of his smoking taverns; for in the 30th year of Elizabeth's reign, Raleigh obtained a patent to make licenses for the keeping of taverns and retailing of wines throughout England, and this being one of the taverns licensed by him, it is thought that the "Queen's Head" was adopted as the sign of the house, out of respect to Elizabeth. Whatever the true origin of the house, there can be no doubt it was one of the most perfect specimens of ancient domestic architecture in the vicinity of London, being a strong wood and plaster building of three lofty stories, projecting over each other in front, and forming bay windows supported by brackets and carved figures. When it was pulled down the floor of the front parlour was four feet below the level of the highway, though at one time it is stated that people went up steps into it. The interior apartments consisted of oak-panelled wainscots and stuccoed ceilings. The ceiling of the principal parlour was ornamented with carved dolphins, cherubs, and acorns, and surrounded by borders of wreathed fruit and foliage, and in the centre there was a medallion surrounded by cherubims and glory. Plays were formerly acted in this tavern, and a play-bill of the reign of George II., in which it is stated "that the play of the Fair Penitent and the Lying Valet will be acted by a company of comedians at the Queen's Head in the Lower-street, Islington," may still be seen, and is, we believe, in the possession of the landlord.

Tradition states this house as having also been tenanted by Sir Francis Burleigh, and Dr. Ellis observes that in the yard of a neighbouring tenement, two lions, carved in wood, the supports of the Cecil arms, were found buried. Whatever traditionary stories may be attached to the building, it is quite evident that it was erected about the time of Elizabeth. This complete and interesting specimen of an ancient hostelry was pulled down in 1829, and was superseded by the modern tame erection. The oak parlour of the old building is still, however, preserved in the new one, and is well worth the trouble of a visit from the curious. The destruction of the house is thus noticed in the *Courier* of October 21, 1829:—" The exertions of a number of labourers have at last accomplished that which has withstood the encroachments of Old Father Time for three centuries. At the dawn of Monday the work of dissolution commenced, and by the end of the week it is calculated the workmen will have demolished the 'Old Queen's Head' to the ground. On stripping the roof the flooring of a range of rooms was discovered, as also part of a flight of stairs. This fact has induced several antiquarians to think that at one time the house itself was a storey or two higher. The gutters on the roof are of the most spacious description ; they are composed of lead at least a quarter of an inch thick ; that on the roof is said to weigh a ton and a half. The flue of the chimney-parlour was found to be nine feet square throughout, and fifteen thousand bricks were used in its construction. The stone-work of the parlour mantel-piece is eight inches in thickness, the girders, groins, flooring, and other timbers, principally oak, are crooked and rudely hewn from one tree. The building material was sold on Saturday, and antiquarians bought various lots at high prices. The mantel in the parlour, on which is carved the story of Diana and Acteon, was bought by Mr. Bird, of the 'Yorkshire Stingo,' in the New-road, for £60. Beneath the flooring of the ground-floor rooms was found a considerable quantity of sand and a beautifully bright and new gold piece of the reign of William and Mary, being a 5s. 4d. gold coin, which is in the possession of the landlord."

According to the quantity of brick and timber found in the "Queen's Head," it appears that "houses used to be *houses*" in those days, and not the flimsy mushroom things of the present time. The method of erecting buildings in Elizabeth's age was more like ship-building than the construction of a common house, the framework of dwellings being constructed of beams of timber of enormous size laid transversely over one another. The houses in the cities and towns were built in a manner to cause each story to lean over its lower story, so that when the streets were not very wide, the people at the top from opposite houses might not only talk and converse with each other, but even shake hands together.

𝕎ard's 𝕻lace.

WARD'S PLACE in the Lower-road derives its name from a very interesting ancient fabric which stood upon this spot, and which was taken down in the year 1800—once the residence of Robert Dudley, the famous Earl of Leicester. It was a noble mansion of the Elizabethan order of architecture, and its internal decorations consisted of a variety of ornaments, beautifully painted, in stucco, carved work, and stained-glass. A great quantity of the stained glass that adorned this building came into the possession of Samuel Ireland, Esq., of Norfolk-street, Strand, who was also in possession of a book containing drawings of different objects in the house copied previous to its destruction. Some of the windows of painted-glass were especially beautiful, and contained Scriptural and historical subjects. In one of the upper rooms of the house on a glass-window there was the device of a person writing at a table, and apparently taking an account of the money lying before him, one piece of which he held in his left hand. All the apparatus of his employment, such as pen-knife, account-book, ink-horn, and pen, were executed with great faithfulness, as well as the furniture and utensils of the room in which he was seated. This subject was no doubt intended to represent the parable of the "Faithful Steward." On the second-floor was a finely executed stained-glass window of the "Prodigal Son." There were also some very fine figures of saints in an upper-room, some more than half-a-yard long. One of these figures, by the nimbus round his head, and the lion at his feet, was probably intended for St. Mark. In the left hand was borne what appeared to be the foundation of a stone pillar, which, with the sword, lion, and armour, intended to typify the strength, durability, and defence of the Gospel. It is somewhat remarkable, that notwithstanding the variety of ornament and works of art with which the building abounded, not a single date was discovered.

A number of conjectures were started as to the origin of " Ward's Place," but the most probable is that it was built by Sir Thomas Lovel, Knight, a person of considerable note in the reigns of Henry VII. and Henry VIII., and who was a resident of Islington. During its tenantcy by Robert Dudley, Earl of Leicester, it was often, no doubt, visited by Queen Elizabeth; and to this circumstance lies the foundation of all the stories of her connexion with the village ; and it may also serve to account for the introduction of the " Squire Minstrel from the worshipful toun of Islington," mentioned in the Earl's entertainment given to the Queen at Kenilworth.

Like many noble and once flourishing mansious, the house gradually descended in the social scale. About the year 1740 it was rented as a house for the purpose of inoculation, and afterwards became an appendage to the Small Pox Hospital in Cold Bath Fields, first established by Mr. Poole, in 1746. After being used for some time for the purpose above-mentioned, it was taken by the congregation once belonging to the church who now worship at the Independent Chapel. It was next converted into a soap manufactory, after which it was for a time used as the parish workhouse; and for some time before it was finally taken down it was let out in apartments to a number of working people at weekly rents.

Highgate Green.

THE VOLUNTEERS.—" DORCHESTER HOUSE."

THERE are few spots upon the summit of Highgate Hill possessing more interest than Highgate Grove—once known as Highgate Green, and the resort of the villagers for promenading in fine weather. It was once covered with a row of splendid elm trees, a few of which are still remaining exhibiting signs of great age. To fully realize the character attached to this locality, it must be borne in mind that the Grove, or Green, before the "Gate" was erected or the road cut over the hill to Finchley, terminated the public road northward, all beyond being the "Bishop's Wood," a large tract of which still remains, bordering the road on the right hand side, along Hampstead-lane, from Highgate to the "Spaniards' Tavern." There are many evidences of the Green having been the resort of the London folk in the summer time for the purposes of recreation and dancing. In an old comedy, entitled "Jack Drume's Entertainment" (1601,) on the introduction of the Whitsun Morris dance, the following song is given:—

" Skip it and frisk it nimbly, nimbly ;
Tickle it, tickle it lustily !
Strike up the tabour for the wenches' favour ;
Tickle it, tickle it lustily !

" Let us be seene, on Highgate Greene,
To dance for the honour of Holloway ;
Since we are come hither, let's spare for no leather,
To dance for the honour of Holloway."

An interesting incident occurred in connection with Hogarth at one of the inns which formerly stood near the Green. One Sunday, during his apprenticeship, he set out, with two or three companions, on an excursion to Highgate Green. The weather being hot they went into a public-house, where they had not been long before a quarrel arose between two persons in the same room. The quarrel waxed fierce till one of the disputants brought it to a close by striking the other on the head with a quart-pot, which cut him severely, and caused him to make such a hideous grin, that it presented Hogarth with too humourous a subject to be overlooked. He drew out his pencil and produced on the spot one of the most ludicrous figures imaginable, and, what rendered the sketch more valuable was that it exhibited an exact likeness of the man, with the portrait of his antagonist and the figures, in connection with the principal persons, gathered round him.

In the vicinity of Highgate Green formerly stood Dorchester House, once the residence of the Marquis of Dorchester. In the year 1685, one William Blake, a woollen draper in Maiden Lane, Covent Garden, set on foot a scheme to establish a hospital at Highgate, for the maintenance of fatherless boys and girls. He spent £5,000 by purchasing Dorchester House to carry out his plan, and published a very rare book, called "Silver Drops, or Serious Things," being a kind of exhortation to ladies to encourage the undertaking. The boys were to be taught painting, gardening, accounts and navigation, and to wear an uniform of blue lined with yellow. The girls to be taught to read, write, sew, starch, raise paste, and dress. The allowance of the housekeeper per day was one bottle of wine, three of ale, six rolls, and two dishes of meat. Subscriptions were collected and several children admitted. It was called the "Ladies' Charity School." At one time (1667), there were thirty-six boy scholars; and in 1675 the books belonging to the school, consisted of two English, eighteen Latin, and three Greek. The founder, William Blake, was, as will be imagined, rather a quaint character. He carried on his business at the sign of the "Golden Boy," at the corner of Maiden-lane, leading into Bedford-street, Covent Garden. He was exceedingly pious and earnest in the Protestant cause, and the motive which led him to found the school was for the purpose of diffusing the Reformed religion among the young. It did not, however, last long after his death, although it had the support of several ladies of rank. The book, "Silver Drops," had a frontispiece engraving of Dorchester House, as well as his own mansion at Highgate, and it also contained a number of notes, in most of which he lamented the want of encouragement, and complained, that by some people, he was treated as a madman.

THE HIGHGATE VOLUNTEERS OF 1801.

On the occasion of Napoleon's contemplated invasion, the inhabitants of Highgate immediately raised and supported during the war, a battalion of three hundred men, commanded by a field officer with the regulated compliment of captains, subalterns, non-commissioned officers, &c. The government provided the adjutants, the arms, and ammunition, but the clothing and all other expenses were defrayed by the voluntary subscriptions of the inhabitants. The colours were presented by the Countess of Mansfield, and the corps reviewed in 1805 by King George III., at Harrow Weald, and at subsequent periods by his Royal Highness the Duke of Cambridge, General Fox, and others, on Finchley Common, on all of which occasions the commanding generals expressed their thanks for the zeal displayed and their approbation of the efficient state of discipline the corps had attained, and the perfect manner in which they performed their various duties.

Their place of muster was most frequently the Grove, near the church, and their place of exercise Highgate Common, which, on fine summer evenings, used to be thronged by the fair sex to witness their various evolutions. An excellent band was maintained to enliven their proceedings. The colours of the corps were lately in the possession of Mr. Prickett, auctioneer, of Highgate. Only one or two of the 300 volunteers of 1801 are now alive to personally compare the past with the present.

THE "FOX AND CROWN."

Over the door of this inn, situated in the road down the hollow of the hill leading to Kentish Town, many, no doubt, have noticed a royal gilt coat-of-arms. This privilege, if such it can be called, was obtained by an interesting incident. On July 6th, 1837, her Majesty, accompanied by the late Duchess of Kent, was taking an airing round Highgate, when on arriving near to the "Fox and Crown" the horses suddenly became restive and set off at a fearful pace down the hill; fortunately, however, their progress was arrested by the prompt assistance of the innkeeper, and the royal party saved from an accident which threatened alarming consequences. The timely service thus rendered was rewarded by a licence being granted to the landlord, Mr. Turner, to place the royal arms in front of his house, and in addition, a suitable present was forwarded to him.

Union and Islington Chapels.

ROBERT BROWN, THE FOUNDER OF THE "INDEPENDENTS."

IN 1801 there were but one Episcopal and two Nonconformist places of worship in this parish. At that date, however, a number of gentlemen residing in the district, composed of members of the Established Church and of various Dissenting bodies, met together and formed themselves into a church. They first repaired an unfinished chapel which stood in Highbury Grove, and secured the services of the Rev. Thomas Lewis as their pastor, who was ordained to that office at Orange-street Chapel, in April, 1804, by Rowland Hill and others. This edifice, was soon found to be inconvenient for the majority of the inhabitants, and accordingly the present building in Compton-terrace was erected. It was called *Union* Chapel to indicate the union of Nonconformists and Episcopalians that worshipped there, and to maintain this union the Litany of the Church was used on the Sunday morning, and extempore prayer on Sunday evening; the communion was also administered to suit both parties. This arrangement continued till the year 1844, when the Episcopalian form of communion was discontinued, and in 1845 the use of the Liturgy was also given up. From that time the church became entirely Congregational, and is now governed in accordance with the discipline adopted by the Independents.

Union Chapel was first opened for divine service on the 30th of August, 1806, on which occasion two sermons were preached, the one by the Rev. T. Gauntlet, late Vicar of Olney, and the Rev. Dr. Bogue of Gosport. It is a pleasing, though not strictly architectural edifice, with a portico of six Ionic columns supporting an entablature, above which is a turret containing a clock. The interior is appropriately fitted up, and before the enlargement now taking place, contained accommodation for 1,000 persons. The galleries are pannelled with mahogany and inscribed in gilt letters with passages selected from the Bible. At a recent meeting it was resolved to enlarge the chapel by

25 feet increased length, giving 400 more sittings.

Mr. Lewis continued to labour with success till the time of his death on Sunday, February 29, 1852. He was interred in Abney-park Cemetery, and his name is still affectionately remembered by many of the inhabitants of Islington residing in the neighbourhood of his ministry. After having assisted for some years as co-pastor with Mr. Lewis, the Rev. Henry Allon, the present minister, was ordained on June 12th, 1844, by the Revs. Dr. Bennett, Dr. Harris, T. Lewis, J. Sherman, J. Sortain, J. Yockney, C. Gilbert, and J. Morris. His ministry has been greatly successful, there being at the present time 825 communicants in connection with it, including the branch establishments in Ward's-place and Spitalfields. There are also a great many institutions belonging to Union Chapel, all of which are in a flourishing condition. There are nine deacons, and 200 teachers belonging to the Ragged, Sunday, and other schools attached to it. The Bible classes have an average attendance of 250 persons, and some 40 people are engaged in out-door preaching and visiting every Sunday. There are also Maternal Societies, auxiliaries to the various missions, and a Tract Society which distributes 10,000 tracts yearly. Upwards of £2,000 is annually subscribed for the support of these institutions, in addition to the ordinary support of the ministry.

Mr. Allon took a leading part in compiling and editing the new Congregational Hymnbook, now so much in use by Independent churches.

ISLINGTON CHAPEL.

ISLINGTON CHAPEL had its origin in a place of worship erected in Church-street, in the year 1788, on part of a nursery ground in that locality. The building was first commenced by a local preacher named Ives, a blacksmith, residing in the parish, who, not being able to complete it for want of pecuniary assistance, it was for some time left in an unfinished state. Nevertheless it was preached in occasionally until finished and a regular minister appointed. Mr. Ives, it appears, used to accompany a local preacher of some fame at that time, named Jeremiah Garrett, who frequently preached at the " Old Rectifying House" in the Lower-road, and subsequently at the "Old Soap House," near the same spot. He also occasionally preached to the multitude on Islington Green on the Sunday afternoons, mounted upon a moveable rostrum, which was carried about from place to place upon the shoulders of the stalwart Ives. On these occasions Ives acted as assistant by giving out the hymns. Justice Cogan, a magistrate, however, interfered with the preaching of Garrett, and he was obliged to retire. Some time afterwards he became pastor of a chapel in Lant-street, Southwark, and in the title-page to one of his publications he styled himself "The Weather-beaten Watchman of the Lant-street Mountain."

In the year 1793 the building in Church-street became the property of Mr. Welch, a banker in Cornhill, who granted the lease for life to the Rev. Thomas Wills, who then resided in Church-row. This Mr. Wills was a descendant of the Rev. Jonathan Wills of Lantiglos, Cornwall, one of the two thousand ministers ejected in the reign of Charles II. In the year 1800, in consequence of bodily infirmity, Mr. Wills was compelled to retire, and he disposed of his interest in the chapel to the Rev. Evan John Jones, who was ordained pastor February 4th, 1800. The increase of the congregation under this gentleman led to its enlargement, and afterwards to the erection of the present chapel in the Upper-street, the first stone of which was laid on Wednesday, November 16th, 1814, by the Rev. Mr. Wilkes, and opened for divine service September 19th, the following year. It is a plain structure of brick, faced with cement and crowned with a turret, having the inscription, "ISLINGTON CHAPEL," written on its front. It affords accommodation for 1390 persons, of which 493 are free sittings.

The Rev. Mr. Jones died March 28, 1827, having preached the preceding evening as usual, and his place was filled by various ministers until the Rev. Charles Gilbert was appointed. On his resignation Mr. Dormer officiated, who shortly resigned, and the chapel was without any regular minister

for two years, when the Rev. B. S. Hollis, of Edmonton, the present minister, was appointed, who commenced his duties August 6th 1840.

In connection with Islington Chapel there have always been a number of charitable institutions,—a Sick Society, for visiting and relieving the sick at their own habitations, Sunday School, Tract Society, a branch of the London Missionary Society, and a Christian Instruction Society. The services at Islington Chapel have, for many years past, been conducted in accordance with the custom of the Independent or Congregationalist body, with which it is connected. An unfortunate dispute, has, however, lately arisen as to whether the "Liturgy" of the Church of England, which had it appears ceased to be read in the chapel for a number of years, should again be introduced. The minister, Mr. Hollis, appears to think he is justified in reviving the Liturgy because some of the doctrinal articles of the Church of England were formerly part of the regular worship of the place, and it is therefore breaking no law in so doing; upon this, those who disagree with its introduction argue that whatever the subsequent formula prescribed in the trust deed or elsewhere may have been *after* the property came into the possession of the Rev. T. Wills, it is quite certain that upon the *first* foundation of the chapel by Ives, the blacksmith, no formularies of the Church were used. At the same time during the ministry of Mr. Wills, it was stated in a printed address respecting the charity schools in connection with the chapel, that "the doctrinal articles of the Church of England are our basis, not, indeed, because they are articles of the Established Church, but for a much better reason, because they are *Bible truths*, and we love the Church on that account, retaining for the same reason her service in our chapels."

LOWER STREET CHAPEL.

THIS chapel is, we believe, the oldest Nonconformist place of worship in the parish, having been erected in 1744. It is a plain but commodious edifice. Its interior contains a handsome gallery approached by a flight of stairs situate in the body of the chapel. A high pulpit of polished wood stands against its south wall, and on its north side is a tablet to the memory of Mr. William Pearcy, a benevolent donor to the chapel.

For some time after the erection of this

place, the ministry was supplied by various Independent pastors until the year 1761, when the Rev. Mr. Gawsell was appointed minister. In the year 1768 Mr. Gawsell resigned his charge and retired to Bury St. Edmonds, where, almost immediately on his arrival, he died of the small-pox, having left the metropolis to avoid that fatal complaint. Nelson, in commenting upon this circumstance, makes the following striking remarks :—

" A remarkable example of the futility of human endeavours to avoid the all-wise dispensation of Providence was exhibited in the case of this gentleman. Never having had the small-pox he was particularly careful to shun every hazard of receiving the contagion. With this view he left Islington to retire into the country, where he hoped to be more secure from danger, but the very means used to escape the contagion was the cause of communicating it to him. A man whom he had employed to pack up his papers and his books for removal had recently had the complaint in his family, and through such agency it was conveyed to the minister, who had scarcely taken possession of his new habitation, when his mortal career was arrested by the hand of death."

It was during the ministry of Mr. Gawsell that a part of the congregation separated and worshipped in the old building previously described as occupying the site of Ward's-place, but which afterwards united with the old congregation. Upon the death of Mr. Gawsell, the Rev. Mr. Jennings was appointed pastor, during whose ministry the congregation much increased. This gentleman was succeeded by the Rev. John Yockney, of Old College, Homerton, who retained the pastorate for a long time. The Rev. C. Brake is now pastor. The chapel contains sittings for about 800. In connection with Lower-street Chapel is a Benevolent Society for visiting the sick and relieving the poor, a fund for supplying the children of the girls Sunday School with clothes at a reduced price, and auxiliaries to the London Missionary and the Christian Instruction Societies.

The above congregations, in conjunction with the members of the Established Church, and of two old-established Baptist churches, caused Islington to occupy a leading place in the history of religious progress in England, and has subsequently obtained for it the reputation of being the *quartier*-evangelical of the metropolis. Aided by a number of useful and benevolent laymen connected with the various churches and chapels, the parish has been rapidly supplied with the means of worship, and there is no district of London where the spiritual wants of the population are better attended to.

In connection with the subject of Congregational or Independent churches, it will be interesting to mention that Robert Brown, the founder of that influential body, was one of the earliest and most remarkable lecturers of this parish. The duty of lecturer consists in preaching a sermon every Lord's Day, either in the afternoon or evening as the ease may be, to ease the minister. This office Robert Brown held for some years at the parish church, though he afterwards separated himself from Episcopacy, and sternly opposed the discipline of the Church, which led to his being severely persecuted. A short history of this remarkable man will be found interesting.

ROBERT BROWN,

THE FOUNDER OF THE INDEPENDENTS.

AMONGST the early opponents of the Church of England after the Reformation the Brownists were, for a period of fifty years, the most considerable and powerful. While the Puritans in general allowed the Church of England to be a true church, though faulty in matters of discipline, Brown represented her " government as anti-Christian, her sacraments as superstitious, her Liturgy as a mixture of popery and paganism, and the mission of her clergy as no better than Baal's priests in the Old Testament." During the reigns of Elizabeth and James, while the Puritans vigorously assailed the Church, the Brownists, with even greater warmth, assailed the Puritans.

The first leader of this party was Robert Brown, born at Northampton in the middle of the 16th century. After studying divinity at Cambridge, he took a schoolmaster's situation at Southwark. He was then promoted to the office of lecturer to Islington, though at the time he had embraced the principles of the Puritans. He was of good family and related to the Lord Treasurer Burleigh, whose grandfather had obtained the singular privilege of wearing his cap in the king's presence. Brown was possessed of a very vehement temperament, which often carried him beyond the bounds of discretion and caused him to be severely treated.

However, such is the imperfection of our nature that in the most zealous a tincture of intoleration is often exhibited, and which, for the sake of such earnestness, ought not to be too severely condemned. His zeal established a body who firmly set themselves against the leanings which the church in the early days of the Reformation, had to Popery

In the year 1571 Robert Brown was cited before Archbishop Parker, at Lambeth, for inveighing against Episcopacy, but escaped punishment through the influence of his relatives. He nevertheless continued to preach against the discipline of the Church, and travelled through England, lecturing against bishops, ceremonies, ecclesiastical courts, ordaining of ministers, &c., until, after repeated arrests, excommunications, and imprisonments, he fled to Middleburgh, in Holland, where, in 1582, the first Independent church on record was formed under his pastoral care. Within three years, however, owing to some misunderstanding with his newly-formed church, he returned to England, when he was cited to appear before the Bishop of Peterborough. It is said that the solemnity of the censure passed upon him on that occasion, had such an effect upon him that he renounced his principles, and through the influence of the Earl of Exeter, a kinsman, obtained the rectory of Archarch, in Northamptonshire. The statement of the entire renunciation of his principles, may, however, be doubted, for he continued to the day of his death to be objectionable to the Church.

Fuller, the historian, who had some knowledge of Brown, in describing his last days, speaks in a very contemptuous tone of him. He says, " Robert Brown had a wife with whom he never lived, and a church in which he never preached; and as all the other scenes of his life were stormy and turbulent, so was his end. For, being poor and proud, and very passionate, he struck the constable of his parish for demanding rates; and being beloved by nobody, the officer summoned him before Sir Rowland St. John, a neighbouring justice, in whose presence he behaved with so much insolence, that he committed him to Northampton gaol. The decrepid old man, not being able to walk, was carried thither upon a feather bed, in a cart, where, not long after, he sickened, and died in 1630 aged upwards of eighty years, and boasting that he had been committed to two-and-thirty prisons, in some of which he could not see his hand at noon-day."

Fuller's account, as a staunch churchman, and therefore opposed to the principles of the Brownists, must only be regarded as his own view of the character of Brown. That he was quick-tempered, hasty, and even intolerant in many things, is not to be denied, but from the fact that he had been committed to " two-and-thirty prisons, in some of which he could not see his hand at noon-day," and also to glory in such, serves to prove the willingness with which he suffered in order to maintain what his conscience considered to be true and in accordance with the principles of the Gospel.

Though Brown had given up his connection with the sect he had formed, his followers increased with amazing rapidity, and for consistency, energetic zeal, and dauntless courage under cruel sufferings, the " Brownists" were behind no other sect whatever. In 1588 Francis Johnson, an eminent Brownist, was imprisoned and expelled from the University of Cambridge, for maintaining in a sermon the following :—

" 1st. That a particular form of Church government is prescribed in the Word of God.

" 2nd. That no other ought to be allowed.

" 3rd. That the Church of God ought to be governed by elders.

" 4th. That we have not this government.

" 5th. That the neglect to form this government is one of the chief causes of great ignorance and idolatry.

" 6th. That there ought to be an equality amongst ministers, which the Popish hierarchy and all who belong to it, do not like."

These principles were rapidly diffused and gave great uneasiness to the State. Desertion from church was punished as sedition, an enactment was passed which punished with a penalty of £25 a month, every absentee from the parish church. The weight of this enactment fell heavily upon the Brownists. A great number died in gaols, others were tried and sentenced to cruel deaths. Copping and Burke, clergymen of Suffolk, were, after seven years' imprisonment, hanged at Bury St. Edmonds, with Brown's books tied round their necks, the charge against them being " that they read, and induced others to read, Brown's writings." The Brownists then held their meetings in the fields and woods, and under the hottest persecution they increased rapidly. In 1590, in the reign of Elizabeth, they were said to have numbered twenty thousand, and in that year another act was passed in which all persons found at a conventicle or meeting, under pretence of religion, were to be committed to prison till they should conform. Again the oppression of this statute fell heavily upon the Brownists. Hiding themselves from the Bishop's officers and pursuivants, those in London met at a retired place in the fields at Islington, where a Protestant congregation had formerly assembled under similar circumstances in the reign of Mary. About fifty-six were apprehended on the Lord's Day while singing hymns, and sent two by two to different prisons in London. They suffered a long and miserable confinement, and many died under their barbarous usage, amongst whom was Roger Rippon. He expired in Newgate, and his fellow prisoners placed the following inscription upon his coffin :—

"This is the Corpse
of
ROGER RIPPON,
A servant of Christ, and her Majesty's faithful subject; who is the last of sixteen or seventeen which that great enemy of God, the Archbishop of Canterbury, with his High Commissioners, have murdered in Newgate within these five years, manifestly for the testimony of Jesus Christ. His soul is now with the Lord, and his blood crieth for speedy vengeance against that great enemy of the Saints."

The Brownists, notwithstanding, continued to increase, and in 1604 John Robinson, a Norfolk divine, who had suffered much for his nonconformity, emigrated to Leyden, in Holland, and formed a church on the model of the Brownists. This Robinson was a man of great piety and catholicity of spirit, and while he adopted the discipline of the Brownist sect, at once renounced the narrow prejudice that there was no true church but his own. Robinson is generally considered to be *the father* of the Independents, in whom the Brownists emerged, the latter, as a separate sect, disappearing after the Restoration.

The Independents maintain as a fundamental principle, that every society of believers united for religious worship is a perfect church within itself; that it possesses full power to regulate and control its affairs independent of all external control, such discipline being supposed to be a complete restoration of the primitive churches. When a church is about to be gathered, such as desire to become members make a confession of their faith in the presence of each other, and, signing a covenant, oblige themselves to walk together in the order of the Gospel. The whole power of admitting and excluding members, and the decision of controversies are in the brotherhood. Church officers for preaching and taking care of the poor are chosen from among themselves and separated to their several offices by prayer. They have the like power to depose any officer whom they find incapable or unfaithful in his duty. When the number of communicants is larger than can be accommodated at any one place, the church generally divides, and choosing new officers from among themselves, live together as sister churches. Any lay brother is allowed to give a word of exhortation in the church assembly.

Such are the principal points of government in the present Independent churches, first founded by Robert Brown. In 1851, according to the census then returned, they had 3,244 places of worship in England, with accommodation for one million and sixty-eight thousand persons,—in the nine years preceding 1851 Congregationalism adding one-third to the number of its chapels. Since the last-mentioned period it has, we believe, increased in a similar ratio. In point of faith there is no difference between the Independents and the Established Church, but only in matters of church form and government.

The "Three Hats."

IN the beginning of the present century, the group of taverns around the Turnpike Gate were visited by thousands of Londoners on account of their famous amusements and tea-gardens. In reference to the little interest and popularity which such places now-a-days enjoy it must be remembered that at that period the outskirts of London, within a walking distance, were the only places available for a day's pleasure in the country; there were no conveyances of any kind except a daily stage-coach, and as for a trip down the river, a sail to Gravesend and back in the lugger took a couple of days. Islington especially, was a favourite resort, and amongst the most frequented places near the part mentioned, were "Dobney's Tea Gardens," and the "Three Hats," which was rebuilt in 1839 in consequence of its roof being destroyed by fire. The latter is particularly alluded to by Mawworm in Bickerstaff's comedy of the "Hypocrite," wherein he says—"Till I went after him (Dr. Cantwell) I was always roving after fantastical delights. I used to go to the 'Three Hats' at Islington. It is a public-house. May be your ladyship may know it?"

In a field behind the "Three Hats" there used to be some noted entertainments of horsemanship and equestrian exercise, which for a long time were very popular, being visited not only by the people but also by the aristocracy. In the *Advertiser* of July 17, 1766, there appeared the following :—

"Yesterday his Royal Highness the Duke of York was at the 'Three Hats' at Islington, to see the astounding feats of horsemanship exhibited there. There were near 500 spectators."

In 1767 a celebrated equestrian named Sampson exhibited himself there, and issued the following notice to the public on the subject, which will give a tolerable idea what the "astounding" entertainments were :—

"*Horsemanship, April 20*, 1767.

"Mr. Sampson will begin his famous feats of horsemanship next Monday, at a commodious place built for that purpose in a field adjoining the 'Three Hats,' at Islington, where he intends to continue his performance during the summer season.

"The Doors to be opened at 4, and Mr. Sampson will mount at five.

"Admittance 1s. each.

"A proper Band of Music is engaged for the entertainment of those ladies and gentlemen who may be pleased to honour him with their company."

Another placard is as follows :—

"At Mr. Dingley's the 'Three Hats,' Islington.

"Mr. Sampson begs leave to inform the public, that besides the usual feats which he exhibits, Mrs. Sampson, to diversify the entertainment, and to prove that the fair sex are by no means inferior to the male, either in courage or agility, will this and every evening during the summer season, perform various exercises in the same art, in which she hopes to acquit herself to the universal approbation of those ladies and gentlemen whose curiosity may induce them to honour her attempt with their company.

"July, 1767."

"Mr. Coningham presents himself to the public, and as he has bought Mr. Sampson's horses, he will perform during this week every evening, at the 'Three Hats' at Islington.

"1st. He rides a gallop, standing upright on a single horse, three times round the room without holding.

"2nd. He rides a single horse at full speed, dismounts, fires a pistol, and performs that boasted feat of Hughes, leaping over him backwards and forwards forty times without ceasing. Also flies over the horses in full speed, leaps over one and two horses on full speed as they leap the bar, plays a march on the flute, without holding, upon two horses standing upright.

"The public are desired to take notice that I do not throw myself over the horses with my feet touching the horses' hind legs, but my feet over the saddles, and will perform every other feat that is performed by any horseman.

"Mr. and Mrs. Sampson will perform, to make these nights the completest in the kingdom,

"*The Tailor and the Sailor*,

Upon the drollest horses in the kingdom. The doors to be opened exactly at five and to mount at a quarter after five.

"Admittance front seats 2s; back seats, 1s.

"Mr. Coningham will engage to fly through a hogshead of fire upon two horses' backs without touching them, and for a single person will perform activity with any man in the world."

Mrs. Sampson was the first female equestrian, and these entertainments were also the first of the kind we read of in this country.

Near to the "Three Hats" was a place called "Dobney's Tea Gardens," kept by a Mrs. Ann Dobney, were there was a rival equestrian named Prince. These latter gardens occupied the ground between White Lion-street and Winchester-place, and were established as far back as 1728. They were also known as the "Jubilee Gardens." In the year 1771 the famous Hughes and Astley establishing themselves in St. George's Fields, Southwark, for exhibitions of a like nature, the popularity of the places at Islington greatly fell for equestrian entertainments, though they kept up their reputation as tea-gardens. In 1770 the house was shortly taken for a boarding-school, but it was soon changed to its original place of amusement, for in 1772, a man named Daniel Wildman, exhibited his bees here :—

"June 20, 1772.

"Exhibition of Bees on Horseback.

"At the 'Jubilee Gardens,' Islington, (late Dobney's) this and every evening until further notice (wet evenings excepted.)

"The celebrated Mr. Daniel Wildman will exhibit several new and amazing experiments, never attempted by any man in this or any other kingdom before. The rider standing upright, one foot on the saddle the other on the horse's neck, with a curious mark of bees on his head and face. He also rides standing upright in the saddle, with the bridle in his mouth; and by firing a pistol makes one part of the bees march over the table, and the other part swarm in the air and return to their hive again, with other performances too tedious to insert. The doors open at six, to begin at a quarter before seven. Admittance: Box and gallery, 2s., the other seats, 1s."

Highgate Hermitage and Pond.

THERE was formerly a hermitage or chapel on the summit of Highgate Hill, which Norden supposes stood on the site now occupied by Sir Richard Chomley's School. The hermitage was in the gift of the Bishop of London. In 1386 "Bishop Braybrooke of London, gave to William Lichfield, a poor hermit, the office of keeping our chapel at Highgate, and the house annexed to the said chapel, hitherto accustomed to be kept by other poor hermits." In 1531 William Forte was hermit. This William Forte was probably the last hermit, as in the year 1565 Queen Elizabeth granted the chapel, or hermitage, to Sir Richard Chomley, and in 1578 an entirely new chapel was built contiguous to the school which that knight had founded. It was erected as a chapel of ease for the inhabitants of Highgate.

In the registry of the Dean and Chapter of St. Paul's is a conveyance of this chapel to Sir Roger Chomley by Edmund Grindall, Bishop of London, in 1565. It was a brick building, of humble architectural character, with a small square tower at its western end. According to an inscription which was placed under the tower, the structure appears to have been enlarged since its first erection by "the pietie and bountie of divers honourable and worthie personages'" and it was likewise repaired at a considerable cost in the year 1772. The interior consisted of a chancel, nave, and south aisle. On the south wall was the monument of William Platt, Esq. (the founder of "Platt's Gift" to the poor), who died in 1637. At a short distance from this was a monument to the memory of Dr. Lewis Atterbury, LL.D., who was preacher at Highgate Chapel. On the chapel being pulled down, this monument was removed to Hornsey Church, of which Dr. Atterbury had been Vicar.

Old Highgate Chapel stood till 1832, when it was pulled down and the present church erected.

HIGHGATE POND.

THE present pond, near the Gate-house, was formed and excavated by the hermits of the old chapel, and the gravel they dug out was used by them for forming the roadway leading down the hill into Holloway. Fuller, in his "Worthies of England," says, "that the old Highgate hermits, by thus making this pond, did a two-handed charity. By digging out a hollow on the top of the hill a place was made to catch water where it was wanted, and plenty of material was had to make the valley clean and passable in winter."

Lauderdale-house.

LAUDERDALE HOUSE is situated on the left side of the hill-road, nearly opposite Cromwell House, and just on the borders of the parish. It is supposed to have been built about the year 1600, and for many years was the residence of the Earls of Lauderdale, eminent as statesmen and warriors. It is a fine old-fashioned mansion, its windows and terraces commanding extensive prospects of the metropolis. For some time it was the residence of Nell Gwynne, mistress of Charles II., and mother of the first Duke of St. Albans. A tradition is related concerning her while living there. She was very desirous of obtaining a title for her son, which she had for a long time been unsuccessful in gaining. The father, Charles II., being there one afternoon, it is stated she held the child out of the window, exclaiming, "If you do not do something for it, I will drop it." He immediately replied, "Save the Earl of Burford!" This story, however, is scarcely probable, the incident being opposed to Nell Gwynne's general character, and it might possibly have originated in some striking but less melodramatic method of putting an alternative.

FITZROY HOUSE.

THE above house was formerly the seat of Lord Southampton, and situated in the park adjoining Caen Wood. Lord Southampton was the Lord of the Manor of Tottenhall, or Tottenham Court, in whose family it still remains. In the rooms of the old mansion were portraits of Henry, the first Duke of Grafton, George, Earl of Euston, and Charles Duke of Grafton. The Duke of Buckingham resided at Fitzroy House in 1811. In 1828 the mansion was taken down and the park sub-divided and improved by the erection of several elegant villas.

Hagbush Lane.

A VERY small portion of this ancient and very interesting highway is yet remaining, but what there is left is known only to a few out of the many thousand inhabitants in Islington. At the south-east corner of the bridge which passes over the Great Northern Railway in the Caledonian-road, there is a little strip of a muddy lane which leads past the back of what is called the Grove in Pocock's Fields, and enters that place some little distance down. This road is still bordered by many noble old elm trees, and to the lover of local reminiscences a stroll down the narrow way will be found interesting, although in wet weather he must be careful to provide himself with a pair of stout boots, as the parish seems to have ignored this old public road and left it to take care of itself. With the exception of a few shovelfuls of cinders which the inhabitants of the Grove now and then throw down, that they may be enabled to enter their houses by the back way, nothing is ever done to render it passable to the ordinary foot passenger.

A few years ago, between the south end of Paradise-row, in the Liverpool-road, and a detached residence called "Paradise House," another part of this ancient thoroughfare was in existence, running westward of the Liverpool-road; it has, however, been intercepted from the part yet remaining.

Hagbush-lane derives its name from the old Saxon word *hæg*, which became corrupted into *hawgh*, and afterwards into *haw*, and is the name for the berry of the hawthorn; also the Saxon word *haga* signified a hedge or enclosure. *Hag* afterwards signified a bramble, and hence for instance the blackberry bush, or any other bramble, would be properly denominated a "hag." Hagbush-lane may therefore be taken to signify either Hawthorn-bush-lane, Bramble-lane, or Hedge-bush-lane, but more probably the latter. It was most probably an old Roman road. Its precise course is now with much difficulty determined, but from good authority it appeared to proceed from London at the distance of a few feet from the "City Arms" public house in the City-road, and then wound circuitously through Islington somewhere in the neighbourhood of the Liverpool-road, as far as Paradise-row, then turning westward through the fields, in the direction of "Old Copenhagen House," and, avoiding Maiden-lane, came into Upper Holloway at the foot of Highgate-hill, and from thence went across in the direction of Hornsey. The term "Packhorse-lane," by which name it is remembered by a few old inhabitants, shows that it was used as a bridle-way by packmen for the conveyance of their wares.

Mr. Hone, who in 1827 visited the remains of this lane, says, "North of Copenhagen House the visitor will find that the widest part of Hagbush-lane reaches from a mud cottage to the road now cutting from Holloway.* Crossing immediately over this road, he comes again into the lane, which he will there find so narrow as only to admit convenient passage to a man on horseback. This was the general width of the road throughout, and the general width of all English roads made in olden times. They did not travel in carriages, or carry their goods in carts as we do, but rode on horseback and conveyed their wares merchandise in pack-saddles on horses' backs. They likewise conveyed their money in the same way. In an objection raised in the reign of Elizabeth to a clause in the 'Hue and Cry Bill,' then passing through Parliament, regarding some travellers who had been robbed in open day in one of these lanes in the County of Berks, 'that they were clothiers, *and yet travelled not with the great troop of clothiers*; they also carried their money openly in wallets upon their saddles.' Thus inferring that travellers had no business to travel alone in those days, and they must expect to be robbed if they did so. The customary width of the roads was either four feet or eight feet."

In a very graphic account of this old bridle-way, constructed as it probably was before any road in the parish, Hone, in his "Every Day Book," speaks thus of it, as well as of a mud cottage, for many years belonging to a poor labourer :—

"From the many intelligent persons a stroller may meet among the thirty thou-

* The Camden-road.

sand inhabitants of Islington on his way along Hagbush-lane, he will perhaps not find one to answer a question that will occur to him during his walk: ' Why is this place called Hagbush-lane ?' Before giving information here to the inquirer, he is informed that, if a Londoner, Hagbush-lane is, or ought to be, to him, the most interesting way that he can find to walk in; and presuming him to be influenced by the feelings and motives that actuated his fellow-citizens in the improvement and advancement of their city, by the making of a *new* north road,* he is informed that Hagbush-lane, though now wholly disused, and in many parts destroyed, was the *old* or rather *the oldest* north road, or ancient bridle-way to and from London and the northern parts of the kingdom.

"Hagbush-lane is well known to every botanizing perambulator on the west side of London. The wild onion, or clowns-wound, wort, wake-robin, and abundance of other simples—lovely in their form, and of high medicinal repute, in our old herbals and receipt-books—take root and seed and flower here in great variety. How long beneath the tall elms and pollard oaks, and the luxuriant beauties on the bushes, the infirm may be suffered to seek health and the healthy to recreate, who shall say? Spoilers are abroad!

"Through Hagbush-lane every man has a right to ride and walk; *in* Hagbush-lane no one man has ever a shadow of right to an inch as private property. The trees, as well as the road, are public property, and the very form of the road is public property; yet bargains and sales have been made and are said to be now making, under which the trees are cut down and sold, and the public-road thrown bit by bit into private fields as pasture. Under no conveyance or admission to land by any proprietor, whether free-holder or lord of the manor, can any person legally dispossess the public of a single foot of Hagbush-lane, or obstruct the passage of any individual through it. All the people of London, and indeed all the people of England, have a right in this road as a common highway. Hitherto, among the inhabitants of Islington, many of whom are opulent, and all of whom are the local guardians of the public right in this road, not one has been found with sufficient public virtue, or rather with enough of common manly spirit, to compel the restoration of the public plunder, and in

---

* Referring to the Euston-road, about which there had been a great noise, and which, even then, was in some parts bordered by fields.

his own defence, and on behalf of the public, arrest the *highway robber.*

"Building, or what may properly be termed the tumbling-up of tumble-down houses to the north of London, is so rapidly increasing, that in a year or two there will scarcely be a green spot for the resort of the inhabitants. The preservation of Hagbush-lane therefore is, in this point of view, an object of much public importance. Where it has not been thrown into private fields, from whence, however, it is recoverable, it is one of the loveliest of our green lanes, and though persons from the country smile at Londoners when they talk of being *rural at the distance of a few miles from town,* a countryman would find it difficult to name any lane in his own county more sequestered or of greater beauty."

Mr. Hone, who was intimately acquainted with Charles Lamb, appears to have caught something of the genial spirit of the latter. He was evidently as proud and as fond of the few green lanes and sequestered nooks, which forty years ago were so plentiful in our parish, as Charles Lamb was of Fleet-street and the Strand. With reference to the mud cottage mentioned, Mr. Hone writes as follows:—

"Crossing the meadow west of Copenhagen House, to the north-east corner, there is a mud-built cottage in the widest part of Hagbush-lane. It stands on the site of one still more rude at which, until destroyed, labouring men and humble wayfarers, attracted by the sequestered and rural beauties of the lane, stopped to refresh themselves.

"This cottage stands no longer; its history is in the simple annals of the poor. About seven years ago an almost decayed labouring man, a native of Cheshunt, in Hertfordshire, with his wife and child, lay out every night upon the road-side of Hagbush-lane, under whatever bough or branch they could creep for shelter, till the winter's cold came on, and then he erected this mud edifice. He had worked for some great landholders and owners in Islington, and still jobbed about. Like them, he was, to this extent of building, a speculator, and to eke out his insufficient means, he profited in his humble abode by the sale of small beer to stragglers and rustic wayfarers. His cottage stood between the lands of two rich men; not upon the land of either, but partly on the disused road and partly on the waste of the manor. Deeming him by no means a respectable neighbour for their cattle, they 'warned him off.' Not choosing, however, to be houseless, nor conceiving that their domains could be injured by his little enclosure between the banks of the road, he refused to accept this notice and remained. For this offence one of the landlords caused his labourers to level the miserable dwelling to the earth, and the 'houseless child of want' was compelled by this wanton act to apply for his family and himself to be taken into the workhouse. His application was refused, but he received advice to build again, with information that his disturber was not justified in disturbing him. In vain he pleaded incompetent power to resist; the workhouse was shut against him, and he began to build another hut. He had proceeded so far as to keep off the weather in one direction, when wealth again made war upon poverty, and while away from his wife and child, his scarcely half-raised hut was pulled down during a heavy rain, and his wife and child left in the lane shelterless. A second application for a home in the workhouse was rejected, with still stronger assurances that he had been illegally disturbed, and with renewed advice to build again. The old man has built for the third time, and erected another hut wherein he dwells, and sells his small beer to people who choose to sit and drink it on the turf seat against the wall of his cottage. It is chiefly in request, however, among the brickmakers in the neighbourhood, and the labourers on the new road cutting across Hagbush-lane from Holloway to Kentish-town, which will ultimately connect the Regent's-park and the western suburb with the eastern extremity of this immensely-growing metropolis. Though immediately contiguous to Mr. Bath, the landlord of 'Copenhagen,' he has in no way assisted in obstructing this poor creature's endeavour to get a morsel of bread. For the present he remains unmolested in his almost sequestered nook, and the place and himself are worth seeing, for they are perhaps the nearest specimen to London of the old country labourer and his dwelling."

A few years ago the line of the old road could be traced across the fields on the north side of the Cattle Market, by the rows of elm trees which ran in an angular direction, but which have since been cut down. A coffee and fruit stall has for many years stood at the entrance of the present strip of lane, near to the bridge of the Great Northern Railway.

Lines written in Hagbush-lane, 1827.

A scene like this
Would woo the care-worn wise
To moralize,
And courting lovers court to tell their bliss.
Had I a cottage here
I'd be content; for where
I have my books
I have old friends,
Whose cheering looks
Make me amends
For coldnesses in men; and so
With them departed long ago,
And with wild flowers and trees,
And with the loving breeze,
And with the "still small voice"
Within, I would rejoice,
And converse hold, while breath
Held me, and then—come Death!

POCOCK'S FIELDS.

THESE fields, now almost covered with buildings, derive the above name from George Pocock, Esq., who purchased forty acres of freehold ground in the neighbourhood from Lord Northampton. Cornwall - place and George's-place were commenced about the year 1800. In the year 1809, in consequence of the inhabitants of Holloway experiencing great difficulty in the procuring of water, Mr. Pocock expended nearly £2,000 in digging a well in a field at the south end of Cornwall-place, over which he erected a steam-engine for the purpose of supplying the entire neighbourhood. This well produced water of excellent quality, and a company was formed to supply the neighbourhood, an Act being obtained for that purpose. No sooner, however, did the New River Company find that such a scheme found favour with the Legislature, than they went to work and carried their pipes with great expedition through Holloway, which they had previously withheld, notwithstanding repeated solicitations from the inhabitants to do so. The new company then dropped.

The Old "Pied Bull."

THE above inn, situated in Upper-street, was another of those old mansions built in the reign of Elizabeth. The old building was taken down about thirty years ago. Its site was a little to the back of Frederick-place, which is now covered with modern houses. It was a long irregular-built house of plaster and wood, with a thatched roof in which were several windows. A wooden paling railed in an enclosure to the left, as far out as the roadway, and a parlour on the right hand of the entrance was ornamented in a peculiar manner, and appeared to be a principal room. On a window looking into the garden were the arms of Sir John Miller, knight, of Islington and Devon, impaling those of Griegg, of Suffolk. In the kitchen were the remains of the same alms, with the date 1624. The first-mentioned arms in the parlour-window were enclosed within an ornamental border consisting of two mermaids, erect, holding globes, and sea-horses supporting a bunch of green leaves over a shield; the lower part contained a green and grey parrot, the former eating fruit. Adjoining this was another compartment in the window representing a green parrot perched on a wreath under a pediment within a border of figures and flowers.

The chimney-piece of the parlour was a marvel of carving. It contained the figures of Faith, Hope, and Charity, with their usual insignia, in niches, surrounded by a border of cherubim, fruit, and foliage. The centre figure, Charity, was surmounted by two Cupids supporting a crown, and beneath was a lion and unicorn couchant. This was probably designed in compliment to Queen Elizabeth. The ceiling displayed a personification of the five Senses, with Latin mottoes underneath. An oval in the centre contained a female holding a serpent, which was twining round her left arm and biting her hand; her left hand held a stick, the point of which rested on the back of a toad at her feet. The motto to this was "Tactus." Around the above, in smaller ovals, was a female bearing fruit under her left arm, of which she was eating; an ape rested at her feet, with the word "Gustus." Another figure held a vigard, and at its feet were a cat and a hawk, with the motto, "Visus." A figure playing on the lute with a stag listening, and the motto, "Auditus." The last figure was standing in a garden, holding a bouquet of flowers, at her feet was a dog, and the motto "Olfactus."

It is a very general tradition that this house was once the residence of Sir Walter Raleigh, and after an examination of the reasons which strengthen the tradition, the reader will no doubt think so too. That Sir Walter Raleigh should have lived in Islington is not to be wondered at when we know of Elizabeth's partiality for the place, and recall the fact of the Earl of Leicester, her particular favourite, having a residence in Ward's-place. It is true that the arms of Sir Walter Raleigh had never been found upon the premises, while those of Sir John Miller, who it is certain resided there in the days of King James, were in existence at the time they were taken down; yet, the arms of the latter bear date eight years after Sir Walter was beheaded, which was the time when Sir John Miller came to reside there. It is deemed very probable that the arms of Sir Walter occupied the same position as those occupied by Sir James Miller, as the latter knight could have easily substituted his own in a leaden casement window. This conjecture is strengthened by the border, inasmuch as it was composed of sea-horses, mermaids, parrots, &c., which bear a most appropriate allusion to the character of Sir Walter Raleigh as a great navigator and discoverer of unknown countries. The bunch of green leaves has been generally assented to represent the tobacco-plant, of which he is said to have been the first importer into this country.

The time when Sir Walter Raleigh lived in this house must have been when he was in high favour with the Queen, and, perhaps, when his various avocations allowed him but little opportunity of being the permanent inhabitant of any place, or otherwise he might have built a house at this part for his future retirement; and this alone would be sufficient for tradition to connect his name with the premises, although they might never have been inhabited by him. The author of the "Life of Sir Walter Raleigh," relates the following circumstances, which may be considered corroborative as to what has been inferred of his having resided in this house:—

"There is," says the author, "no farther from London than *Islington*, about a bow's shot on this side the church, which, though I think, it has no such evidences remaining on its walls, ceilings, or windows, that will prove Sir Walter to have been its owner, the arms that are seen there, above a hundred years old, being those of a succeeding inhabitant, it is yet popularly reported to have been a villa of his, for the present tenant, his landlord, was possessed of some old account books, by which it appears, beyond all doubt, this house and fourteen acres of land, now let at £10 per annum, did belong to Sir Walter Raleigh, and that the oldest man in the parish would often declare his father had told him Sir Walter had purposed to wall in that ground with intention to keep some of his horses therein; further, that some husbandmen, ploughing up the same a few years since, found several pieces of Queen Elizabeth's money, whereof they brought (whatever they might reserve to themselves) about four-score shillings to their master, the said tenant, in whose hands I have seen the said coin. As for the house, it is, and has been, an inn for many years, so that what it was is not clearly to be judged from its present outward appearance, it being much impaired, or very coarsely repaired, and diminished, perhaps, from what it might have been, when persons of distinction lived in it. However, there are within some spacious rooms. The parlour was painted round the uppermost part of the wainscot in about a dozen pannels with Scripture history, but now so old and decayed as to be scarcely discernible. There is also a noble dining-room, the ceiling whereof is all wrough over in plastic or fret work, with representations of the five Senses, and the chimney-piece with the three principal Christian Virtues. But the arms in the windows, as well as those in the hall, are by the present inhabitants erroneously called Sir Walter Raleigh's, there being a date under one of the coats which shows it was annealed six years after his death, so we are not sure the decorations aforesaid were done by his direction, *or that others more rich and elegant were not in their stead before them.*"

Altogether, it appears clear that Raleigh was in some way or other connected with the old house, which is now represented by a modern structure at the corner of Theberton-street. His name is also connected with several of the old inns in the district, which, it is said, he used to make use of as smoking-houses. The "Pied Bull," was not converted into an inn until about the year 1750, and, therefore, it is likely that while the latter was his residence he frequently visited the former, and indulged in the narcotic weed in the presence of the company assembled at such places.

Camden, in his "Annals of the Reign of Elizabeth," says, "that to the best of his knowledge the first tobacco seen in England was brought from Virginia by Sir Walter Raleigh in 1583, and in *a few years after* tobacco-taverns, or smoking-houses, were as common in London as beer-houses or wine-taverns. Such was the rage for this narcotic on its first introduction, that it was even smoked in the theatres and other places of public amusement both by men and women. On the other hand, it was so disgusting to some that one Peter Campbell in his will dated October 20th, 1616, desired that his son should be disinherited of the property bequeathed him *if at any time he should be found taking of tobacco.*"

The following pleasant story is related of Raleigh in reference to the custom he introduced:—

"Sitting one day in deep meditation, with a pipe in his mouth, he, without thought, called to a waiter to bring him a tankard of small ale. The waiter carried the liquor upstairs, but on entering the room where Sir Walter was sitting smoking, he immediately threw all the liquor in his face, and in a state of great consternation ran down the stairs, crying out, '*Fire! fire! help! Sir Walter has studied till his head is on fire, and the smoke bursts out of his mouth and nose!*' After this Sir Walter made it no secret, for he took two pipes just before he went to be beheaded."

The author of the "Life of Sir Walter Raleigh," says, "Being at Leeds, in Yorkshire, after Mr. Ralph Thoresby, the antiquary, died, 1725, I saw his museum, and among it Sir Walter Raleigh's tobacco-box. From the best of my memory I can resemble its outward appearance to nothing more nearly than one of our modern snuff-cases, about the same height and width, covered with red leather and opened at top with a hinge like one of those. In the inside there was a cavity or a receiver, of glass or metal, which might hold half-a-pound or a pound of tobacco, and from the edge of the receiver at top to the edge of the box a circular collar with holes in it, to plant the tobacco about, with six or seven pipes in it."

Mr. Boughy, a tobacconist, who lies buried in Islington churchyard, kept for many years in his window in Bishopsgate-street, the painted sign of Sir Walter Raleigh and the waiter, taken from the story just mentioned.

The execution of this remarkable man took place October 29th, 1618. He has been called the English Xenophon, for while he excelled in feats of arms and strength of counsel, he surpassed in all those arts which belong to peace and retirement—history, oratory, philosophy, politics, and poetry. In short, he was " a warrior both by sea and land, a statesman, navigator, and discoverer of new countries, an accomplished orator, a scholar, an elegant writer, a sweet and true poet, and a munificent patron of letters. There is scarcely one of the aspects in which we view him where he does not shine with a remarkable brightness."

" Raleigh, the scourge of Spain, whose breast
   with all
The Sage, the Patriot, and the Hero burned;
Nor shrunk his vigour, when a coward
   reign
The warrior fettered, and at last resign'd
To glut the vengeance of a vanquished foe.
Then active still and unrestrained, his
   mind
Explored the vast extent of ages past,
And with his prison hours enriched the
   world,
Yet found no times in all the long research,

So glorious or so base, as those he proved,
In which he conquered and in which he
   bled."

THE VICARAGE HOUSE.

NEAR the " Old Pied Bull" was the Vicarage House, yet standing behind Woodifield's, the brush-maker, in the Upper-street. It is a square brick and plaster erection, and is supposed to have been built by Dr. William Cane, Vicar, who held the living from 1662 to 1691, for his initials were found in the front of the building when the premises were undergoing some repairs. It appears to have been erected in the garden of an old adjoining house, which was the original rectory or parsonage attached to the living, as by a lease dated March 22, 1755, it is stated that " all that messuage or tenement called the parsonage-house, stables, out-houses, &c., abutting on the vicarage-house," was granted by the Rev. S. Stonehouse, Vicar, to a Mr. Burton. This Mr. Burton was a bricklayer. It was afterwards rented by a Mr. Thompson, who held the cattle-pens, which then stood behind the " Pied Bull" (now Gibson-square.)

The Vicar now resides in Barnsbury-park. He receives a modus of fourpence per acre for land, twopence per cow, and twopence per calf. Attached to the living is a glebe of nine acres, part of which, situated on the north side of Sermon-lane, in the Liverpool-road, was let by Dr. Strahan upon building leases; the remaining five acres is at Ball's-pond, and has also been let. The old vicarage house is now partly occupied by the brush-maker named.

Kingsland Hospital and Chapel.

THIS chapel, formerly connected with the Hospital for Lepers at Kingsland, is still in existence. It is a small stone building at the south-east corner of the road near Kingsland-green, and at the eastern boundary of this parish. It is of a very ancient character, about twenty-seven feet in length and eighteen feet broad, and on the outside not more than twenty feet high, the road about it being so raised that the bottom of the pulpit is on a level with the highway, and the floor of the area three feet below it. It is supposed to have been erected about the period of the Reformation. It had a communication with the original Lazar-house whereby the patients entered to attend divine service, and it is said to have been so contrived, that when in the chapel, they could neither see nor be seen by the rest of the audience. Its interior is exceedingly diminutive and ancient. Five single pews comprise the whole of the gallery, and in the area are seven double pews and two single ones. The communion-table is formed of a plain deal falling slab, and the Decalogue is painted on a large board in gilt letters on a black ground. There was lately in the chapel an old pewter salver on which the arms of St. Bartholomew's Hospital were engraved; and in former days, in a closet in the chapel there was an old folio Bible, strongly secured with brass, having Psalms at the end set to music in the ancient square character, not divided into bars, and which, from the appearance it carried with it, had remained in the place from the days of Henry VIII. or Elizabeth. This book cannot be found at the present day, nor is anything known as to what has become of it.

The foundation of a house at Kingsland for persons afflicted with leprosy is of considerable antiquity. So early as the year 1437 John Pope " citizen and barber, by his will, gave to the master and governors of the House of Lepers, called Le Nokes* at Kingeslond without London, an annual rent of 6s. 8d., issuing out of certain houses situate in Shirborne-lane, towards the sustenation of the said house at Kingeslond for ever."

The disorder of leprosy, so common in ancient times, has been termed the "lack-linen" disease, and is supposed to have been caused through inattention to personal cleanliness. Lazar-houses or hospitals for lepers were once established in every suburb of the metropolis —Whitehall, Clerkenwell, Highgate, Lambeth Marsh, and Kingsland.

From the records of St. Bartholomew's Hospital, it appears that soon after the foundation of that charity in the reign of Henry VIII., certain lock or lazar hospitals were opened for the reception of persons afflicted

with syphilis at a distance from town, to which place persons were sent who applied to Bartholomew's to get cured of that complaint, and thus they were kept apart from all other patients. Each house was under the care of a surgeon, a chaplain, a sister, a nurse and helper, and each contained about twenty beds.

The hospital at Kingsland was one of these receptacles so established, and it superseded the old "House of Lepers" which first stood there. The Governors of St. Bartholomew's Hospital afterwards added to the old building a more commodious edifice of brick, which, although now occupied by several tenants, has still over the door the arms of the hospital. It continued, however, to be an appendage to St. Bartholomew's Hospital, until the committee of that institution recommended in Jan. 27, 1751, "that in future convenience be found for persons with all such complaints in the new wing of their own hospital, and that no more be sent to the *outhouses*."

In consequence of this order the Kingsland Hospital and Chapel were ordered to be let to some other use, but a petition was presented in February 17, 1761, by a Mr. Cookson, who had been chaplain to the hospital, from the inhabitants of Kingsland, praying " that he might continue the duty for their accommodation." The committee afterwards ordered that Mr. Cookson should have the use of the " chapel " as desired on paying a yearly acknowledgment of " sixpence" into the poor's-box with leave to take down the patient's pew in the gallery and raise the seats at his expense under the direction of the hospital surveyor.

From this time the office of chaplain was discontinued, and Mr. Cookson being no longer upon the establishment, was, by way of recompense, permitted to have free use of the chapel, and to receive what he could collect from persons attending public worship on condition of keeping it in repair. In this manner the chapel has been kept open till the present time, the Governors of St. Bartholomew's Hospital continuing to nominate a preacher on vacancy.

The congregation attending the chapel is not above twenty or thirty persons at the present time. The Islington boundary line crosses the floor of the edifice, entering it by what was formerly the patients' door on the south side and passing out by the public entrance on the north; consequently, so much of the edifice as stands eastward of this line, including the altar and the pulpit, is within

---

* This word was probably derived from the Saxon word *loc* or *loke*, which implies shut or confined, perhaps alluding to the restraint under which the patients were kept at these houses, and which from the nature of the disease, was necessary. Stow calls a similar house, the *Loke*, from whence we have the modern term 'Lock,' as applied to hospitals of a particular class, by which name the hospital at Kingsland was afterwards called.

the parish of Hackney. It is said that an ecclesiastical or parochial custom exists, that "whensoever the parishioners of Islington beat the bounds, prayers are read from the pulpit by the clergyman who attends the procession.

St. Paul's Church, Ball's Pond.

THIS church, near Ball's-pond Gate, was designed by Charles Barry, and is one of the three built under the arrangement made with the parish of Islington in the year 1825, the other two built at the same date being Holy Trinity, Cloudesley-square, and St. John's, Holloway. The site was given by the Marquis of Northampton for the sum of £50, little more than a mere nominal consideration. The first stone was laid September 15th, 1826, and it was consecrated by the Bishop of London, October 23rd, 1828. It contains 1,793 sittings, of which 817 are free, and was erected at an expense of £11,000.

The church is built of brick and stone, and is of the pointed collegiate style of architecture. Its principal front is to the east. The upper story of the tower is clear of the church, and fronting the road is a very handsome clock dial with antique figures. On each side, in the interior, are five arches, and the trusses which sustain the ceiling are of an ornamental character. The decorations of the altar are very handsome. In the lower part of a lofty arch is a handsome screen of imitation stone, in seven divisions made by buttresses, each covered by a canopy in the style of the altar-tombs of the fifteenth century. In the recess, which has a groined ceiling, is placed the altar. The decalogue is beautifully executed with red initial letters, illuminated with leaves and flowers, the small letters black, and the figures denoting the number of the Commandments, blue. The recess above the altar is lighted by a magnificent stained-glass window, containing the arms of George IV. The present incumbent is the Rev. John Sandys, M.A.

In 1839 the congregation, in order to testify their attachment to their minister, raised a fund for the purpose of endowing a perpetual exhibition, to be called "the Rev. John Sandy's Exhibition," to be in the gift of Mr. Sandy's, to one or more undergraduates of the Universities of limited means. The proceeds of this fund are now paid to the nominee of Mr. Sandy's for life, and the patronage afterwards reverts to the minister and churchwardens for the time being. In the vestry-room of the church a tablet is erected to record the fact, and at a public breakfast, which took place October 22, 1839, a folio volume, elegantly bound in morocco, was presented to Mr. Sandys, containing, besides the autographs of the contributors to the fund, a MS. history of the proceedings in beautiful ornamental writing and characters.

Attached to the church are Infant and National Schools, also various other institutions.

Islington Spa;

OR, "NEW TUNBRIDGE WELLS."

THIS place, though not in the parish, belonged to what was in former times called the *village* of Islington. It stood upon the site of Lloyd's-row, near the New River Head, and at the present time the well may be seen in the rear of the house of Mr. Moore, in the row mentioned. It is not exactly known at what date the well was first opened to the public. As early as the year 1685, however, it was much frequented, and in 1700 was in high favour, when dancing and music were introduced as additional inducements for the people to visit it. In the summer of that year we find a notice to the effect that "dancers were admitted during the whole of Mondays and Thursdays, provided they did not appear in masks." Hampstead Wells and other places became neglected through the thousands that used to flock to Islington Spa, and in 1733 it was visited by royalty itself. "In June, 1733, their Royal Highnesses the Princesses Amelia and Caroline frequented these gardens daily, for the purpose of drinking the waters, when such was the concourse of the nobility and others that the proprietor took about £30 in one morning!" "On the birthday of one of the Princesses," says the *Gentleman's Magazine*, "as they passed through the Spa Field, which was generally filled with carriages, they were saluted with a discharge of twenty-one guns, —a compliment which was always passed them on their arrival—and in the evening there was a great bonfire, and the guns were again discharged several times." On ceasing to visit the gardens the Princess Amelia presented the master with twenty-five guineas, and to each of the other attendants one guinea. The visits of these Princesses are also alluded to in a lyric poem published in 1734, entitled "The Humours of New Tunbridge Wells, at Islington," and among other persons described as visitants is the celebrated Beau Nash, "King of Bath."

The owners at this time appear to have conducted the "Well" with great propriety, for among other inducements offered to inva-lids to make a trial of the place, it is stated in the *London Chronicle* of 1760, that "the present proprietor has taken effectual care to have everything provided for the accommodation of the company who come hither to drink the waters or to breakfast, or drink tea or coffee at other times of the day; and ladies and gentlemen may depend upon having the best tea, coffee, or chocolate with due attendance and the most civil and obliging treatment.—N.B. There are very pleasant and commodious lodgings to be let, with the convenience of walking in the gardens, which are laid out in an agreeable and elegant taste, with boarding if required. The price for breakfasting is ninepence each person, and for drinking tea in the afternoon sixpence, and coffee, eightpence; and no other liquors are sold at this place, which enables the proprietor to keep out all bad and improper company."

About the year 1780 the reputation of the Spa began somewhat to decline, though it was still visited by a great many people, and it continued to be partially used till within the last thirty years. In the year 1803, Malcolm speaks of the gardens attached to the Spa as being "really beautiful; pedestals and vases are grouped with taste under some extremely picturesque trees, whose foliage is seen to much advantage from the neighbouring fields." Nelson, who wrote in 1811, says, "the gardens are still frequented by persons for the benefit of the waters; the subscription is one guinea for the season, or sixpence per glass with capillaire. The spring is enclosed with an artificial grotto, composed of flints and shells, which is entered by a rustic gate. Here is also a lodging-house, where invalids may be accommodated with bed and board, and in the garden is a breakfast-room, about forty feet long, having at the end a small orchestra. In this room is a printed comparative statement, dated May 1, 1737, of the specific gravity of the most celebrated of the mineral waters, in which that of this spring is said to be 3 ozs. 4 degs. 36 grains lighter than common water.

Here are also some testimonials of the virtues of the spring, said to have been written by persons who experienced its salutary effects, of which the following is a specimen, which a gentleman left in his apartment who had been restored to health by this water, after having been ill thirty years, and having tried every other mineral water in the kingdom without effect :—

"' For three times ten years I travelled the globe,
  Consulted whole tribes of the physical robe.
  Drank the waters of Tunbridge, Bath, Harrowgate, Dulwich,
  Spa, Epsom (and all by the advice of the College),
  But in vain—till to *Islington* waters I came
  To try if my cure would add to their fame ;
  In less than six weeks they produced a belief
  This would be the place for my long-sought relief.
  Before six weeks more had finished their course,
  Full of spirits and strength I mounted my horse,

  Gave praise to my God and rode cheerfully home.
  Overjoyed with the thought of sweet hours to come.

  May thou, Great Jehovah! give equal success
  To all who resort to this place for redress !' "

As late as the year 1828 the gardens, though limited, continued open. They are now all built upon. The spring, however, as has been stated, is still preserved in the rear of the premises of Mr. Moore, Lloyd's-row, Clerkenwell, over whose house is written the inscription, " Islington Spa, or New Tunbridge Wells." Mr. Moore kindly permitted the writer to view this interesting spring and also to drink the water, which has a slight saline taste and a whitish hue. The yield is now only about two pailfuls per day. Mr. Moore took some of the water a short time ago to the Polytechnic and had it analyzed, when it was found to contain magnesia and iron.

Old Sadler's Wells and Music House.

THE above place was, at first, a wooden building erected on the north side of the New River Head, some time prior to 1683. It derives its name from a well of mineral water discovered by a Mr. Sadler, District Surveyor of the Highways, in a garden belonging to a house which he had opened for the public entertainment about the year above named. In the olden time this well belonged to the monks of the Priory of Jerusalem, who dispensed its waters mendicinally, the deluded recipients being persuaded that upon drinking them their cure would follow by the intercession of the Virgin and the Saints. When, however, the Priory was suppressed by Henry VIII., the well was covered over, and thus all remembrance of it was lost for nearly a century and a half.

In a pamphlet, published in 1684 by Thomas Maltus, at the sign of the " Rising Sun," in the Poultry, there is an interesting account relating to the manner in which this well was discovered by Sadler, from which the following is extracted :—

" The new well at Islington is a certain spring in the middle of a garden belonging to the Music House built by Mr. Sadler on the north side of the great cistern that receives the New River water near Islington, the water whereof, before the Reformation, having been much famed for several extraordinary cures performed thereby ; it was also accounted sacred and called ' *Holy-well.*' The priests belonging to the Priory of Clerkenwell used to attend there and make the people believe that the virtues of these waters arose from the efficacy of their prayers ; but upon the Reformation the well was stopped up, and so by degrees it grew out of remembrance, and was wholly lost until found out and the fame of it revived again by the following incident : Mr. Sadler being made a Surveyor of the Highways, and having good gravel in his own garden, employed two men to dig there, and when they had dug pretty deep one of them felt his pickaxe strike upon something very hard; whereupon he endeavoured to break it, but could not; whereupon, thinking within himself that it might be some treasure that was hid there, he uncovered it very carefully and found it to be a *broad flat stone*, which, having loosened and lifted up, he saw was supported by four oaken posts, and under it a large well of stone, arched over and curiously carved. Having viewed it he called his fellow labourer to see it likewise, and asked him whether they should fetch Mr. Sadler and show it him, who having no kindness for Sadler, answered, 'No! he should not know of it, but as they had found it so they would stop it up again and take no notice of it.' To which he that found it at first consented, but he found himself strongly inclined to tell Sadler of the well, which he did one Sabbath evening.

" Upon hearing this, Sadler went down to see the well, and observing the curiosity of the stone-work that was about it, and fancying within himself that it was a mendicinal water formerly held in great esteem, he took some of it in a bottle, and carrying it to an eminent physician and telling him how the well was found, desired his judgment on the water; who, having tasted and tried it, told him it was of a very strong mineral taste, and advised him to brew some beer with it, and carry it to some persons whom he would recommend, which he did accordingly. And some of those who used to have it in little bottles found so much good by it that they desired him to bring it in 'roundlets,' which was done the most part of the last winter, and it continued to have so good an effect upon those who drank it, that at the beginning of this summer Dr. Morton advised several of his patients to drink the water, which operates so near Tunbridge water that it has obtained a general approbation, and great numbers of those who used to go thither, drink it. There are few physicians in London but have advised some or other of their patients to drink it, by which means it is so frequented that there are five or six hundred patients there every morning."

The pamphlet then gives an account of the qualities of the water thus discovered and the diseases it is good for, and directions for those drinking it, concluding with stating that "those who please may eat carraways while they drink the water, and drink a glass of Rhenish or White wine after them, and it is very convenient for those who smoke tobacco to take a pipe or two whilst the water works."

After the death of Sadler the Music House came into the successive occupancy of two individuals named Forcer and Miles, who produced a variety of low entertainments; for instance, on the 23rd of May, 1799, the public were invited to witness the disgusting exhibition of a man *eating a live cock*. In the *Protestant Mercury* of that date the feast is recorded as follows:—

" On Tuesday last a fellow at Sadler's Wells, near Islington, after he had dined heartily on a buttock of beef for the lucre of five guineas ate a live cock, feathers, ' guts,' and all, with only a plate of oil and venegar for sauce, and half a pint of brandy to wash it down, and afterwards proposed to lay a wager of five guineas more that he would eat the same again in two hours' time. This is attested by many credible people who were eye-witnesses of the same."

Another advertisement in the paper of the same date says:—

" The man who ate the live cock at Islington, proposes to eat another, with the feathers, bones, and garbage, at ' Stand-up Dicks,' Newington Butts. Twopence admission."

This same man is also stated to have eaten a live cat at a singing saloon near the Tower, on the 24th of January, 1800, for the *amusement* of the company!

At this time Sadler's Wells' Music House and grounds became very low, rope-dancing, tumbling, and other entertainments were introduced to gratify the company, and the house was repaired and improved. In 1753 it assumed the rank of a regular theatre, having been licensed for such, the spectators paying for a ticket on admission which entitled them to its value in liquors and refreshments. After the death of Forcer, Rosoman purchased the theatre, and in 1764 the old wooden building was pulled down and the present one erected in its stead at a cost of £4,225. In fitting up the interior accommodation was provided for supplying the audience with liquors during the performance by means of a shelf at the top of the back of each seat, and this very reprehensible practice was the cause of much disturbance.

The well which Sadler discovered appears to have ceased to draw company about this date, and was covered in during the various improvements and rebuildings. For a long time it was hidden from view, until it was accidentally discovered in the open space between the stage-door and the New River. It is said to be encircled with stone, and has a descent of several steps. In the year 1788 the whole of the inside of the house was taken down and materially improved, and about the same period Dibdin composed several pieces for the theatre which raised the character of the house, so that it began to be frequented by a more respectable class. Several novel spectacles were introduced, such as the representation of dramatic spectacles upon water, for which purpose an immense trough, occupying the whole space of the stage, was filled with water from the New River. By these means, it is said, " the besieging of fortifications by sea, naval engagements, &c., were introduced with unusual effect."

On the evening of the 15th of October, 1817, a fatal scene took place in Sadler's Wells' Theatre. The exclamation, "a fight!" vociferated by some person in the theatre, was construed by a part of the audience into the word fire, and though neither flame nor smoke were seen, a frenzy took place in the gallery which it was impossible to control. The entreaties and cries of the managers, who, through speaking trumpets, declared that there was no fire, availed nothing. Some of the audience, regardless of their lives, threw themselves into the pit, and eighteen died from pressure and suffocation on the gallery stairs, while a great number were bruised and maimed by the extraordinary pressure of the crowd in their endeavour to leave the theatre. A prosecution was entered into against the person by whose exclamation the terror was excited, and the produce of two benefits were divided amongst the families of those who had suffered.

Since the time of Rosoman the theatre has passed through the hands of various persons : Thomas King and Wroughton, comedians, of Drury-lane Theatre, were managers in the early part of the present century. It is now under the sole management of Mr. Phelps.

It is curious to read the old bills and advertisements relating to Sadler's Wells, at the end of which were notices to the public, stating that protection from being robbed would be afforded to those who came from the city or the west-end to visit the playhouse. At the bottom of a bill in the year 1790 is the following notice :—

" A horse-patrol will be sent in the Newroad for the protection of the nobility and gentry who go from the squares and that end of the town. The road also towards the city will be properly guarded."

Another of the same date was worded as follows :—

" Patrols of horse and foot are stationed from Sadler's Wells along the New-road to Tottenham-court Turnpike, likewise the City-road to Moorfields ; also to St. Johnstreet, and across the Spa-fields to Rosomanrow, from the hours of 8 till 11."

The following specimen of a bill given away at Bartholomew Fair some forty years ago, for the purpose of drawing an audience to Sadler's Wells, will bring to the recollection of many the character of the entertainment given at that time :—

SERIOUS NOTICE !

In Perfect Confidence ! !

The following extraordinary Comic Performance at

SADLER'S WELLS

Can only be given during the present week; the proprietor therefore most respectfully informs that fascinating sex, so properly distinguished by the appropriate appellation of

T H E   F A I R,

And all those well-inclined gentlemen who are happy enough to protect them, that the amusements will consist of a romantic tale of mysterious horror and broad grin, never acted, called,

Enchanted
G I R D L E S,
or,
Winki the Witch,
and the
LADIES OF SAMARCAND.

A most whimsical burletta, which sends people home perfectly enchanted from uninterrupted risibility, called,

THE LAWYER, THE JEW,
and
THE YORKSHIREMAN;

With, by request of seventy-five distinguished families and a party of five, that never-to-be sufficiently praised Pantomime, called,

MAGIC IN TWO COLOURS,
or,
FAIRY BLUE AND FAIRY RED,
or,
Harlequin and the Marble Rock.

It would be perfectly superfluous for any man in his senses to attempt any more than the mere announcement in recommendation of the above unparalleled representations, so attractive in themselves as to threaten a complete monopoly of the qualities of the magnet, and though the proprietors were to talk nonsense by the hour, they could not assert a more important truth than that they possess

The only Wells from which you may draw
WINE!
Three Shillings and Sixpence
a full quart.

Those whose important avocations prevent their coming at the commencement will be admitted for

HALF PRICE AT HALF-PAST EIGHT.

Ladies and Gentlemen who are not judges of the superior entertainments announced, are respectfully requested to bring as many as possible with them who are.

N.B.—A full Moon during the week.

The Fleet Brook.

THE ancient Fleet Brook, which had its origin in the high grounds of Hampstead and Highgate, was anciently denominated "Turnmill Brook," also the "River of Wells." Some years ago, on making the excavation necessary for arching over the Brook, at Battle Bridge, an anchor was found, from which it is inferred that vessels must have originally passed from the Thames down to that place. Stow, the historian, in his survey of London, says, "that the Fleet Brook was clear and sweet as far down as Old Borne (Holborn) Bridge." It did not long remain so, however, for in the year 1290, the monks of Whitefriars complained to Parliament of its putrid exhalations overcoming the frankincense burnt at their altar during the hours of divine service, and at a Parliament, held in 1307, Henry Lacy, Earl of Lincoln, complained "that whereas in times past, the River Fleet had been of such depth and breadth that ten or twelve ships, with merchandise were wont to come to the Fleet Bridge and some of them to Old Borne Bridge, now, the same course, by the filth of the tanners, and such others, and by the raising of wharfs, is stopped up." Subsequent to this the stream was frequently cleansed, and in the year 1502 the whole course of the Fleet Dyke, as it was then called, was scoured down to the Thames, so that boats, laden with fish and fuel, were rowed to Fleet Bridge and Holborn Bridge, as was their wont. In 1670 it was again cleansed, enlarged, and deepened sufficiently to admit of barges as far as Holborn Bridge, when the water was five feet deep at its lowest tides, and twenty-three at the fullest. So convenient, however, was the river as a receptacle for filth to the inhabitants, that

the expense of keeping it clear became very burdensome, and in the year 1734 it was ordered to be arched over as far as Farringdon-street by an act of Parliament, and thus became extinct as a navigable river.

Not many years since, however, its stream was sufficiently powerful to give motion to some flour and flatting mills in Clerkenwell, and in the winter time it frequently overflowed its banks and laid the fields in the neighbourhood of Battle Bridge and King's Cross entirely under water.

A local historian who lived in Somers Town in 1812, says : "Such is the increase of water in the channel of the Fleet, after long-continued rains, or a sudden thaw with much snow on the ground, by reason of the great influx from the adjacent hills, that sometimes from this place (Battle-bridge) it overflows its bounds, breaks up the bridges, and inundates the surrounding neighbourhood to a considerable extent. Several years ago an inundation of this kind took place, when several drowned cattle, butts of beer, and other heavy articles were carried down the stream from the premises on its banks, in which the flood had entered and made great devastation."

The most considerable overflow that has happened within the memory of many now living, occurred in January, 1809. At this period, when the snow was lying very deep, a rapid thaw came on, and the arches not affording a sufficient passage for the increased current, the whole space between Old Pancras Church, Somers Town, and the bottom of the hill at Pentonville was in a short time covered with water. The flood rose to the height of three feet from the middle of the highway; the lower rooms of all the houses within that space were completely inundated, and the inhabitants suffered considerable damage in their goods and furniture, which many of them had not time to remove. For several days persons were obliged to be conveyed to and from their houses, and receive their provisions, &c., in at their windows, by means of carts.

The Clothworkers' Almshouses.

THESE almshouses, situated in Frog Lane, were founded by Lady Margaret, Countess of Kent, widow of Richard, Earl of Kent, in the year 1538. By the will of the Countess she devised four tenements at Queenhithe, and one at Fenchurch-street, in the City of London, to the Clothworkers' Company, and also granted the residue of her part of a lease of garden-ground within the precincts of Whitefriars, with an almshouse, &c., built thereon by her, to the said Company; for which gift and the payment of a certain sum, the Master and Wardens of the Clothworkers agreed to pay £11 7s. a year in weekly payments of 7½d. each to seven poor almswomen resident in the Countess's almshouses; and 20s. a-year to an honest poor man to keep the gate of the almshouses and to assist in certain superstitious uses. The Master and Wardens were directed to fill up all the vacancies that occurred after the Countess's death, giving a preference to the wives of clothworkers.

The original almshouses at Whitefriars, however, long since became dilapidated, and in the year 1770 the Clothworkers' Company took them down and erected the present ones upon their own land at Islington, they owning more than sixty acres of land in the neighbourhood of Frog-lane. The almshouses are eight in number, one having since been added to the original seven founded by the Countess of Kent. Each house contains two rooms and has a garden in the rear. The eight women are chosen by the Court of Assistants from among the freemen of the Company not under the age of fifty-five. Besides the emoluments to which they are entitled by the foundresses grant, there are several benefactions which have augmented their pensions, and they now receive £20 per annum each and ten chaldrons of coal divided among them annually.

The Clothworkers' Company's land is situated between the Shepherdess Fields and the High-street. Included in this estate are 23 acres, bequeathed by Dame Ann Packington to the Company by her will dated Nov. 24, 1559. The rents of the latter land thus bequeathed, amounted at that time to £16 16s., which she directed was to be divided by the Company as follows:—

	£	s.	d.
To poor inhabitants of St. Dunstan's in the West, between Nov. 1 and Feb. 1 . . .	3	13	4
To poor inhabitants in the parish in which Dame P. should be buried*	3	0	0
For teaching poor people of the same parish	3	0	0
For alms to poor people on the anniversary of the day of her burial	2	0	0
To a learned man in the Scriptures of God for a sermon on Feb. 15, in St. Dunstan's Church	0	6	8
To a like learned man for a sermon in the church she should be buried in, on the anniversary of that event	0	6	8
To the Company for their trouble	4	10	0

This charity estate, after the lapse of a certain time, got mixed up with the other portion of the estate belonging to the Company, but by an order of the Court of Chancery the Master of the Company was ordered in 1825 to make out an account of the proceeds and define the situation of the trust, which was done, and the report stated that the annual income was £400, which was directed to be applied in accordance with the will of the testatrix. The Master of Chan-

---

* She was buried in St. Botolph, Aldersgate.

chery also ordered that the Clothworkers' Company should get preachers for the sermons, and directed that their charity lands in Islington should be divided by boundary stones.

DAVIS'S ALMSHOUSES.

ON the south side of Queen's Head Lane is a row of almshouses founded by Mr. Davis. Mr. Davis was a carpenter residing in Islington, who died in 1793, leaving the sum of £2,000 to endow this charity. In the year 1805, Mr. Robert Careless left £100 towards improving the charity, but his benefaction was greatly lessened by the insolvency of one of the trustees who received the legacy, it being reduced to £30. A portrait of Mr. Davis is preserved, we believe, in one of the almshouses. The almshouses are open to both male and female parishioners, who receive £10 per annum each. On a stone in front of the building are recorded the following particulars :—

"In the year of our Lord
1794,
These eight Almshouses were erected and endowed
For the reception and maintenance
Of aged poor persons,
By Mrs. JANE DAVIS,
In pursuance of the will of her deceased husband,
Mr. JOHN DAVIS,
Late of this parish.
The Rev. George Strahan, John Jackson, Esq., Edmund Clutterbuck, Esq., Mr. Edward Martin, Mr. Thomas Craven—Trustees."

Holloway.

HOLLOWAY appears to have been so called from its situation in the *hollow* or valley at the foot of Highgate Hill. The high road is now studded on each side with numerous detached residences of every form and style in architecture. Some of the villas are, however, very elegant, Loraine-place, built in 1832, Lansdowne-place, and Walter's-buildings, being the most deserving of notice. One of the houses opposite Loraine-place was, for several years occupied by Sir Richard Phillips, sheriff of London, and a very celebrated publisher of his day. He established the *Monthly Magazine* in July 1, 1796. John Thurston and Robert Branston, two eminent artists, also resided in the same part of Holloway.

The "Mother Red Cap," a public house of some note at Upper Holloway, and rebuilt some time ago, is celebrated by Drunken Barnaby in his "Itinerary;" and the "Half Moon," an equally famous house, was celebrated a century ago for its famous cheesecakes, which, as has been stated in a previous page, was one of the London cries by a man on horseback. This circumstance, with others relating to Islington, is noticed in a poem entitled, "A Journey to Nottingham," in the *Gentleman's Magazine* for September, 1743, from which the following is extracted :—

"Now we set out, for sages have decreed
That fair and gently brings the greatest speed.
Now straggling Islington behind we leave,
Where piety laments her learned Cave ;*
Now Canonbury's tower rises to view,
No costly structure if the tale be true †
Here Humphreys breathed his last, the Muse's friend ;
Here Chambers found his mighty labours end ;
Here City doctors bid the sick repair,
Only, too often, to die in better air.
Through Holloway, *fam'd for cakes*, we onward tend,
While much St. Michael's hermit we commend,
Whose care a double charity bestowed,
Supplying water as he raised the road !
To Highgate hence the long ascent we gain,
Whose varied prospects will reward our pain."

---

* Vicar of Islington.

† Reported to have been built for 1d per day.

Cross Street.

FISHER HOUSE.

MANY of the houses in Cross-street and its neighbourhood, were, in former times, occupied by the principal inhabitants of the village. The house No. 41, was once the residence of Sir Thomas Fowler, knight, lord of the manor of Barnsbury, which has since passed into the Tuffnell family. The family of Fowler appears to have been one of the most noted in the parish during the reigns of Elizabeth and James, and even antecedent to that their name frequently occurs in records connected with Islington. Sir Thomas Fowler, knight, was one of the Deputy-Lieutenants for the County of Middlesex. He married Jane, daughter of Gregory Charlot, citizen and tallow-chandler of London, and died January 14, 1614. He was one of the jurors who sat at the trial of Sir Walter Raleigh at Winchester, in November, 1603. His son, Sir Thomas, was created a baronet in 1628, but the title became extinct at the death of Sir Edmund Fowler, brother to Sir Thomas. The house in Cross-street in which this family resided, has been much altered from its original state, though it still retains some evidence of its former grandeur. It appears to have been erected in the reign of Elizabeth, the ceiling of a back room on the first floor being decorated with the arms of England in the reign of that princess, with the date 1595 in stucco; also the initials of Thomas and Jane Fowler in the same style as those at Canonbury House. At the extremity of a garden which belonged to the mansion is a small building, but not now connected with the house, called Queen Elizabeth's Lodge. It appears to have afforded access to the house through the grounds, and was probably built as a summer-house or porter's lodge at the entrance of the garden about the time the mansion-house was erected.

FISHER HOUSE.

THIS mansion, which stood nearly opposite the end of Cross-street in the Lower-road, was taken down in 1845. It was a spacious well-built house erected by Sir Thomas Fisher about the beginning of the seventeenth century. It bore in front the initials " P. W. F. " and in the building were the arms of the Fowlers and of Fisher. These were placed over opposite doors on the landing-place of the large staircase.

Amongst the various residents of the house may be mentioned Ezekiel Tongue, author of some celebrated tracts against the Papists, and some treatises upon natural history. About the year 1660 this person kept an academy at the house for the purpose of teaching young ladies Latin and Greek. During the beginning of the present century it was appropriated by Dr. Sutherland, of St. Luke's Hospital, for the reception of insane patients; the grounds adjoining it were then very spacious, and beautifully laid out in lawns and shrubbery, flower-gardens, &c. For some time previous to its demolition it was uninhabited.

Highbury Barn.

THE "SLUICE" AND "EEL PIE" HOUSES.

THIS place derives its name from occupying the site of the barn-house originally belonging to the Manor House at Highbury. The house adjoining the tavern was originally a farm-house, called Highbury Farm, and was considered as the manor-house until the present mansion was erected by the late John Dawes, Esq. Each of the farms in the neighbourhood, Highbury Farm and Cream Hall, were extensive dairies, from which the London milk dealers obtained their chief supply, and which, from time immemorial, was the principal article dealt in by the Islington farmer. The name *Cream Hall*, doubtless originated from this circumstance, and the term *barn* amongst milk dealers is, as is well known, applied to the measure of milk.

Highbury Farm came into the possession of a Mr. Willoughby about the year 1770, who also kept a cake and ale-house upon a very limited scale in connection with the farm. In process of time this ale-house, from its pleasant situation, being much resorted to by persons from the metropolis, the trade increased beyond the accommodation the place afforded, and an extensive barn belonging to the farm was added to the premises, which, being handsomely fitted up, gave the name to the whole place. This barn during the present year (1861) has been pulled down, and houses, fronting the road, are about to be erected which will occupy its site, another " barn " being erected in a different part of the grounds.

In connection with Highbury Barn, a society now extinct, but which deserves remark from several curious customs it originated, was held there for many years during the last century. It was formed by a few *Protestant Dissenters*, who first combined together at the time when the privileges of that body were eminently endangered by the proposed "Schism Bill," which was directly levelled against all those who would not conform to the Established Church. The day on which this Act was to have received the royal sanction Queen Anne died, in consequence of which important event the "Highbury Society" was instituted in commemoration of their deliverance. Their meetings were originally held at Copenhagen House, but, it appears that so far back as the year 1740, Highbury was the place at which they met, and where, "with no penalties to enforce attendance and governed by a set of rules which may be inscribed on the palm of the hand, they continued their uninterrupted meetings, whilst societies, splendid in establishment and powerful in influence, were forgotten." The following particulars, extracted from a printed report published in 1808 by the committee, on the "Rise and Progress of the Highbury Society," will not be found uninteresting to lovers of local curious customs. It appears that a number of Dissenters used to meet at a certain spot in the outskirts, after which they walked together to Highbury for the purpose of an afternoon's recreation. After a few preliminary remarks the report states :—

"About the year 1740, the party of Dissenters who walked together from London had a rendezvous at Moorfields at one o'clock on a certain day, and at *Dettingen Bridge* (where the house known by the name of the "Shepherd and Shepherdess" now stands) they all chalked the initials of their names upon a post for the information of such as might follow. They then proceeded to Highbury, and to beguile the way to that place it was their custom in turn to bowl a ball of ivory at objects in their path. This ball has lately been presented to the society by Mr. William Field. After a slight refreshment they repaired to the field for exercise, but in those days of greater economy and simplicity, neither wine, nor punch, nor tea were introduced, and eightpence was generally the whole expense incurred.

"A particular game, denominated ' hopball ' has from time immemorial formed the recreation of the members of this society at their meetings. On a board which is dated 1734, which they use for the purpose of marking the game, the following motto is engraven :—

    "' *Play justly, play moderately, play cheerfully ; so shall ye play to a rational purpose.*'

    " It is a game not in use elsewhere in the neighbourhood of London, but one resembling it is practised in the west of England. The ball used in this game, consisting of a ball of worsted stitched over with a packthread has from time immemorial been gratuitously furnished by one or another of the members of the society. The following toast is always given at their annual dinner in August, viz.,—' *The glorious first of August, with the immortal memory of King William and his good Queen Mary ; not forgetting Corporal John ; and a fig for the Bishop of Cork, that bottle-stopper !*'

    " How this toast first originated has not been ascertained, but it seems strongly tinctured with the spirit of the times in which it is supposed to have been first adopted. John Duke of Marlborough, the great friend of Protestant and Whig interest, was, in all probability, the person designated as ' Corporal John.' The society dine together weekly ; and it consists at this time of between forty and fifty members."

When this society ceased to hold its meetings at Highbury, is not now known ; probably about the year 1820.

From a simple country dining and refreshment-house, Highbury Barn has become a tavern for giving public dinners on a large scale. Dancing and music in the evening have lately been introduced, which attract a certain class of company. The present proprietor is Mr. Giovanelli.

THE "SLUICE" AND "EEL PIE" HOUSES.

THE little building across the New River called the "Sluice House," has long been famous with the lovers of the piscatorial art as a spot whose neighbourhood was always sure to yield some sport, and even now the rod and the line are pretty frequently employed in its vincinity. It has, however, lost much of its former rurality, and buildings are making rapid strides towards the banks of the river near this spot. Some time ago the "Sluice House" used to contain a ma-

chine for the purpose of supplying water to the neighbourhood of Holloway. It was this portion of the New River, now carried above the level of the ground by high banks, that in former times was nicknamed the *Boarded River*, from being enclosed in a wooden aqueduct.

Near to the "Sluice House" stands what in former times was called the "Eel Pie House," but which has now assumed the former appellation. It used to be famous for its eel pies, supposed to be made from the eels caught in the New River, and for aught we know to the contrary, pies are still made of them. Nelson, writing in 1811, just fifty years ago, says:—" Such is the resort of the lower order of people from the metropolis to the 'Eel Pie House ' on Palm Sunday on their way to Hornsey Wood to procure palm, that the host and servants are obliged to be on the alert at *two* o'clock in the morning in order to receive their numerous guests ; who, even at this early hour begin to call for refreshment. Generally, on that day more than an extra butt of beer is drawn at the house, with gin and liquors in proportion."

At the above period the wholesome regulation of closing public-houses on Saturday night at twelve o'clock was not in force, and it was the custom for apprentices and others to be out on Sunday morning before daylight to collect palm in Hornsey Wood.

The road which runs in the hollow on the west side of the New River between the bottom of Highbury Vale and the "Sluice House" towards the Seven Sisters-road, appears to have been an ancient public way (some suppose part of the Hermann-street constructed by the Romans). The reason why this road has for many years been closed at the Highbury end is that its right as a public way was successfully opposed by James Colebrooke, Esq. When in possession of the manor he erected gates for the purpose of stopping the passage, and this act gave rise to a law-suit, an account of which appeared in the *Gentleman's Magazine* for October, 1784, as follows :—

"There was one Jennings, a Quaker, originally by profession an ass-driver, afterwards he became the proprietor of some donkeys in fee simple, and latterly became a farmer at Crouch End, Hornsey. This man became acquainted with Richard Holland, a leatherseller in Newgate-street, who had a villa at Hornsey, and was at great pains to obtain the suppression of some tolls in Smithfield Market. These two persons determined to oblige Mr. Colebrooke to open the road. Accordingly, one day, they sent several teams down the road. When they came to the Boarded River, not finding anybody to open the gate, they, without further ceremony, cut it down, drove across the fields to the next gate, and did the same there; thence, passing by Cream Hall, they came to Highbury Barn, where they found a third gate, whereupon they despatched a messenger to Mr. Wallbank, farmer at Highbury, requesting him to open the same, which he, refusing to do, they pulled it up with their horses and drove it in triumph down the road to Hopping-lane, and from thence to *Islington*, where they proclaimed aloud that they had come along the old road which was a thoroughfare. Upon this Wallbank commenced a suit, and, in order effectually to stop the passage, by Mr. Colebrooke's desire, took off the crown of the arch at the Boarded River and laid it open, railing in the opening to prevent mischief. At length the suit was brought to an issue, and the plaintiff examined one Richard Glasscock, who had long dwelt at the Boarded River House as a servant to the New River Company, who swore that there had always been a bar there. The defendant did not appear, and the cause was determined in the plaintiff's favour."

Highbury Place.

ABRAHAM NEWLAND. — JOHN NICHOLS.

THE ground upon which this fine row of houses stand was the freehold estate of the late John Dawes, Esq.; they were erected about the year 1780 by Mr. John Spiller. They are now occupied by some of the wealthiest families in Islington, though for a considerable time after they had been built, they remained unoccupied and the first tenants of Nos. 2 to 8 inclusive, had leases granted them at from £34 to £36 per annum; they now fetch thrice that amount of rent.

At various times some of these houses have been inhabited by characters well known both locally and generally. No. 38 was the residence of Abraham Newland, the celebrated cashier of the Bank of England. A short sketch of the history of this somewhat remarkable man, rising as he did by his own industry and integrity from a very humble position to that of one of the heads of the commercial world, will be found interesting : —

He was the son of William Newland, a baker, of Castle-street, Southwark, where he was born on the 23rd of April, 1730. Being educated for the counting-house, and showing great aptitude in the application of the rules of arithmetic, at the age of eighteen his father contrived to get him an appointment as junior clerk in the Bank of England.

His business-like habits, punctuality, and sagacity, soon gained for him the notice of the directors, and by a regular gradation, from one post to another, he was, in the year 1782, appointed chief cashier, with a handsome salary annexed to the situation, and in that important office he continued until the day of his resignation. When he was nominated chief cashier the bank was being enlarged, and a handsome suite of rooms was entirely set apart for his use; and so much was he attached to his employment, and so punctually did he acquit himself in relation to it, that for a whole quarter of a century in which he held office, he never slept one night out of the building. His mind was totally absorbed in his duties; he appeared to exist only for the service of the Bank, and he had been known to declare that he derived " more happiness from a single hour's attendance on the duties of his office than a whole day spent in the most convivial and entertaining company."

The services he rendered were, indeed, of the most important nature, and greatly assisted in placing that institution in the position it now holds. The Company of Directors, however great their experience, were always a fluctuating body, and on every occasion of importance Newland was consulted by them as the senior of the institution, and his opinion on doubtful questions used generally to be decisive. On the occasion of the Directors of the Bank ceasing to pay the amount of their notes in specie, by virtue of an order of the Privy Council, in 1792, he rendered great service to the public and the government by the information he afforded as to the circumstances which led to that measure.

Owing to the rigid economy of his habits, and to some successful speculations, Newland acquired a handsome fortune, and though not parsimonious to those immediately surrounding him, his public bounty and munificence were seldom or ever exhibited. Though in the latter period of his career he possessed a handsome house in a pleasant and inviting neighbourhood, he seldom enjoyed the pleasures it afforded for many hours at a time. His usual practice was to repair to his house at Highbury, after dining in his apartments at the bank, drink tea with his housekeeper, walk in the garden, or along the pathway in front of Highbury-place, or the gravel way leading to Highbury Barn, and then return in the evening to the Bank to sleep. He was remarkably careful as regarded his household expenses. Before the close of the day the domestic transactions were entered in a book, cast up and checked, so that, to a farthing, the rich man might see that the outlay and receipts balanced correctly.

After a constant and faithful discharge of his official duties at the Bank for nearly sixty years, twenty-five of which he had been cashier, Newland was induced, on the 17th September, 1807, to resign by reason of the infirmities of age, on which occasion he declined taking an annuity, but agreed to accept a service of plate valued at one thousand guineas ; before, however, he was put in possession of this valuable gift, he died at his residence at Highbury, his health having began rapidly to decline from the moment he gave up his duties.

Newland was never married, but he had, for several years previous to his death, received into his house a person of the name of Cornthwaite, whose attention relieved him from every domestic trouble, and with whom a friendship was cemented which conduced to the comfort of his declining years. This lady became his housekeeper, and his gratitude for her kindness was expressed in his will. He left her £5,000 in cash, and the interest of £60,000 in the stocks, in addition to his carriages, furniture, and other personal estate. His property at the time of his decease was valued at £200,000, besides £1,000 a year from his landed estates, the whole of which, with the exception of the above legacies to his housekeeper, he bequeathed among his relatives, who were for the most part in necessitous circumstances.

The method by which Newland gained his wealth was not by investing in the stocks, as many supposed, but by participating in shares of loans to the government. The latter was the principal source of his wealth, and from the nature of his situation he could speculate on pretty safe grounds. Notwithstanding his retired and saving habits, it is said that some time previous to his death he projected a plan to receive company, intending to spend £4,000 a year on his domestic establishment, and £2,000 on *extraordinary gratifications*. The infirmities of age, however, hastening upon him, he felt himself ill-qualified, under their pressure, to change the direction of the habits of a life; and like many others whose soul has been absorbed in the acquisition of wealth, he left, as stated, his immense fortune to be enjoyed by those who had no hand in building it up. Thus, while on the one hand Newland's life is an example of industry and successful perseverance, it exhibits the danger of being entirely absorbed in the pursuit of business to the exclusion of all things else.

The celebrity which Newland attained from his name being a prominent feature on the paper currency of the day, gave rise to the following humourous and satirical song, from the pen of the celebrated Charles Dibbin, who was then manager of Sadler's Wells' Theatre :—

There ne'er was a name so bandied by fame,
Thro' air, thro' ocean, and thro' land,
As one that is wrote upon every bank note :
You all must know Abraham Newland !
    Oh, Abraham Newland !
    Noti-fied Abraham Newland !
I've heard people say, sham *Abraham* you may,
But you musn't sham *Abraham Newland !*

For Fashions or Arts should you seek foreign parts,
It matters not wherever you land,
Jew, Christian, or Greek, the same language they speak,
That's the language of Abraham Newland.
    Oh, Abraham Newland !
    Wonderful Abraham Newland !
Though with compliments crammed,
You may die and be d——d,
If you hav'nt an "Abraham Newland."

The world is inclined to think Justice is
  blind,
But lawyers know well she can view land ;
But lor, what of that—she'll blink like a bat
At the sight of an " Abraham Newland."
    Oh, Abraham Newland !
    Magical Abraham Newland !
Tho' Justice, 'tis known, can see through a
  millstone,
She can't see through Abraham Newland.

You Patriots who bawl for the good of us all,
  Kind souls! here like mushrooms they
  strew land ;
Though loud as they drum, each proves
  Orator Mum,
If attacked by stout " Abraham Newland."
    Oh, Abraham Newland !
    Invincible Abraham Newland !
No arguments found in the world half so
  sound,
As the logic of Abraham Newland.

If a maid of threescore, or a dozen years
  more,
For a husband should chance to sigh thro'
  land,
I'm greatly afraid she would not die a maid
If acquainted with " Abraham Newland."
    Oh, Abraham Newland !
    Deluding Abraham Newland !
Tho' crooked and cross, she'd not be at a
  loss
Through the friendship of Abraham New-
  land !

Another celebrated resident in Highbury-
place was John Nichols, Esq., a gentleman
held in affectionate remembrance by many of
the inhabitants of Islington. He was, for
nearly half a century, editor of the *Gentleman's Magazine*, and his whole life was devoted to literary pursuits. He was born at
Islington, on the 2nd of February, 1744, and
ever retained a great affection for the parish,
residing in it the greater part of his life. His
parents first resolved that he should enter
the naval service, but that design being
abandoned through the death of his uncle, a
lieutenant in the navy, under whom he was
to have been placed, he was apprenticed to
William Bowyer, a printer. Mr. Bowyer
being a kind and indulgent master, en-
couraged young Nichols' taste for poetry,
which he observed him cultivate, and when
in his sixteenth year he enjoined him, as an
evening's task, to translate a Latin poem,
which he did with so much success as to
gain his more especial favour. Before the
expiration of his apprenticeship he was sent
by Mr. Bowyer to Cambridge, to treat with
that University for leave of their exclusive
privilege of printing Bibles, which he completed with great tact and success. At
length, in the year 1766, he was taken by
his master into partnership, and afterwards
became his successor.

Mr. Nichols wrote a great number of
works, the first of which, on the " Origin of
Printing," gained him many friends and considerable fame. In 1788 he obtained a share
in the *Gentleman's Magazine*, which, as
stated, he edited for a period of fifty years.
In 1780 he began to publish the " Biblio-
theca Topographica Brittanica," which took
ten years in completing—a work which contains a collection of all articles of British to-
pography, manuscript or printed, that were
in danger of being lost or becoming scarce.
From 1792 to 1815, besides collecting material for the " History and Antiquities of the
Town and County of Leicester," he edited
and wrote no less than forty-seven publications and works, among which may be men-
mentioned " Bowyer's Greek Testament,"
" Bishop Atterbury's Correspondence," " The
History and Antiquities of Lambeth," " The
History and Antiquities of Canonbury, with
some account of the Parish of Islington," &c.
During the same period he also published an
edition of the *Tatler*. The extent, however,
of his literary labours, did not prevent his
engaging in some of the duties of public life ;
for many years he was a member of the
City Corporation, and in 1804 he attained
what he himself called " the summit of his
ambition," being elected Master of the Stationers' Company, the duties of which he
performed in an exemplary manner. On the
8th of February, 1809, Mr. Nichols experienced a great calamity in the destruction
of the whole of his printing-office, in Red
Lion-passage, Fleet-street, by fire, with the
warehouses and their valuable contents.
This great blow, however, did not discourage
him ; supported by his friends and the consoling influences of religion, he applied himself with redoubled energy to the pursuits of
literature, and completed several other important and valuable works. His death,
which was very sudden, took place on the
26th of November, 1826. At ten o'clock at
night he was retiring to rest, and having ascended a step or two of the lower staircase of
his residence, assisted by his eldest daughter,
he sunk down quietly on his knees, and expired without a sigh or a groan at the pa-
triarchal age of eighty-two. He was interred in Islington Churchyard, where his
parents, and those of his children who had

died before him, lay sleeping, and at the time of his death he was probably the oldest inhabitant of the parish. His funeral was attended by Sir Henry Ellis, of the British Museum, Alexander Chalmers, W. Tooke, and many other celebrities.

Of Mr. Nichols' social qualifications, all who ever came in contact with him bore testimony to his excellent temper, obliging disposition, and benevolent heart. He was a humble but fervent believer in the doctrines of Christianity, and no writer, at the close of his life, could have affirmed with greater truth than himself, that he knew of nothing he had written of which he had reason to repent.

In the preface to a memoir written of him by his friend Alexander Chalmers, the following stanzas by George Daniel, of Islington, are inserted:—

Sovereign parent, holy earth,
 To thy bosom we commend
Nichols, full of years and worth,
 Johnson's last surviving friend.

He was of that glorious time,
 Of bright transcendent age,
When immortal truth sublime
 Dropped like manna from the sage.

Called to fill that honoured chair
 Johnson once so nobly graced,
He assayed, with pious care,
 Still to guide the public taste.

Attic wit and sense profound,
 Mid the Muses humbly lay,
Truth divine, with Science crown'd,
 All their various powers display.

Many a name to learning dear
 Bears his faithful fond record:
Greet his memory with a tear,
 Give his name the like reward.

Rich in antiquarian lore,
 Pageants quaint and deeds of arms,
He from history's ample store
 Drew its most romantic charms.

Blest with candour, liberal praise,
 Years beheld his fame increase,
Cheerfulness and length of days,
 Friendship, competence, and peace.

To no quibbling sect a slave,
 His religion was from heaven,
And to Want he freely gave
 What to him was freely given.

Thoughts of *those* that once had been,
 Sweet remembrance of the past,
Cheer'd him through life's closing scene,
 Of those honoured names, the *last!*

Among other remarkable inhabitants of Islington who have resided in this neighbourhood, may be mentioned Dr. Hugh Worthington, for forty years minister of the congregation worshipping at Salter's Hall; also the Rev. John Clayton, minister at the King's Weigh House, East Cheap.

Highbury College.

HIGHBURY COLLEGE is erected on a piece of ground purchased by the late Thomas Wilson, Esq., of Highbury-place for the sum of £2,100, and presented by him to the institution established for the education of ministers of the Independent denomination. The institution was first established in the year 1783 at a house in Mile End, under the superintendence of Dr. Addington. In 1791 premises were obtained at Hoxton, where the students were transferred, and in ten years their number increased from four to forty. This rendered a change of situation necessary, the premises being incapable of enlargement. The committee of the institution then decided upon the erection of a new building, and the present spot was selected and purchased in the manner described. Mr. Wilson, also, with great generosity, in the year 1834, when some land adjacent to the college was announced for sale which it was deemed advisable to purchase in order to prevent the annoyance from the erection of buildings, bought it for £430 for the use of the institution; it now forms a fine exercising ground.

On the 28th of June, 1825, the foundation stone was laid by Mr. Wilson and on the 5th of September, 1826, it was opened for the reception of students, having cost £15,000.

The Independents however, disposed of the building and grounds some time since, when they were purchased for the purpose of forming a Normal Training College on the principles of the Established Church, the Independents removing to St. John's Wood. The Rev. C. R. Alford, M.A., is the present principal of the " Metropolitan Training College," as it is now called, and also afternoon lecturer at Christ Church, Highbury. A large number of the Islington youth attend the college.

The Chapel of Ease.

THIS massive brick structure in the Holloway-road, was erected in the year 1814, the increase of buildings in the neighbourhood of that district rendering it necessary that some accommodation should be provided in addition to that afforded by the parish church. In the year 1811 an Act was passed " for providing a Chapel of Ease and an additional burial ground for the parish of St. Mary, Islington, in the county of Middlesex." By this act the trustees were empowered to raise by annuities the sum of £15,000 for the purposes of building, with power to raise another like sum if found insufficient. The expenditure incurred in the erection of this chapel caused great stir in the parish at the time in consequence of the trustees borrowing a larger sum of money than they were authorised to raise by the Act of Parliament, and also by the enormous expense incurred. It appears, according to a report published at the time, " that one of the trustees purchased land from their own body contrary to law, and were charged besides with purchasing more land than was requisite for the site of the building, having other land, the property of the parish, fit for a burial ground ; in also building a tower at an expense of £3,000, in violation of the Act, which gave no authority for so doing, the *tower* alone of this ugly chapel costing half as much as the *whole* expense of building the elegant church and spire of St. Mary itself."

The total expenditure of the chapel was £33,000. The tower, which is low and square, has a balustrade round the top. The principal entrance at the west end is under a projecting portico of four Doric columns. The defects of the outside are somewhat compensated by the spaciousness and comfort of the interior. The galleries are neatly panelled and supported on circular Doric columns with plainly moulded capitals ; the pulpit and reading desk are of fine mahogany, and the altar, placed in a shallow recess between pillars of Scagliola marble, has the Ten Commandments in the centre and the Lord's Prayer and Creed at the sides. Over the altar is a well-executed painting of Christ's appearance to Mary Magdalen after his resurrection.

On a tablet in front of the building is the following inscription : " This chapel, erected by authority of Parliament at the expense of the parishioners, was consecrated by the Right Rev. William. Lord Bishop of London, August 17, 1814, Geo. Strahan, D.D., Vicar, Edward Flower, treasurer ; Robert Oldershaw, Vestry Clerk ; William Wickins, architect ; Thos. Griffiths, John Tibbatts, John Patrick, churchwardens."

The first minister appointed to this chapel by Dr. Strahan, the vicar, was the Rev. Joseph Patten Rose. On the decease of Mr. Rose in 1830, the present minister, the Rev. John Hambledon, M.A., was appointed. Mr. Hambledon is the author of several religious works, which are very generally esteemed, " A Brief History of the Soul," and " Sabbath Profanation and Sabbath Sanctification," being, perhaps, the most worthy of mention.

The Caledonian Asylum.

THIS well-known institution is situated in the Caledonian-road, to which highway it has given the name. In the year 1828, when it was erected, it was the only building on the line of road between Thornhill-bridge and Holloway. It is a handsome edifice of Suffolk brick ornamented with freestone, with a boldly projecting portico of four fluted columns of the Doric order supporting a triangular pediment, in the centre of which is a shield bearing the arms of Scotland, and on the apex is a full-length figure of St. Andrew, bearing his cross. Within the portico, over the principal entrance, is the following inscription :—

"This institution, founded by the auspices of the Highland Society, and honoured with the patronage of the King, was incorporated by Act of Parliament, 1828, for the supporting and educating the children of sailors, soldiers, and marines, natives of Scotland, who have died or been disabled in the service of their country; and of indigent Scotch parents resident in London not entitled to parochial relief. The first stone of this building was laid in the 8th year of his most gracious Majesty George VI., on the 17th May, 1827, by his Royal Highness Augustus Frederick, Duke of Sussex, Earl of Inverness, Baron of Arklow, President of the Corporation."

The asylum was erected at a cost, in the first instance, of £10,000, but fifteen years ago it was greatly enlarged to accommodate girls as well as boys, Mr. Matheson, a Scotch gentleman, giving £1,000 towards that object. The building contains school-rooms and dormitories for 200 children, with the requisite offices for the master and superintendents of the establishment. In the committee room of the institution there is a large drawing of the building by the architect, George Tappen, Esq.

The history of the institution is interesting. In the year 1808 the many wealthy Scotchmen residing in London, sensible that there were a great many indigent Scotch poor in the metropolis for whose children no institution had been provided, determined upon establishing the Caledonian Asylum, which should confer upon those children the blessings of education. The measure was well received, but in consequence of the circumstances of the country at that time it was postponed till the year 1813, when the Highland Society prosecuted it with so much energy that £10,000 was subscribed. In the following year the management was transferred to the Society and a place was procured in Cross-street, Hatton-garden, which, in December, 1819, was opened for the reception of children. The number admitted was twelve which was afterwards increased to forty, the utmost the premises in Hatton Garden could accommodate. . The establishment was removed to the new building at Islington in the year 1828.

The boys are admitted from the age of seven till ten, and remain till they are fourteen, when they are apprenticed or otherwise provided for. They wear the kilt made of the royal Stuart tartan, and their whole dress is picturesque and appropriate. They breakfast off Scotch porridge every morning. The education imparted is of a varied character, and the children are examined by the Scotch Presbytery once every year when prizes are awarded. The number of children in the institution at the present time (1861) is 119.

The Angel Inn.

THEATRICAL PERFORMANCES IN THE TIME OF CHARLES I.

THE Angel Inn, though not in the parish, is so identified with Islington, that it would not be proper to pass it over without some mention. There is a tradition that the whole of the ground from the corner of the Liverpool-road (formerly known as the Back-road) to the Angel, was forfeited by this parish and united to that of Clerkenwell in consequence of the refusal of the Islington authorities to bury a pauper who was found dead at the corner of the road in question ; the corpse was taken to Clerkenwell, and, as a consequence, the district above described was claimed, and ultimately retained by that parish. This might possibly have happened before a single house stood on the disputed ground ; certain it is, that on the opposite side of the way, the parish of Islington extends to the corner of the City-road, exactly facing the Angel.

The Angel is said to have been established upwards of two hundred years, during the greater part of which period it was usual for travellers coming from the north, to welcome it as their final resting place previous to entering London ; particularly if they happened to reach Islington before nightfall, few travellers would encounter the remaining perils of their journey till the morning, the roads, as before stated, leading thence to the City being, even less than half a century ago, infested with robbers.

The ancient house, which was pulled down in 1819, presented the usual features of a large old country inn, having a long front with an overhanging tiled roof and two rows of windows, twelve in each row, independent of those on the basement story. The principal entrance was beneath a projection which extended along a portion of the front, and had a wooden gallery at top. The inn-yard, approached by a gateway in the centre, was nearly a quadrangle, having double galleries, supported by plain columns and carved pilasters, with caryatides and other figures. Here were the principal evidences of the antiquity of the building. These galleries, no doubt, had been often thronged with spectators of dramatic entertainments at the period when inn-yards were customarily employed for such purposes. At Islington it was customary to hold these dramatic entertainments at several of the inns, as is evidenced in the account given of the Islington Reformers, who used to assemble at an inn under the pretence of seeing such performances. These public theatres were only open during the day in the summer time. The central part was open to the sky, the public occupied the galleries round the inn-yard ; a platform for a stage was erected at one end, round which the *groundlings*, as those who sat in the area were called, witnessed the performance. The stage was generally strewed with rushes, and separated from the groundlings, or occupiers of the pit, by a simple wooden paling. At the rear of the stage was a balcony, about eight or nine feet above the platform, in which a mock audience sat when a play within a play was exhibited, as in Hamlet, the actors in that case addressing themselves to the balcony, and turning their backs upon a great portion of the real audience. From beneath this balcony the performers made their entrance and exit, through a pair of curtains which opened in the centre and were drawn backwards and forwards on an iron rod. Matted walls, or tapestry, were the general interior decoration. When these theatres began to be covered in, as they appear to have been in the time of Charles I., candle-light performances, as well as day-light, were adopted.

The present Angel Inn does not occupy the exact space of its predecessor, the two shops in the High-street to the north being erected on part of its ancient site.

Concerning the origin of the name of this celebrated inn there are several traditions. The reference made in the proclamation of Henry VIII. to "our Ladye of the Oke at Iseldon," is thought by some to have alluded to an image of the Virgin placed amidst the branches of an oak-tree by the wayside, near to the " hermitage at Islington's town's end" (mentioned in Sir Richard Cloudesley's will, dated January 13, 1518), to excite the adoration of the passers' bye. This hermitage was situated on the land belonging to the Knights of St. John of Jerusalem, and on their suppression fell into lay hands, and from some documents in the archives of the Brewers' Company, it appears the site of Dame Alice Owen's Almshouses in the Goswell-road, was formerly the Hermitage field. The " Angel" nearly opposite being established as an hostelrie for "travellers

at Islington's town's end" might have taken its name from the image thus placed in the tree in question.

It is known that in the old Church of Islington, dedicated to the Virgin Mary, there was a figure designated as " Our Ladye of Islington," to which allusion has before been made, but we think the " Ladye of the Oke" mentioned in the above proclamation, could not have referred to that which was in a building, but rather belonged to the hermitage which it is known existed in the neighbourhood referred to.

Colebrook Row.

"STARVATION FARM" — ALEXANDER CRUDEN.

COLEBROOKE-ROW was built on land belonging to the family whose name it bears. On the west bank of the New River, near to the place where it formerly emerged from the arch beneath the road to the north end of Colebrooke-row—(now covered in)—there stood, in the beginning of the present century, a yard and a barn known to the inhabitants by the name of *Starvation Farm.* The singular individual who obtained for his property this unpleasant cognomen was the Baron Ephraim D'Aguilar, whose private residence was at No. 21, Camden-street, in the same neighbourhood. He was by birth a Jew, and born at Vienna about the year 1740. Succeeding to the title and estate of his father, who died in England in the year 1760, the Baron became a naturalized British subject, and about that time he married the daughter of Moses da Costa, a rich merchant, by which lady, who had an immense fortune, the baron had two daughters. In 1770 the Baron married a second wife with whom he also had a large fortune. During his first marriage and the former part of his second, this baron lived in great splendour at a house in Broad-street Buildings, City, keeping an elegant equipage and between thirty and forty servants. Soon after his latter marriage, however, he began to change his mode of living; he removed from Broad-street, became careless both in his person and manners, and affecting the appearance of poverty, totally withdrew himself from his family connections and the world. Although abounding in wealth he contracted habits of the most mean and pernicious kind, and acted with the greatest cruelty towards his second wife. She died several years before the Baron. Previous to her death he took a house in Shaftesbury-place, Aldersgate-street, whither he usually retired to sleep, also the one in Camden-street, Islington, together with the farm described, in which latter place he spent a considerable portion of his time during the day. He had several houses in various parts of the metropolis filled with rich furniture which he kept shut up. His house in Aldersgate-street became a scene of great licentiousness by the characters he contrived to decoy into the place.

His farm-yard at Islington, in consequence of the wretched pittance of food which he allowed his cattle, was denominated by the inhabitants "Starvation Farm." Frequently he suffered the animals to linger and die from want through a morbid love of cruelty and delight in witnessing their anguish. When remonstrated with on the inhumanity of the practice, he would answer "that he did it in order to make them know their master." Whatever was given to the wretched animals was apportioned by himself and frequently bestowed by his own hand ; and although in one sense penurious he allowed nearly the whole of his live stock to perish for want of provender. In the heap of dung and dirt which he permitted to accumulate on his premises from the time he commenced farming (he never suffered the place to be cleansed) between thirty and forty carcases of different animals were supposed to have been deposited, all of which had dropped from starvation. It is to be regretted there were no Sanitary Inspectors or Society for the Prevention of Cruelty to Animals in those days! A man whom he employed to look after his cattle on the farm had directions, when any of his stock died, to bury them in the general heap. This man, having on one occasion, sold the body of a starved calf to a vendor of catsmeat, and the transaction coming to the ears of the Baron, he was instantly summoned before him to answer the serious charge of embezzling his master's property, which, however, ended in the man having to pay the sum of 1s. 10d. out of his wages, that being the amount he received for the dead carcase. His cows he would sometimes send from his farm to a field he possessed at Bethnal-green, whither he would despatch his servant every morning to fetch the milk for his own use. Such, indeed, was the state of famine to which the live stock belonging to the Baron on his Islington Farm were reduced, they frequently devoured each other; his hogs were often observed to be making their meals upon the poor starveling fowls.

As may be supposed the wretched situation of these poor animals frequently aroused the indignation of the neighbourhood, who assembled in crowds to hoot and pelt the Baron, for he was often to be seen about the premises in a very mean and dirty state. Upon these occasions he would take no notice of the incensed multitude, but at the first opportunity quietly effect his escape. Upon the farm he kept an old favourite coach, a large and cumbrous machine, which, when in use, was drawn by six horses, the latter being a part of the live stock on his farm.

This odious character, apparently a fit subject for a lunatic asylum, is said to have been an excellent scholar, and to have written with great elegance and facility. During the latter years of his life, he forsook all society, and scarcely ever allowed any of his family or former connexions to have an interview with him. In his last illness, which was occasioned by an inflammation in his bowels, notwithstanding the severity of the weather and the dangerous nature of his complaint, he would not allow a fire in his house, nor

admit a doctor into his presence. He, however, followed the prescriptions of a medical man, to whom he would send a fee by his servant. His youngest daughter affectionately sent several times to him in his last moments, begging permission for an interview, but the unnatural father, with oaths declared she should never enter his presence. He died at his house in Shaftesbury-place on the 11th of March, 1802, at the age of 62. His body was afterwards removed to Islington and from thence to the Jew's burying-ground at Mile-end, where he was interred. He left two legitimate daughters and a number of illegitimate children; the former, upon his dying intestate, administered to his property and came into the possession of the whole.

The Baron's effects at Islington were sold by auction which lasted two days; his coach which scarcely held together from decay, fetched only £7, and his stock of horses, cows, and pigs, £128. At Shaftesbury-place his valuable library, consisting of Hebrew, English, and foreign literature, was also sold. His diamonds and jewels were computed to be worth £30,000, and he was possessed of seven cwt. of silver plate. He had, moreover, hoarded up in a lumber room of his house 40 bags of cochineal and 12 bags of fine indigo, probably worth £10,000, and which he had purchased years before his death upon speculation, intending never to part with them till he could get a good profit by their sale. The whole of his personal property was estimated at £200,000.

ALEXANDER CRUDEN.

A HOUSE in Camden-passage, in this neighbourhood, was once the residence of the amiable but eccentric writer, Alexander Cruden. He had been an occasional resident at Islington for a number of years before he took the house in Camden-passage, having previously lived in Upper-street and Paradise-row.

He was the second son of William Cruden, a merchant of Aberdeen, at which place he was born, in the year 1701. Having received an education at the Grammar School at that city, he took the degree of M.A., with the view of entering the ministry, but before the time arrived for taking upon himself such profession, he exhibited symptoms of insanity, and was put in confinement, which afterwards settled into the belief that he was delegated by Heaven to "reform the guilty world," and his meritorious acts in numerous instances proved his ardour and zeal for the good of his fellow-creatures. At the age of eighteen he came to London, and after serving as a private tutor, opened a bookseller's shop under the Royal Exchange, where he also employed himself as a corrector of the press. It was in the following year, after he had opened this shop, that Mr. Cruden commenced his great and laborious work, " A Complete Concordance of the Holy Scriptures of the Old and New Testament," a work which required an amount of labour, patience, and perseverance, which few men have ever been known to possess. The first edition was published in 1737, and was dedicated to Queen Caroline, whose patronage he was unfortunately deprived of by her death. This, together with other disappointments, occasioned some embarrassment in his affairs, and some time elapsing before his valuable work was properly appreciated, he was compelled to give up his business. He became melancholy, and was sent to a lunatic asylum at Bethnal Green. His disorder, however, was always of a very harmless kind, and on his release he published a pamphlet with the following singular title :—" The London Citizen extremely injured, giving an account of his adventures during the time of his severe and long campaign at Bethnal Green for nine weeks and six days ; the citizen being sent there in March, 1738, by Robert Wightman, a notoriously conceited whimsical man, where he was chained, handcuffed, straight-waistcoated, &c."

He commenced an action against Dr. Munro, the physician of this place for his cruel treatment, but was unable to make out a case. He shortly afterwards assumed the title of " Alexander the Corrector," and maintained that he was divinely commissioned to reform the manners of the age and to restore the due observance of the Sabbath. Among other singularities of Mr. Cruden's life may be mentioned that, in September, 1738, after his release, he tried to persuade those who had been the means of his confinement, to be imprisoned in Newgate as a compensation for the injuries they had brought upon him. To his sister he proposed what he thought were very mild terms, viz., Newgate, Reading, and Aylesbury jails, or the prison in Windsor Castle. On her refusal to be incarcerated he commenced an action against her and three others, which was tried in February, 1739, when a verdict was given for the defendants. Upon the occasion of his visit to Oxford and Cambridge, he in person exhorted the young persons whom he found in the public walks on the Sabbath, to keep

that day holy. Such advice from the pulpit would be deemed orthodox, but under such circumstances, in Mr. Cruden, it was deemed madness. Though it cannot be questioned that Mr. Cruden was in many ways very singular, it has too often been the fashion in all ages to account those as mad who through extraordinary zeal, do good in ways not generally adopted by mankind. Paul, the apostle of the Gentiles, in his appeal to Festus, was under the same condemnation, and Rowland Hill was once accused of insanity upon enthusiastically proclaiming the Gospel in the open street. " Mad !" replied the celebrated divine, in answer to the accusation, " if I were to shout and cry aloud to bring assistance to save the life of a poor creature which was in danger, you would commend me for the act, but because I am in earnest in crying to men to save their eternal souls from everlasting perdition, through the blood of Jesus, I am counted insane."

Mr. Cruden made application for the honour of knighthood, which was refused him. He frequently traversed the streets, and with a piece of sponge which he carried in his pocket, would efface from the walls all expressions contrary to good morals, and he would enter any mob or tumultuous assembly with the authority of a magistrate, and strenuously exhort the contending parties to depart quietly to their homes, which advice, from his respectable appearance, and the gently reproving manner in which it was delivered, frequently produced the desired result.

From the second edition of his " Concordance " he realized £500, and he presented a copy in person to his Majesty. In private life Mr. Cruden was exceedingly affable and polite ; under the influence of a philanthropic spirit of the most exalted kind, he spent his days in doing good. In the year 1762, by his fervent application to the Earl of Halifax, then Secretary of State, he succeeded in rescuing from the gallows a poor ignorant sailor named Richard Potter, who had forged a seaman's will. His benevolence did not stop here ; he visited the man in prison, prayed with him, instructed him, taught him the principles of religion, and, in fact, made a convert of the wretched prisoner. He also continued his labours among the other felons of Newgate, gave them copies of the Bible, Catechisms, &c., questioned them himself, and bestowed small pecuniary rewards upon the most apt scholars. Upon one occasion he was the means of inducing a man who intended suicide, to return to the bosom of his family. He died at his lodging in Islington, on the morning of November 1st, 1770, in his 69th year. When the house-keeper went to inform him that breakfast was ready, he was found dead on his knees, in the posture of prayer.

Mr. Cruden was firm in his religious opinions, which were Calvinistic, and when-ever an attack was made upon them, he would reply with considerable warmth. He never neglected, however, to shew his faith by his works. To the poor he was as liberal of his money as his advice, and seldom, indeed, separated the one from the other. It is well known that he often gave more than he re-tained for his own use. Mr. Cruden wrote several other works beside his "Concor-dance," but it is on the latter that his fame rests.

Highgate Archway.

GEOLOGICAL FORMATION OF HIGHGATE HILL.

IN the year 1809, in consequence of the vast coach traffic which at that period passed over Highgate Hill, it was felt desirable that some road should be made so that the steep ascent, with its consequent wear and tear of horseflesh and material, might be avoided. Accordingly, Mr. Robert Vazie, an engineer, projected a plan for forming a subterranean arched tunnel twenty-four feet wide, eighteen feet high, and three hundred yards in length, through the body of Highgate Hill, and an Act of Parliament was obtained incorporating the proprietors by the style of the " Highgate Archway Company, with power to raise £40,000 by shares of £50 each, and an addi-tional sum of £20,000 if necessary." Upon the necessary funds being raised, the work was commenced and the tunnel formed to the length of 130 yards, when, owing to the bad construction of the brickwork, the greater part fell in on the morning of the 13th of April, 1812, fortunately before the workmen had commenced their labours for the day. Hornsey-lane, which now runs across the archway, and which bounds the parish of Islington on the north, presented a curious spectacle on the occasion. The road had sunk as if by some inward convulsion of the earth, and a row of trees on the north side of the lane were all thrown together in sin-gular confusion

The idea of forming a tunnel, was, after the accident, abandoned. The plan was altered, and on the 21st of the ensuing year, a road in the line of the intended tunnel was formed, by which the hill and village of Highgate are avoided, making the latter much more retired than formerly In con-structing this road the company at first neg-lected to provide a way across the cutting which had severed Hornsey-lane, and pedes-trians were obliged to descend one side and ascend the other of the incline. The inhabitants, however, compelled the com-pany to erect the present arch, which forms so agreeable an object in the surrounding landscape. It is built of stone, flanked with brickwork, and surmounted with three semi-arches supporting a bridge with open battle-ments of stone. It was erected in the year 1812. During the progress of the cutting of the road a vast number of fossil shells, sharks teeth, and scales of different fish were discovered. Also fossil wood and fruits, and a peculiar resinous substance which emitted an odour when heated and melted into a limpid fluid. These fossils were found at a depth of eighty feet from the surface, and the specimens have been classed by Mr. Wetherell, F. G. S., of Highgate, who read a paper on the subject on the 13th of June, 1832, at the Geological Society of London.

The cutting open of this road threw much light upon the geology of Hampstead Heath, which belongs to the same range of hills. The top of the heath, near Jack Straw's Castle, is situated about 410 feet above high-water mark at London-bridge. and is covered with a large stratum of sand. Various speculations have been indulged in as to the origin of the sand at so high an altitude, and a thoughtful person on visiting Hampstead Heath might put the question, "How is it that we do not find sand in or on the strata of any other part of the London basin in the neighbourhood?" There is, according to geological science, scarcely any doubt that by some extraordinary operation of nature, that portion of land now known as Hampstead Heath, was once the bed of a pre-existent ocean. James Parkinson, Esq., in a letter to a fellow-student on the subject, says, " Does the sand at Hampstead Heath differ much from the sea-sand? I think not. Indeed, there is no doubt of its being deposited from the waters of some former sea or immense lake, which deposit may have been carried by the mechanical agency of the water into heaps. How to explain the partial deposit in a place so far distant from the sea, except by the agency of the winds or the action of the waters, which might have brought deposits of sand and left them in a heap, so that after being bereft of its covering waters it remained in the spot deposited, there is not sufficient data to determine.

"In support of the strong evidence in favour of this supposition, in the blue clay beneath the sand, have been found the teeth of fish and shells, and in Dr. Woodward's collection at Cambridge College, is a shark's tooth, and the spiral bodies of several marine animals. Pieces of wood pierced by the " teredines " or ship worms, and which had become petrified, and numerous fossils, exactly agreeing with those of Southend in Essex and the Isle of Sheppy, besides several of the genus nautilus of a large size, were also discovered in the yellow clay-stone in excavating the road for Highgate Archway."

Notwithstanding the length of time which the heath formerly supplied the metropolis with sand, the average depth is now about 10 feet, though in some cases it averages more than 25. Mr. Abrahams, an auctioneer, who lived in the neighbourhood in 1803, says, " Upwards of 20 cartloads of sand pass through Hampstead every day, which sells at 4s. 6d. per load and gravel at 6s."

The view from the summit of the Archway is very extensive and picturesque.

Stroud's Green.

AT the bottom of the Hanley-road, Upper Holloway, is a place called Stroud's Green, which was formerly a long piece of land in Highbury Manor, but now nearly all enclosed. One side of Stroud's Green is in Hornsey parish, and on the side belonging to Hornsey, there stood an old country residence called Stapleton Hall, originally the property and residence of Sir Thomas Stapleton, of Oxon, Bart., a very ancient family. The building contained in various parts the initials of the baronet and his wife, with the date 1609, and a century ago had on its front the following inscription :—

" Ye are welcome all,
To Stapleton Hall."

This building was for some time converted into a country inn, but Mr. William Lucas, a proprietor of the place some forty years ago, divided it into two houses, and erecting a handsome frontage, gave it a modern appearance. Some time ago there was a society which held its meetings at the " Queen's Arms," Newgate-street, who were accustomed to dine at Stapleton Hall annually, and who styled themselves the " Lord Mayor, Aldermen, and corporation of Stroud Green." The occasion of their visit invariably drew to the spot an immense concourse of people, and a kind of fair or country wake was observed during the day. This society has long ceased to exist.

St. James's Church.

ALL SAINTS'. — ST. STEPHENS'. — ST. PETERS'. — HOLLOWAY CONGREGATIONAL CHAPEL. — FRIENDS' MEETING HOUSE.

ST. JAMES'S CHURCH, situate at the northern termination of the Liverpool-road, was the first of the three churches built by subscription in accordance with the plan of the late Bishop of London. The site was given by Miss Sebbon, and £1,000 was granted in aid of its erection out of the Metropolis Church Fund. It was consecrated for public worship on the 19th June, 1838, at a cost of £3,600, and in 1839, the accommodation proving insufficient for the numbers who attended, a wing was added at a further cost of £2,398. It is a neat brick edifice, with a handsome south front of four Ionic semi-columns, executed in Bath stone, the entablature and cornice being erected on the model of the temple of Erectheus at Athens. The interior is plain but neatly-arranged, and is lighted by a range of five circular-headed windows in the north side, the upper portion of which light the galleries and the lower the body of the church. Against the south wall is a board containing the following inscription :—

"This church was enlarged in the year 1839, by which 385 additional sittings were obtained ; and, in consequence of a grant from the Incorporated Society for promoting the enlargement, building, and repairing of churches and chapels, 226 of that number are hereby declared to be free and unappropriated for ever, in addition to 824 sittings formerly provided, 100 of which are free. Rev. W. B. Mackenzie, minister."

The present minister is the Rev. William Bell Mackenzie, M.A., who has been so from its commencement. There are the usual benevolent institutions in connection with St. James's, including the Infant and National schools in St. George's-place.

ALL SAINTS' CHURCH.

THE above church, situate near Thornhill-bridge, in the Caledonian-road, was opened for public worship on the 3rd of July, 1838, at a cost of £4,412. The contribution of £3,500 made in October, 1836, from the Metropolis Church Fund Committee to the Islington fund for building three new churches in the parish, was granted on the condition that one of those edifices should be at Battle-bridge. An eligible piece of ground was therefore selected and purchased for £200 from George Thornhill, M.P. for Hunting-don, the proprietor of the large estate which bears his name, which reaches from near King's-cross to the south side of the Offord-road, and includes Thornhill-square, Hemingford-terrace, Richmond-road, and the streets adjoining. Mr. Thornhill gave £30 as a donation to the fund.

All Saints' Church is a plain edifice of brick in the later style of English architecture, with a turret surmounted by a small crocketted spire. The walls are strengthened by plain buttresses. Its interior is commodious and neat There is a range of eight narrow lancet-shaped windows bordered with stained glass. The altar is placed in a recess under the east window between two columns, the Decalogue, Lord's Prayer, and Creed, being painted on tablets within the recess. The present minister is the Rev. Theophilus Saulez, M.A. By an order in Council, £48 per annum was allotted out of the fund raised by the suspension of certain canonries, to augment the minister's income. There are National and Infant schools, a Sunday school, Saving's bank, and many other institutions connected with the place. The schools are situated in Rodney-street, and are built of red brick in the Elizabethan style.

ST. STEPHEN'S CHURCH.

This church, situated on the west side of the New North Road, is one of the three churches whose erection was aided by the grant from the Metropolis Churches Fund. It was consecrated in June, 1839, by the Bishop of London, in the presence of the Lord Mayor and other dignitaries. The building was erected by Mr. Dove of Islington, at a cost of £4,720, of which £1,500 was granted out of the fund mentioned. It is a neat edifice of Suffolk brick, built in the early English style of architecture. From the tower, which is strengthened by flying buttresses, rises, about twelve feet from the roof, a small octagonal bell-turret. The interior is lighted by five lancet-shaped windows; the galleries are panelled in pointed arches and supported on cast-iron pillars. The altar-piece also consists of three lancet-shaped arches, in the recesses of which are painted the Decalogue, &c. The whole arrangement is pleasing and appropriate, and the tower and spire give to the exterior a stately appearance. The Rev. Thomas Barton Hill, curate of St. Mary's, was the first-appointed incumbent of this church. The present minister is the Rev. H. Deck.

ST. PETER'S CHURCH.

St. Peter's Church, situated on the south side of River-lane, was erected after designs by the same architect as St. Paul's, Ball's Pond—Sir Charles Barry. It is a neat quadrangular edifice of brick in the early English style. At each angle of the building is a buttress, supporting a pedestal, which terminates with octagonal pinnacles of stone. The interior is simple, the gallery is supported on cast-iron pillars, and the roof is panelled-painted in imitation of oak. This church was opened for public worship on the 14th July, 1835, and the expenses were £3,400. Attached to it are day and Sunday schools, which are very efficient and well-managed. The Rev. T. Haslegrave, M.A., is the minister.

HOLLOWAY CONGREGATIONAL CHAPEL.

This place of worship, situated at the northern end of the Caledonian-road, where it emerges into Holloway at the junction of the Camden-road, is a handsome Gothic structure built of Kentish rag stone. Its interior is in keeping with the general style of the building. This church first held its meetings at the chapel in the Holloway-road now being used by the Presbyterians, which was erected in 1808, a former chapel upon the same spot being destroyed by fire, supposed to have been the work of an incendiary, for whose apprehension £200 reward was offered, half by the congregation and half by government. This place was subsequently enlarged when under the ministry of the Rev. William Spencer, and again becoming inadequate to meet the wants of the congregation the present new and commodious chapel was erected about fifteen years ago. The present minister is the Rev. J. Morris. A new school and lecture-room has lately been erected in connection with this place situate in the lane opposite the north-end of the chapel.

FRIENDS' MEETING HOUSE.

A little to the east of the National schools in St. George's-place, Holloway, is a Quaker's Meeting House. It was formerly a Wesleyan Chapel, and had a Sunday school attached. In accordance with the unassuming principles of the Society of Friends, the building is exceedingly plain, though neat. In front of the edifice is a zinc covering, and a small wicket-gate is situate at the entrance.

Lady Owen's School and Almshouses.

THE handsome red-brick buildings in the St. John-street-road, known as Lady Owen's Schools and Almshouses (founded for the education of boys and sustenance of poor people belonging to Islington and Clerkenwell) are said to have had their origin from a very remarkable circumstance, of which the following interesting traditionary account is extracted from a record in the possession of the Brewer's Company:—

"Alice Owen was born at Islington in the reign of Queen Mary; her first husband was Henry Robinson, citizen and brewer of London; her second husband was William Elkin of London, alderman; her third and last husband was Thomas Owen, one of her Majesty's Queen Elizabeth's Justices of the Court of Common Pleas; lived and died in Bassishaw; made her will on the 10th of June 1613; in the E. corner of St. Mary's Church is a curious monument erected to her memory.

"In the reign of Queen Mary it was an exercise for archers to shoot with their bows and arrows at butts; this part of Islington at that time being all open fields and pasture land, and on the same spot of ground where the school now stands was a woman milking a cow. The lady Owen, then a maiden gentlewoman, walking by with her maid-servant, observed the women a-milking, and had a mind to try the cow's paps, whether she could milk, which she did, and at her withdrawing from the cow, an arrow was shot through the crown of her hat (at which time high-crowned hats were in fashion) which so startled her that she then declared that if she lived to be a lady she would erect something on that very spot of ground in commemoration of the great mercy shown by the Almighty in that astonishing deliverance. The time passed on till she became a widow-lady; her servant at the time this accident happened being still with her lady, reminded her lady of her former words; her answer was she remembered the affair and would fulfil her promise, upon which she purchased the land from the 'Welsh Harp' to the 'Turk's Head,' Islington-road, and built

thereon, as appears with the arrows fixed on the top."

That the above story is literally true there is no reason at all to doubt, it being testified both by documents and trustworthy historians, such as Stowe and others. The charity now contains about ninety boys, who are taught reading, writing, and accounts, and of whom four-fifths are taken from Islington and one-fifth from Clerkenwell. The master receives a liberal salary, and has a house rent free. The almshouses are for fourteen poor widows (seven from Islington and seven from Clerkenwell) who are required by Lady Owen's regulations to be at least fifty years of age, of good reputation, and to continue no longer on the foundation than while they remain single. Each of the inmates now receives eight shillings per week, together with a donation of ten shillings and sixpence at Christmas, a sufficient allowance of coals, and a gown every two years. The original allowance settled by Lady Owen was 16s. 8d. per quarter for the maintenance of each widow, and 6l. per annum between them in sea-coal; also, one cloth gown each, of three yards of broad cloth, once in three years.

The original free-school and almshouses erected by Lady Owen on the east side of St. John-street-road, consisted of a low range of brick buildings. The almshouses comprised two separate single apartments with a small garden in the rear, for each almswoman, and a court in front; and the school accommodated thirty boys. Over the entrance-gate was a stone bearing the following inscription :—

"These ten Almshouses, with the Free Grammar School adjoining, were built and endowed in the year 1613, by Lady Alice Owen, and by her will left to the government of the Worshipful Company of Brewers, in London. In commemoration of which this stone was placed in the year 1788.

"EDWARD BONBY, Esq., *Master.*

"Mr. BENJAMIN SMITH } *Wardens.*"
"Mr. SAMUEL WALLINGTON }

These buildings having become dilapidated, and the funds of the charity having been increased by the falling in of some leases, the Brewers' Company determined upon erecting new schools and almshouses, under the direction of Mr. F. Tattenall, surveyor. The expense of their erection was about £6,000. On taking down the old building two of the original arrows alluded to, were discovered, and are now, we believe, in the master's care; the more perfect one of the two was found sunken very deep in the wall on which it had been placed upon the erection of the building.

The present building is composed of red brick with copings of stone, in the Elizabethan style of architecture. The schoolroom is a well-arranged apartment 45 feet in length and 20 feet wide. At the upper end is the master's seat, enclosed by panelled oak, and above this are the rules of the school in letters of gold in a framed tablet. At the opposite end of the room is part of Lady Owen's monument, originally erected in old Islington church, and removed into the former school-room on the taking down of that structure: it contains nine out of the eleven figures of that lady's children and grandchildren in a walking attitude. The seats for the scholars are of oak, and furnished with every requisite accommodation for keeping the books.

Facing the school, and equally handsome in their style of building, are the almshouses. In a niche over the entrance, is a full length figure of Lady Owen; at the extremity of each wing of the building are two tablets of marble, one bearing the arms of Lady Owen the other that of the Brewer's Company. There are twelve tenements of two apartments each, and one in the centre, which contains on the ground floor a large sitting-room for two inmates, and above it a separate sleeping-room for each, the whole, as stated, affording accommodation for fourteen persons.

This interesting and useful charity was founded and endowed about 1609, and Lady Alice Owen, on the 22nd of November, in the same year, conveyed to the Brewer's Company in trust for it, upwards of ten acres of ground, called the "Hermitage Fields,"*

* These fields are now covered with buildings, the rents from which support the institution. The ground extends from the "Red Lion," in the St. John-street-road, to Rawstone-street. The fields, no doubt, derived their name from the circumstance of a hermitage being, in olden times, within their proximity.

and the rent-charge of £25, issuing out of certain closes situated on the north side of the road leading from Islington to Paddington; and agreeably also to her request and direction, Sir Thomas Rich, her executor, purchased a farm at Orsett, in Essex, containing forty-one acres, then of the annual value of £22, for the benefit of the funds. Lady Owen also laid down rules for the government of the school and almshouses, and gave the entire management of the charity to the Brewer's Company, the master and wardens of which she enjoined once a year to "take pains and go and visit" the charity and her tomb in Islington Church, allowing thirty shillings for a dinner on the occasion. By these rules it was directed that the schoolmaster should have the school-house for his habitation, and a garden for his recreation rent free, and should be paid £5 quarterly. "Devout and godly prayers" were also to be read at due hours and times, by the master to the almspeople, who were required to be "duly and daily present except when hindered by sickness or some tolerable cause." It was also enjoined that there should be ten widows in the almshouses chosen from Islington parish, and thirty children in the school, twenty-four chosen from the poor inhabitants of Islington and six from those in Clerkenwell. The widows were to have resided in Islington seven years.

THE "OLD RED LION."

On the east side of St. John-street-road, adjoining the site where the old Almshouses once stood, is the "Old Red Lion." This house, which has been recently renovated, was established as far back as the year 1415. It has been used by many celebrated characters; Thompson, the author of the "Seasons," Hogarth, who has introduced the gable end of the house in his picture of "Evening," and Paine, lived there for some time. At the commencement of the present century this inn stood almost alone; opposite were pens in which sheep were folded previous to being taken to Smithfield, in the midst of which stood an old house called "Goose Farm," which is said to have derived its name from being a receptacle for droves of geese.

St. John-street-road used, up to the year 1820, to be called the Islington-road, and the following advertisements taken from papers of the period, will give a tolerable idea of the character of entertainments provided in that neighbourhood for visitors :—

"On Tuesday next, being Shrove Tuesday, there will be a fine 'hog barbecued' whole at the house of Peter Pratt, at the 'Rising Sun,' in Islington-road, with other diversions. It is the house where the ox was roasted whole at Christmas last."—*Mist's Journal,* Feb. 9, 1726.

"At Mr. Stokes's Amphitheatre, in the Islington-road, this present Tuesday, the 16th inst. (March, 1731) the public will have an opportunity of being diverted in a most extraordinary manner by the noble, large, savage, incomparable Russian bear, which was for the first time put to stake on Shrove Tuesday last, in order to be baited to death by six dogs, but by his matchless strength and fury overcoming that number, he was preserved for the day aforesaid, when ten out of the largest and best dogs that can be picked out in town or country, are to engage him for the diversion of some foreign noblemen, who will honour the sport with their presence. Also, the famous Hertforshire bull, dressed in fireworks, will be baited by a like number of dogs, 'farthest and fairest in.' After which a rump and buttock of beef, of 3 stones weight, will be fought for, and that dog that fights fairest to be entitled to one pound. And, to close the evening, the beauty of back sword will be shown, in all its branches, by some of the best proficients."

Parochial Charities.

THE following are the principal parochial charities whose rents and profits are mostly disposed of annually in coals, bread, and money, by the Churchwardens :—

The Cloudesley Charity has already been described.

Alice Owen.—In a book belonging to Christ's Hospital, entitled the "Wills and Benefactions," is an entry which states that "Alice Erskine, *alias* Owen, gave £60 to that institution upon condition that the governors should pay one shilling per week, or £2 12s. per annum, to buy bread for the parish of Islington." This money is regularly paid.

Thomas Hobson.—In the seventh year of King James I. Sir Thomas Fowler, at the instance of Thomas Hobson, granted certain premises, situate in Gloucester-place, High-street, subject to the annual payment of £5 4s., for the use of the poor at Islington, to be paid to the churchwarden upon trust, and to distribute two shillings per week to twelve persons in money (being twopence to each) for ever. The rent charge is regularly paid to the churchwardens.

Nathaniel Loame.—The sum of £5 4s. was devised by this gentleman by will dated July 22, 1625, to the churchwardens, to the intent that they should every Sunday distribute two shillings, half in bread and half in money, amongst twelve of the poorest and most needy inhabitants. The premises from which this charity is derived, are situated in the Old Bailey.

Ephraim Skinner.—This gentleman, by will bearing date May 13, 1678, bequeathed to the governors of Christ's Hospital, the sum of £700 on trust, among other things, to pay to the minister of the parish of Islington 5s. every Sunday for catechising in the parish church in the afternoon, and £5 per annum more, which was to be distributed amongst such of those who should come to be catechised and should deserve it. The sum of £18 per annum is regularly received on account of this legacy by the vicar from the governors of Christ's Hospital ; £13 of this sum is retained for his own use, and the remaining £5 is given by him to the parochial schools.

Dame Sarah Temple.—This lady, by will dated January 8th, 1696, directed her executors to lay out the sum of £350 in the purchase of an estate, the rents and profits of which, with the exception of a legacy of 40s. to the Vicar of Islington and 20s. to the churchwardens, were to be appropriated to the maintenance of as many poor children as possible, such children to be nominated by the churchwardens. In 1702 an estate was bought at Potters Bar, Hertford, the income derived from which is at present £60 a year, and the number of children boarded, educated, and clothed, is three. 40s. is annually paid to the vicar and 20s. to the churchwardens.

Benjamin Smith.—Benjamin Smith, by his will dated September 21, 1688, devised, among other things, as follows :—" I give to the poor of Islington, 32s. for ever, to be paid yearly out of rents and profits of the house Mr. Gregory has of me by lease, situated in Hedge-row, to be distributed every Sabbath day in bread to the poor of the said parish by 12d. per week." There are now no means of ascertaining the premises charged as above, and the charity was discontinued in 1813 in consequence of not being able to determine the place.

Annie Hill.—This lady, on the 5th of October, 1633, bequeathed the sum of £50 to be laid out in the purchase of lands of the yearly value of 50s., 30s. of which were to be given to thirty poor aged persons on St. Thomas's Day; 13s. 4d. to the minister for a sermon, and 6s. 8d. between the sexton and clerk. The land bought with the money comprised three-quarters of an acre of ground upon which the present workhouse was erected in 1777. No payment of this is now made, although properly chargeable to the poor rate.

John Parsons.—The charity bequeathed by John Parsons now amounts to £10 annually distributed by the churchwardens in coals. The proceeds are derived from a close called " Porters Acre," in the manor of Newington Barrowe

William Heron.—William Heron, citizen of London, by will dated July 12, 1580, bequeathed the yearly rent of £8 for ever out of his property, "towards repairing the highways from time to time in most needful places between the Spital House, Highgate,

and the corner of St. James' Wall, Clerkenwell, along the road leading from Highgate, through Kentish-town and Battle-bridge." Islington being one of the three parishes in which this road is situated, receives £30 6s. 8d. per annum from the proceeds of this gift.

The Kingsland Estate. — At Kingsland there is an estate of half an acre of ground belonging to the parish, left by a pauper named Cooper. In 1812 it was let out on a building lease for 61 years at £16 per annum which is distributed in bread and coals. This charity will receive a great increase in value when the lease expires.

Parke's Charity.—Daniel Parke, in the year 1649, charged a house situated near the turnpike-gate, with the annual rent of 40s., of which 10s. was to be paid to some godly minister for preaching a sermon on Christmas day, and the remainder to be spent in bread for the poor people of Islington. This rent is regularly paid.

Margaretta Browne.—This lady, by will dated 1829, bequeathed the sum of £1,400 three per cent. consols to the incumbent of Islington, who, with other trustees, was directed to apply it as follows :—20l. per annum to the officiating minister for once a month (the day not being Sunday) reading prayer and catechizing children, preaching an appropriate sermon on the festival of Epiphany, and conducting an annual examination of such children as have been catechised. 40s. a-year to the clerk and 20s. to the sexton, the remainder to be laid out in the purchase of bibles and prayer-books, to be given away at the annual examination.

The above are the principal charities belonging to the parish ; there are minor ones, and several others have been entirely lost through want of documentary evidence.

Laycock's Dairy.

THE celebrated dairy-farm of Mr. Laycock, in the Liverpool-road, now so well-known as a lair for cattle, is worthy of notice as being the source from whence flowed the greatest supply of milk to the metropolis, when Islington was completely a rural district.

Mr. Laycock's dairy-farm occupied 500 acres of land, and was entirely devoted to the growing of hay for his cattle. The quantity of hay taken from his fields in the year 1811, when it was sold in the London market at the enormous price of 10 guineas the load, amounted to several thousand loads; and a stack of hay made by Mr. Laycock in the summer of the same year, measured 144 feet in length, and contained upwards of 300 loads.

Mr. Middleton, a writer upon the state of agriculture in Middlesex about fifty years ago, says: "The village of Islington and its vicinity during the haymaking season displays a scene of unusual bustle, occasioned by the number of persons (men and women), who have been through the day employed as haymakers in the fields. Several hundreds of persons are thus employed by Messrs. Laycock and Rhodes for the purpose of mowing and carrying the crops." Mr Foot, another writer upon the agriculture of Middlesex of the same period, says: "The farmers of Islington confine their cows during the night in stalls; about three in the morning each cow has given it a half-bushel basket of grains. From four to half past six o'clock they are milked by the dealers who come from town. When the milking is finished a bushel-basket of turnips is given to each cow. In the afternoon the same process is gone through. Those cows that give the most milk are not found fit to be kept above three or four years, after which time they are fattened and sold to the butchers.

"The milk is conveyed from the cow-houses in tin-pails, which are principally carried by strong, robust girls, who retail the milk about the metropolis. It is surprising to witness the labour and fatigue these girls will undergo. Even in the most inclement weather and in the depth of winter, they arrive at Islington in parties from different parts of the metropolis by three or four in the morning, laughing and singing to the music of their empty pails; with these they return loaded to town, and the weight they are accustomed to carry on their yokes is sometimes from 100 to 120 lbs.

"The milk-room is furnished with a pump to which the retail dealers apply in rotation, not secretly, but openly, and as may be expected, it is made to give a very good yield.

"The stock of cows kept on Mr. Laycock's farm amounts to between 500 and 600, and upwards of fifty wagons and 80 horses are kept for fetching turnips and supplying the cattle, when, from draught or other causes, there is not a sufficient supply of fodder."

Pentonville.

THIS large district, most of which is in the adjoining parish of Clerkenwell, received its name from the fact of its being built by a publican of the name of Penton, in the beginning of the present century. The following interesting account of its origin, written by a correspondent lately appeared in the *Islington Gazette*:—

"In the year 1816, I was an apprentice to an eminent medical practitioner in Lambeth, who was surgeon to the workhouse of that extensive parish. As I listened with credulous sympathy to the tales of the poor people who sought shelter in that welcome refuge, I soon became familiar with the autobiography of every inmate. Amongst the impugners of fortune were a quiet unobtrusive couple of the name of Penton, whose story of grief was as follows:—

"They had always been poor, but had worked hard to a late period of their life, when, strength and energy failing, they were obliged to come on the parish. A cousin of theirs, Mr. Penton, had, by industry and frugality, and perhaps penury, accumulated in the wine trade a large fortune, part of which he had expended in building houses above Bagnigge Wells, forming a suburb called Pentonville. In their approaching adversity they applied to their relative for assistance, but he also had become old and feeble, and had fallen completely into the power of one or two dependants and domestics, whose interest it was to separate the old pantaloon from his relatives. The application was consequently refused. The old wine merchant had a confidential cellarman, one Pyke Watts, who married the housekeeper, and their only child, a daughter, married one Russell, another servant of Mr. Penton's. The four became an impenetrable *chevaux de frise* around the virtual prisoner, who made a will in their favour, and the whole of the property fell into their hands.

"In 1816, a Mr. Watts Russell, the grandson of Pyke Watts (the confidential cellarman of the rich old publican Penton,) was the owner of this property, and having a princely income, moved in a highly fashionable circle, had married a sprig of nobility, and was, I believe, an M.P. Similar to this is the fate of many a miser, and the foundation of many a family. Determined to probe the story of the old pauper Penton, I applied to Mr. Field the overseer of Lambeth workhouse, to inquire into the subject, which he did, and succeeded in inducing Mr. Watts Russell to accord them, out of his income of twenty thousand a-year, a pension of fifty pounds annually. In granting this annuity, Mr. Watts Russell acknowledged the truth of the old Penton's statement, and thus afforded one proof that tales of injustice told by the poor, though often exaggerated, are not always unfounded."

The Home for Starving Dogs.

THIS institution, situate in Hollingsworth-street, in the district of St. James's-road Holloway, consists of three cab-stables in a yard at the back of the house No. 14. It owes its existence to a benevolent lady residing at Canonbury, who started by befriending a few stray dogs, and giving them a home in her own house. As their numbers increased the difficulty of keeping them in a private dwelling grew greater, and a local agitation was got up, by which means the Home was established in October, 1860. At present it has fifty annual subscribers and fifty donors. The following are some of the rules and regulations of the society :—

"Any dog found and brought to the Home, if applied for by the owner, will be given up to his master on payment of the expenses of its keep.

"All unowned dogs, after they have been in the home some little time, will be given away ; but, as this is a charitable institution, it is hoped that all who can afford it, will make a donation towards the expenses of the Home, in proportion to the value of the dog selected.

"To prevent dog-stealing no reward will be given to persons bringing dogs to the Home. The committee hope, that to persons of ordinary humanity, the consciousness of having performed a merciful action will be a sufficient recompense.

"None but governors of the institution shall be eligible for the committee, or vote at any meeting of the institution.

"A donation of five pounds constitutes a life-governor, and the yearly subscription of five shillings and upwards, an annual governor of the institution ; and any lady or gentleman collecting small sums to the amount of five pounds, will be considered a life-governor."

Notwithstanding the ridicule and difficulties which have been thrown in the way of this refuge, it is considered to be sufficiently established to be reckoned a permanent London institution. A man is engaged to take charge of the animals, to answer the questions of applicants who brings dogs or claims them, and keep a record of incomers and outgoers. When a dog is brought to the Home, its breed is entered in a book under a particular number, a tin ticket, with a corresponding number, is hung around his neck like a locket, and he is provided with a place in a basket or box. They are generally well-behaved and require much the same attention as poverty-stricken and houseless human beings. The most worthless dogs have the largest appetites and make the most noise, and these are known to the keeper by the title of the "wolves," for they do nothing but eat and yell, and are never likely to be reclaimed or purchased. There are at present about seventy in the Home, the majority of the animals being rough creatures, such as Scotch terriers, mongrels, and a few old fighting dogs who have given up their profession. Some of the animals are knowing street trampers, who offer no objection to be housed during the winter months, but who, on the first signs of summer, get away if they can. Within a period of four months nearly 180 dogs have been taken in, and during the winter months the incomers far exceed the outgoers, which proves that the charity is like a human refuge. The dogs are principally disposed of by being given away; some are reclaimed, and some die. The committee consist of seven ladies and four gentlemen, and its honorary secretary is a clergyman; it has, besides, four lady patronesses, three of them being ladies of title. The following is extracted from the address which the committee put forth on behalf of the institution:—

"Persons walking through the streets of London or its suburbs, can hardly fail frequently to have seen lost dogs in a most emaciated or even dying state from starvation.

"The committee would willingly hope and believe that no one who is capable of appreciating the faithful, affectionate, and devoted nature of the dog, can have seen any of these intelligent creatures in that state without feeling an earnest wish that there were some means established for rescuing them from so dreadful a death, and restoring them to usefulness. The object of the institution is to give humane persons an opportunity to relieve so much misery.

"The parent home is now established in Holloway, and all persons finding dogs in the state above described are entreated to convey them to it, and all persons losing dogs are requested to apply at once to the Home.

"In proportion as the funds will admit of it, receiving-houses will be established in all parts of London, from which dogs will be conveyed to Holloway."

It is to be hoped that the benevolent individuals who have instituted this dog-pauper establishment will be careful not to make it a parody of refuges for human outcasts, but treat the faithful animal as an "animal" only. With such management it will have the countenance and support of all right-minded persons.

Church Missionary Institution.

PRESBYTERIAN CHURCH. — ST. JOHN'S CATHOLIC CHAPEL. — ISLINGTON PROPRIETARY SCHOOL.—THE FRENCH COLONY.

CHURCH MISSIONARY INSTITUTION.

THIS institution, situate in College-street, Barnsbury-road, was opened on the 31st January, 1825, for the reception and education of students for missionary labours. It is the first seminary of the kind established in connection with the Episcopal Church in this country. The Church Missionary Society purchased the ground for £2180, and the building was erected by special subscription. It is a plain but handsome structure of brick, capable of accommodating forty students. A flight of stone steps leads from the hall in the centre of the building to a spacious garden, intersected with retired paths, in every way calculated for the encouragement of study. The students are instructed in the Latin, Greek, and Hebrew languages, and generally remain there three or four years before going abroad.

THE PRESBYTERIAN CHURCH,
RIVER TERRACE.

THIS edifice, situate in River-terrace, is one of the eight churches which form the Presbytery of London in the Synod of the Presbyterian Church in England in connection with the Church of Scotland. It was erected in the year 1834 for the use of the congregation till then worshipping in Chadwell-street, Myddelton-square, under the pastoral care of the Rev. John Macdonald, A.M. It was built at an expense of £1250. It is a neat edifice of brick in the early English style, and will accommodate 700 persons. The interior is simply arranged, and is lighted by lancet-shaped windows on either side above the galleries and square-headed windows below. The Rev. Peter Lorimer was the first minister of the new building, and until lately the Rev. Dr. Weir officiated as pastor. This latter gentleman, however, has lately resigned his pastorate, upon which occasion a handsome testimonial was presented to him by his congregation as an acknowledgment of his services. The church is now without a regular pastor.

There are two other Presbyterian places of worship in Islington beside the one in River-terrace: One in the Holloway-road, a little above the Great Northern Railway Bridge, called the " Caledonian Church," and at which the children of the Caledonial Asylum attend every Sunday in their Scotch costume. This chapel was formerly used by the Congregational Church now moved to the corner of the Camden-road, under the ministry of the Rev. J. Morris. The other Presbyterian chapel is situated in the Caledonian-road opposite the Asylum. It is built of Kentish rag-stone and in the pointed style of architecture. It has not yet possessed any appointed minister. A united free Presbyterian church is also now holding their meetings at Myddelton Hall under the ministry of the Rev. J. Edmonds.

ST. JOHN'S CATHOLIC CHAPEL.

THE foundation-stone of this building, situate in Duncan-terrace, was laid Sept. 27, 1841, and it was opened the following year. It is built in the Anglo-Norman style, the front being composed of fine red brick with mouldings and decorations of Bath stone. The structure is lighted by ten windows on each side, and three at the end filled with stained glass. The interior arrangements are of the same Anglo-Norman character as its exterior. The chancel is enriched by the high altar, with its screen-work, tabernacle, and rich hangings, and its ceiling decorated with fresco-paintings representing the Last Judgment. The Catholic schools attached are situate in the rear of Duncan-terrace, and comprise, on the ground-floor, a large school-room for boys and one above it for girls. It is a substantial building of the same style as the church.

ISLINGTON PROPRIETARY SCHOOL.

THIS school, situated in Barnsbury-street, was opened on the 16th February, 1830, for the purpose of providing a classical educa-

tion for youth, and in conformity with the doctrines of the Church of England. The institution consists of a proprietary of 200 shares of £15 each. Every proprietor is at liberty to nominate one scholar in respect of each share he may possess. A sum not exceeding £11 per annum is paid for the tuition of each scholar.

The building, which is a neat red-brick Elizabethan structure, cost £2,000. It comprises, in the upper portion, four spacious and handsome school-rooms, and apartments for the head-master. The covered playgrounds under the school-room are well-arranged and afford ample space for recreation. The president is the Rev. D. Wilson, the vicar.

THE FRENCH COLONY.

SOME few years ago, on the west side of the Caledonian-road, there stood an extensive collection of cottages, each cottage surrounded by a garden fenced in with wooden palings, and called the " Experimental Gardens," or French colony. They were established by a Mr. Peter Henry Joseph Baume, who originally intended to found a community on the principles of Robert Owen, the rationalist. The attempt, however, failed; the cottages rapidly deteriorated and became the residences of the poorest class of people. The district was never lighted, neither were the roads properly mended, and its whole appearance was more like a colony in the wilds of Canada than a suburb of London. Part of this collection of tenements is still in existence, at the bottom of Bingfield-street, near St. Michael's Church. They are, however, in a very dilapidated state, and as the leases have but three or four more years to run from this date (1861), they will soon be numbered among the things of the past.

In connection with the neighbourhood of the Caledonian-road, it may not be uninteresting to state that some forty years ago it was customary for the Irish packmen of that period to assemble in great numbers on the sloping fields on its east side, upon the site now occupied by Hemingford-terrace, to play at football, dressed in their knee-breeches and worsted stockings. The games on these occasions generally wound up with a fight.

The " Thatched House."

DR. HAWES, THE FOUNDER OF THE ROYAL HUMANE SOCIETY.

THE "Thatched House" Tavern, in the Lower-road, occupies the site of one destroyed by fire in November, 1729. The original inn, however, called "Job's House," or the " Old Thatched House," was burned down, on the 4th of August, 1742. It was kept by Mr. Hawes, the father of Dr. William Hawes, who was born near this spot on the 28th of November, 1736. This benevolent and useful man received his education at a school in the parish, upon leaving which he was placed under the care of a medical practitioner, a Mr. Dicks, in the Strand, whom, upon the expiration of his apprenticeship, he succeeded in the business, and soon acquired a reputation.

In the year 1772, Dr. Hawes displayed great zeal in calling the attention of the public to the resuscitation of persons apparently dead from drowning, many thousands of valuable lives having been lost through ignorance previous to his time. Like other public benefactors, Dr. Hawes, for a long time, had to contend against much opposition and ridicule on account of his efforts, but gradually these gave way as society became more and more aware of the fruits that were constantly appearing through his noble exertions. He would advertise rewards to persons who, between London and Westminster-bridges, should, within a certain time after the accident, rescue drowned persons from the water and bring them to places appointed for their reception, and give immediate notice to him. Many lives were thus saved, and Dr. Hawes, at his own expense, paid rewards in these cases, to a considerable amount. At length his friend, Dr. Cogan, remonstrated with him on the injury his own means were sustaining, and urged him to call upon the public to pay their share in such rewards. Dr. Cogan and he then agreed to work together, and each promised to bring fifteen friends, to meet together at the Chapter Coffee House, which they did, and they then and there laid the foundation of the Royal Humane Society. This took place in the year 1774. The Society's or-

ganization, however, chiefly devolved upon Dr. Hawes, whose indefatigable labours contributed to its firm establishment. From this noble institution many similar ones have been established in nearly every country in Europe, in addition to those in India and America. Our Royal Humane Society at home is supported by the subscriptions of the highest in the land, and is under the patronage of Royalty itself. Dr. Hawes thus affords another example of what can be attained by perseverance in a noble cause. He did not, however, confine his benevolence to the establishment of the Royal Humane Society. In 1793, when the manufactory of cottons began to lessen the quantity of silks used, so as to occasion great distress amongst the weavers in Spitalfields, Dr. Hawes, by his own individual exertions, rescued 1,200 families from ruin and starvation. His address on that occasion, to a popular clergyman, was afterwards made public, to the great benefit of the industrious sufferers, and as it perhaps shows his philanthropy in a nobler light than mere encomiums would do, it is worthy of perusal :—

"REV. SIR,—Permit me to address you on the present occasion, and to return you my most sincere thanks for your voluntary exertions on behalf of the distressed weavers. Believe me, sir, it is not in the power of language to describe their long and continued miseries; miseries not brought on by idleness, intemperance, or a dissolute course of life, but human wretchedness absolutely produced by want of employment. My profession obliges me daily to be an eye-witness of the severe distresses and afflictions of these much-to-be-pitied of our fellow creatures. Whole families without fire, without raiment, and without food; and, to add to the catalogue of human woes, three, four, and five in many families languishing on beds of sickness. I assure you, sir, and you will believe me, when I declare that such scenes of complicated woe are too affecting to dwell upon, and shall therefore conclude with my most earnest wishes that by your pleading in their behalf, other divines may be animated by the same undertaking, as I am certain that public benevolence will prevent the premature death of many, will restore health to hundreds, and afford the staff of life to thousands.

> "I am, &c.,
> "WILLIAM HAWES,
> "*Physician to the London Dispensary.*
> "Spital-square, Nov. 16, 1793."

This gentleman died in Spital-square, December 5th, 1808, and was buried in the new cemetery attached to Islington churchyard. His funeral was attended by the managers and directors of the Humane Society, and a handsome marble tablet was erected to his memory in Islington Church by that corporation. Dr. Hawes was noted for singular Christian simplicity of character, self never appearing to enter into his contemplation. Like Nathaniel, he was "without guile," and was an honour to the parish in which he was born.

His brother, Benjamin Hawes, was also a native of Islington, and was likewise noted for his benevolence. By unflagging industry he amassed an ample fortune as an indigo merchant. He chiefly bestowed his gifts anonymously to those whom he heard were struggling with poverty, and whom he always used to keep in ignorance as to who was their benefactor. In the same modest spirit he was a large but anonymous contributor to all the public charities, and at his death he left 24,000*l.* amongst twenty-four different charities. To promote the abolition of the slave trade he contributed very large sums, and in a letter to Wilberforce he offered to sacrifice several thousands to the cause of emancipation.

𝕱𝖊𝖛𝖊𝖗 𝕳𝖔𝖘𝖕𝖎𝖙𝖆𝖑.

THE above noble charity is situated on the east side of the Liverpool-road. It is built of red brick with stone facings, and comprises a centre building, with two wings, the latter being connected by corridors on either side. On the centre building are the words "The London Fever Hospital." It is surrounded by a spacious and well-laid-out garden, and a light iron railing encloses the ground from the high road. The hospital will hold two hundred patients; a detached central house is the residence of the resident officers, and this is connected with open corridors on either side, through which a fresh draught of air passes into the inner open squares, with the detached wards for the men on the one side and the detached wards for the women on the other. The building contains some very large double wards, separated by open arches, well lighted with windows opposite each other, so as to admit of good ventilation. Over these wards, on either side, a narrower single ward is built, so as not to impede roof ventilation of the rooms on the ground floor. The hospital throughout is excellently ventilated, and an allowance of two thousand cubic feet of space is allotted to each bed. Baths, and all necessary appliances are attached, as also an engine house and a laundry—the latter separated from the building—in which the linen is soaked three times, then boiled and afterwards washed by a machine.

When a patient is admitted his bed is placed by the side of a bath, in which he is cleansed, after which the bed is wheeled to the part of the ward assigned to it. Besides the public, there are private wards, admittance to the latter being granted upon the payment of two guineas. These private wards often prove a great boon to those who, keeping large establishments or a number of domestic servants, desire, to prevent contagion, the removal of some poor fever-stricken creature. Indeed, the hospital gives shelter and health and life to numbers of such cases. Such a provision must have been the means of preventing desolation in many a household, and on these, and on the broader grounds of its general charity, it ought never to lack support.

The history of the hospital is interesting. From the very nature of the object for which it was called into existence, it met with much opposition, people, especially those residing near the building, dreading infection. The first house that was opened for the reception of the fever patients was No. 2, Constitution-row, Gray's Inn-lane. At that time Gray's Inn-lane, north of Guildford-street, was a kind of country road, there being but few houses between the street named and the row in question, so that the hospital had the advantage of, comparatively, pure air. Notwithstanding threats and indictments by those residing near to its precincts, the hospital was allowed to remain, and in its sixth year its benefits were so far appreciated that ninety-three persons were admitted, and there were two remaining when the year began. Of this number (ninety-five) fourteen died, eighty were cured, and one remained.

In consequence of this influx of patients it was considered necessary to look out for a more convenient house. In October, 1811, ground and premises in Coldbath-fields, including the bath-house and garden-ground in the centre of Coldbath-square, about to be sold by action in three lots, were considered eligible, and were bought by the institution for £3,830, the princpal. of this money, viz., £3,000 being a grant made by Parliament. The committee had still £2,000 in hand, with which, and from what they hoped to derive from public subscription, they trusted they would be enabled to erect a new building. The erection of the hospital, however, in Coldbath-square, was strenuously opposed by the Clerkenwell Vestry, who declared that its proximity would be dangerous to the Workhouse, the House of Correction, and a crowded neighbourhood. The committee were therefore compelled to give up their idea of building on their Coldbath estate; they resolved at once to turn it to the next best account, and it is now yielding £150 a-year to the revenues of the institution.

A short time after Sir Thomas Bernard, who was much interested in the success of the hospital, stated " that there was a disposition in some of the governors of the hospitals for the small pox, for inoclutation and vaccination, at King's-cross, to appropriate the building next the Hampstead-road, containing about eighty beds, with furniture, to use as a fever house upon moderate compensation, if the fever committee was disposed to apply for it. The suggestion was at once acted upon, the building was inspected, and except for the want of a kitchen, which could easily be added, was considered remarkably well suited to the object in view. So it came to pass that for £4,000, with the payment of incidental charges and the cost of building boundary walls, the western building and garden of the old Small-pox Hospital became converted into the London House of Recovery, for the Cure and Prevention of Infectious Fevers." This house at King's-cross opened for sixty patients, but was afterwards enlarged, and in the year 1848 it had afforded an asylum to one thousand four hundred patients. The old house may be remembered by many an inhabitant of the present day; it formed a companion to the Small-pox Hospital, which now stands in an open ground, a pleasing and elegant building, situated about halfway up the hill at Highgate.

The hospital, however, was soon destined to another removal. The Great Northern Railway Company wanted its site for their terminus, and the result was a settlement of compensation in May, 1847. The Company agreed to pay £20,000 wherewith to build a new hospital, and £1,000 to cover law expenses; they also agreed to pay £5,000 towards the purchase of the land abutting on the Liverpool-road, on which the present hospital stands. The whole cost of the ground was £7,500. The amount thus paid by the Great Northern Company was in all £26,000, so that "after the purchase of the site, £17,500, together with £180 out of the thousand paid to cover lawyer's bills, remained in hand as a building fund. This, with the help from interest, while the cash remained in hand, was raised to about £18,000, the whole of which sum, except about £500 left to meet occasional changes and additions, was fairly and well spent between the middle of the year 1847 and the beginning of the year 1849, in building the admirable New Fever Hospital in the Liverpool-road, which is not only the single hospital of its kind in London, but probably the best of its kind in Europe."

We are sorry to hear that this excellent institution is much in want of funds; indeed, it is assumed that unless additional subscribers are added to its list, in less than twenty years this refuge for the fever-stricken will have to be broken up.

Colebrooke Cottage.

CHARLES LAMB.—WEBB'S MINERAL WATER WORKS.

AT the back of Mr. Webb's mineral water works, Islington Green, there stands a cottage in which the genial-hearted Charles Lamb resided for about the space of three years. This distinguished prose-writer and critic, about whom so many anecdotes and stories are told, was born in London in February, 1775, and educated at Christ's Hospital. In 1792 he obtained an appointment in the East India Company's service, where he remained above thirty years, until his salary gradually rose to 700l., when he was pensioned off with 450l. per annum. Being thus in easy circumstances, and living as a bachelor, with a mind possessing a keen relish for literature, he was able to gratify his cravings and enjoy the society of men of genius, and throughout life he boasted of the friendship of Coleridge, Wordsworth, Southey, Hazlitt, Rogers, and others, who used often to enjoy the feast of reason at his fireside. As a prose writer for periodical works he stood unrivalled, and his " Essays of Elia" may be said to have formed an era in magazine literature. For nearly a quarter of a century were the public delighted with his papers. Lamb, as is well known, was very fond of his native city, and, like Johnson, would not exchange Fleet-street or the Strand for the most beautiful country scenery in the world. It appears, however, he often enjoyed a residence in the suburbs, for besides his cottage at Colebrooke-row he also had a residence at 45, Chapel-street, Pentonville. In a letter to Bernard Barton, dated September 2, 1823, he thus pleasantly and graphically describes his place of abode at Islington :—

" When you come Londonward you will find me no longer in Covent Garden. I have a cottage in Colebrooke-row, Islington—a cottage, for it is detached; a white house with six good rooms in it; the New River (rather elderly by this time) runs (if a moderate walking pace can be so termed) close to the foot of the house, and behind is a spacious garden, with vines (I assure you), peas, strawberries, parsnips, leeks, carrots, and cabbages, to delight the heart of old Alcinous. You enter, without passage, into a cheerful dining-room, all studded over and rough with old books, and above is a lightsome drawing-room, with three windows, full of choice plants. I feel like a great lord, never having had a house before."

In November following, in a letter to Robert Southey, he also informs him that he is at "Colebrooke Cottage, a detached whitish house, close to the New River, end of Colebrooke-terrace, left hand coming from Sadler's Wells."

WEBB'S MINERAL WATER WORKS.

LAMB'S cottage is now used in connection with the large soda-water manufactory which was established about thirty years ago by Mr John Webb, and is now conducted by his son Mr. John G. Webb. The works for carrying on the business of this establishment are very extensive, a steam-engine of 10-horse power, which is connected with some beautiful and peculiarly-constructed machinery, being employed for the generation of the carbonic-acid gas.

The most scrupulous attention is paid to the purity of the water, which is procured from a well 225 feet deep (25 feet deeper than the famous well at Carisbrook Castle), and bored at an expense of nearly 400l. The water, which is of excellent quality, and is rendered still more pure by artificial means, formerly rose to within 95 feet of the surface ; but it is a remarkable fact, that after the boring of the well at the Model Prison, the water in the pump at the above manufactory fell 25 feet, and it was consequently found necessary to lengthen the suction-pipe in proportion. The water now rises to within 110 feet of the surface, and for the last eight years the supply has been good, and no alteration observed in its level.

The well is situated within the manufactory, and Mr. Webb informed the writer that its temperature displays but little variation the year round. The following table shews the thickness of the several strata (downwards) through which the boring was made, and which may be taken as a specimen of the geological strata of the greater part of Islington :—

Sand and gravel	.	.	.	12 feet.
Blue clay	.	.	.	48 ,,
Mottled clay	.	.	.	70 ,,
Light sand with shells	.	.	10 ,,
Dark blue clay	.	.	.	7 ,,
Dark sand and pebbles	.	.	18 ,,
Green sand and oxide of iron	.	10 ,,
Black sand and shells	.	.	3 ,,
Flints	.	.	.	3 ,,
Chalk and flints	.	.	44 ,,

225

To hold the water there are tanks containing 4,600 gallons each ; to these sufficient carbonate of soda, in fine crystals, is added, so as to obtain a solution which, when charged with gas, each bottle shall contain fifteen grains of bicarbonate of soda, so that the article produced at this manufactory is actually *soda* water, and not mere gas water, as is the case with the generality of manufacturers. The solution of carbonate is transferred in certain proportions called charges, into very strong cylinders of bell-metal, thickly plated with silver inside, where it is ready for the reception of the carbonic-acid gas. These cylinders form part of the machinery, and very much resemble brightly polished guns. The carbonic-acid gas is generated in a vessel constructed of slate, so that not a particle of any metal can come into contact with the gas, which is conducted through earthen tubes into a gasometer made also of slate. Before entering the gasometer, the gas is well washed by being made to pass through a tank of water. From the gasometer it is drawn through an earthern tube by the force-pumps which are set in motion by the engine and forced into the solution of carbonate of soda in the silver-lined vessels already mentioned, called the impregnators, which are provided with safety-valves loaded to 700 lbs. on the square inch. To prevent the gas from acquiring any bad taint from the oil which must be used for lubricating the solid plungers of the pumps, they are most ingeniously washed at each ascending and descending stroke by a jet of water caused to play around them. When the pressure of the gas lifts the valves, the action of the pumps is suspended, and the carbonated soda-water awaits the bottler.

The operation of bottling is attended with some danger in consequence of the liability of the bottles to burst, which they frequently do. The bottler is therefore obliged to wear a wire mask to protect his face, and also to shelter his hands with a leathern flap. The purity of the materials used, and the general excellence of the manufacture, has, as may be imagined, resulted in Mr. Webb having a large trade.

The Model Prison.

THE foundation stone of the Model Prison in the Caledonian-road, was laid on Friday, April 10, 1840, by the Marquis of Normanby, accompanied by the Marquis Lansdowne, several members of Parliament, and others interested in the improvement of prison discipline. It is built of brick with stone facings, its principal feature being a central structure, in which are contained the chapel, hall, and other offices, and four large wings, which contain the cells. The total cost of the prison, with all its fittings, was 200,000l.

The building contains cells for 560 prisoners, who are confined upon the separate system, each cell being provided with a hammock, a stool, a table, a stone water-closet, with a cover or lid of wood, and other conveniences. The doors of the cells—the two uppermost rows of which open upon galleries—are formed of iron and wood, having in the centre of the upper part a small eyelet-hole, so arranged that the warders may, by looking through from the outside, observe all that is passing in the interior without being seen by the inmates. In these cells the prisoners are confined during the day and night, with the exception of the time occupied in divine service and bodily exercise. The prisoners are never allowed to converse with each other, and if found doing so are punished by a stoppage of their usual rations; so strictly is this rule enforced, that precaution is taken to furnish the pipes connecting the water-closets with valves, that all communication through such channels may be cut off. The convicts are supplied with such work as can be carried on without noise, as tailoring, brush, rug, and mat making. The articles they make are very strong, and are contracted for by Messrs. Schoolbred and other firms. The prisoners are well and liberally dieted, and are furnished periodically with books from a good library, to amuse themselves with in their spare hours and on Sundays. Their dietary is as follows:—

Breakfast—¾ pint cocoa, 10 oz. bread.
Dinner—¼ lb. meat weighed when cooked, without bone; 1 lb. potatoes; ½ pint soup; 5 oz. bread. (The soup is made with the liquor of the meat the same day, strengthened with three ox heads, barley, carrots, onions, and pepper for every 100 pints.)
Supper—1 pint of oatmeal gruel and 5 oz. bread.

The punishment diet consists of 1 lb of bread and three pints of cold water per diem. The prisoners rise at a quarter to six, work twelve hours per day exclusive of meal time, and go to bed at a quarter to nine all the year round. To manage the prison there are thirteen discipline warders, fifteen trade instructors, two principal warders, deputy-governor and governor. The present governor is Captain Craig. Each prisoner costs the state on an average, 29*l*. per annum.

The chapel, which is in the centre of the building, used to be so constructed that while the preacher could see all the prisoners present, the prisoners could not see each other, and upon the conclusion of the service they were marched out one at a time, each to his cell, by means of a circular-numbered signal, which corresponded with the number of the cell or box in which the prisoner was standing, no commands being given in spoken words. The separate cells in the chapel, have, however, lately been abolished.

Part of the exercising ground is so constructed that a single prisoner walks up and down between high walls, the only objects visible being the warders. There is also a more open exercising ground in which the prisoners walk in a circular path, each catching hold of a rope which has knots or handles twenty or thirty paces apart, thus being kept at a certain distance from each other.

The system of separate confinement, if not carried too far, has been found to be a salutary one, but if endured beyond a certain length of time, disposes to lunacy. There is no doubt that it is a far greater punishment to a confirmed thief than any mere corporeal infliction. Convicts are generally acute and cunning in their way, but have very little resources within themselves, and if taken out from the path in which they are accustomed to walk, are ignorant, superstitious, and cowardly to a remarkable degree. Such persons in solitary confinement are the most helpless and resourceless creatures that ever lived—without energy to look forward or courage to look back—without religious principle to support them, or knowledge to direct them in the search of that peace which religion only can afford to the guilty man, the mind preys upon itself, and such cannot be supported long without affecting mind and body. Memory and reflection may supply the place of society to an educated man, but it is very dreadful to an ignorant being, who only derives his sensations from the eye and ear, to be shut out from his kind. The term of imprisonment in the Model Prison is generally limited to nine months.

St. John's, Holloway.

CALEDONIAN ROAD CHAPEL. — WESLEYAN CHAPEL. — ST. MARY'S PAROCHIAL SCHOOLS.

ST. JOHN'S, HOLLOWAY.

ST. JOHN'S CHURCH is situated on the western side of the road at Upper Holloway, and from its commanding position on the slope of the hill, forms a very agreeable object from the adjacent neighbourhood. The foundation-stone of this fine ecclesiastical edifice was laid by the late Archbishop of Canterbury in the presence of a very distinguished assemblage, on the 4th of May, 1826, and was consecrated by the Bishop of London on the 2nd of July, 1828, being the first completed of the three district churches then in progress. It cost 11,980*l.*, and contains 1,872 sittings, of which number 700 are free. It is built of fine white brick, the ornamented portions being of Bath stone; a square tower, surmounted with four crocketted pinnacles, is situated at the north end of the building, in which is the principal entrance; the whole is built in the pointed English style from designs by the late Sir Charles Barry. The interior is simple and chaste. On each side of the nave are six arches, and both the aisles have galleries, the fronts of which are varnished in imitation of oak and ornamented with square panels. The altar-end of the church is decorated by a magnificently-painted window, presented by Mr. Bacon, of Great Russell-street. It contains a representation of the Saviour after the resurrection, together with the apostles with their crowns of martyrdom. In the centre is a royal coat-of-arms. The first minister appointed to this church was the Rev. William Marshall, who on his death was succeeded by the Rev. H. Venn. The present incumbent is the Rev. C. W. Edmonstone. The National Schools attached to St. John's were erected in 1830, at a cost of £1,000. There is an infant school in Grove-lane, a Sunday school, and numerous other excellent institutions in connection with this district parochial church, the neighbourhood of which is increasing its population every year.

CALEDONIAN - ROAD CONGREGATIONAL CHAPEL.

THE above chapel, situated at the corner of Bingfield-street, was opened for public worship in June, 1851, upon which occasion the Rev. James Bennett, D.D., the Rev. Alexander Fletcher, D.D., the Rev. T. W. Jenkyn, D.D., and other eminent ministers preached sermons. It is a handsome and commodious structure, built of Suffolk brick with stone facings. An elegant portico, consisting of four columns — the two outside square and of brick, the two inner fluted with ornamental capitals, supporting a triangular pediment of stone—stands over the entrance, which is approached by a flight of stone steps. The interior arrangements are simple but pleasing. The pulpit and reading-desk, together with the pews, which are open, are of stained wood; the latter will afford accommodation for about 1,000 people. The galleries, which are also stained, are supported by light columns with ornamental capitals, and the whole is lighted by a row of six circular-headed windows on either side. The whole expense was £3,000.

At the time this chapel was erected there were only two places of worship between King's-cross and Holloway in the neighbourhood of the Caledonian-road, one of these being the little Wesleyan chapel in Charlotte-street, built by Mr. Eckett, and capable of accommodating only a limited number of people. The Rev. Ebenezer Davies, the pastor, who first originated the idea of a chapel in this locality, felt there could be no better spot for usefulness than the rapidly increasing district of west Islington. Indeed, it is well-known that while the City is becoming less populated, the suburban districts exhibit a great increase, and none more so than Islington. In his endeavours Mr. Davies was assisted by a committee consisting of Mr. Alderman Wire, Rev. John Liefchild, D.D., W. Spicer, Esq., of Highbury-place,

J. K. Starling, Esq., John Jones, Esq., and other well-known gentlemen of local influence. The undertaking was also warmly supported by the Revs. H. Allon, T. Lewis, Charles Gilbert, and other neighbouring ministers. The Rev. Mr. Davies, who commenced his labours without even the nucleus of a congregation, is still the minster, and was formerly pastor of the mission church at New Amsterdam, Berbice. In connection with the chapel, there is a Sunday School in which upwards of 2,000 children have been taught, and 600 at present receiving instruction. There are also a Dorcas Society, a Temperance Association, and other valuable institutions sustained by the congregation.

THE WESLEYAN CHAPEL, LIVERPOOL-ROAD.

THE Wesleyan Chapel on the east side of the Liverpool-road is a striking building in the collegiate style of architecture. It was erected in the year 1849, the former chapel standing upon the site being burnt down in 1848. Its interior is very elegant. A magnificent stained-glass window adorns the eastern end of the nave, and there are two oriel lights of coloured glass over the galleries. Underneath the centre window, painted in illuminated gold and colours, are the Decalogue, the Lord's Prayer, and the Creed, and in the centre, on a gold ground, are the words, "For as often as ye eat this bread and drink this cup, ye do show the Lord's death till he come." The pulpit and reading-desk are beautiful specimens of symmetry and carving, the pews are also ornamented with carved mountings. Four stone pillars divide the aisles, and support the roof, the ceiling of which is carved and panelled oak; in the upper story on either side of the roof are windows filled with stained glass. In the aisles are three monuments, one of which is erected to George Chubb, Esq., the inventor of the patent lock, who was a great

benefactor to the church, and mainly instrumental in the enlargement of the chapel in 1844.

The succession of ministers, as is usual with the Wesleyans, is appointed by conference, the management of the chapel being regulated by the trustees. The form of worship used is in accordance with the common prayer book of the Episcopal Church. Attached to the church is a very efficient Sunday school, also many other institutions. The chapel which formerly stood here was a neat edifice of brick erected in the year 1827 at a cost £4,000.

ST. MARY'S PAROCHIAL SCHOOLS.

THESE schools, situated in Little Cross-street, were opened in Nov. 1859, at a cost of £3,600, Alexander Gough, Esq., architect. The building is of white brick with stone facings, in the Elizabethan style of architecture. The schools contain at the present time 220 boys and 160 girls, who are taught by a staff of ten teachers. Mr. W. Fairmaner is the master, and Mrs. Lee, the matron.

The parochial schools were first founded in the year 1710, for the instruction and clothing of 24 boys and 24 girls. A building was then erected opposite the burial ground in the Liverpool-road in the the year 1815, at a cost of upwards of £3,000, on a piece of freehold ground given to the charity by Mr. Samuel Rhodes, and containing about half an acre. These schools, being used conjointly with the Chapel of Ease, becoming unable to meet the wants of the district, it was resolved at a meeting held in the Vestry of the parish church in Nov. 1841, that separate parochial schools should be established for the parish church of St. Mary's, and a house on the south side of Church-street was obtained for the purpose. From this place the schools have been removed to their present permanent erection in Little Cross-street, while those belonging to the Chapel of Ease remain in the Liverpool-road.

The Vestry Hall and Workhouse.

LOCAL MANAGEMENT.—DIET OF THE POOR.

THE new Vestry Hall in the Upper-street was erected at an expense of £5,863 2s. 9d., exclusive of the cost of land, which amounted to £1,550. The architect was Thomas Allom, Esq., and the builder, W. Dove, of Islington. It was opened for the transaction of public business in August, 1859. It is a handsome and commodious building erected in the Grecian style of architecture. A portico, containing six Corinthian columns, and supporting a small balustrated gallery, covers the entrance, and the upper range of windows have Corinthian pilasters on either side. The roof of the whole building is balustrated, a line of ornamental stucco-work running beneath. The interior is spacious and convenient. On the ground-floor are the various offices belonging to the Vestry Clerk. The principal hall is approached by a handsome flight of double stairs, and the hall itself is designed to accommodate the 120 vestrymen who conduct the affairs of the parish. This room is an oblong square, neatly fitted up. The windows, which are eight in number, are ornamented with crimson drapery. The floor is carpeted, and the seats cushioned with green morocco leather. The chairman's seat is a handsome high-backed piece of furniture, with a beautiful carving of the arms of the parish and other ornamentation. A ratepayer's gallery, having a light iron railing in front, is situated at its southern end. At night the hall is lighted by gas sun-burners placed in the ceiling.

The Vestry are elected by the ratepayers, so many being sent from the eight wards into which the parish was divided upon the passing of Sir Benjamin Hall's Local Act. The Churchwardens are elected by the Vestry every Easter Tuesday. The Vestry have the power of levying all rates and taxes for the relief of the poor, for lighting, repairing and paving the highways and footpaths, for the payment of annuities for monies expended for building the Chapel of Ease and other district churches, as well as for other purposes.

THE parish workhouse is a large brick edifice, situated at the west end of Barnsbury-street, in the Liverpool-road. It was erected in the year 1777, agreeably with the Act 17 George III., c. 5, at an expense of £3,050. The building at first consisted of a centre and two wings, but an enlargement being found necessary an addition was made in the year 1802. The ground on which it stands was given to the parish by Mrs. Annie Hill. Before the erection of the present building, the poor were maintained in an old house in the Lower-street, and previously to that in a workhouse situated on the north side of the road at Holloway, and in the year 1726, in a building at Strouds Green, conjointly with the poor of Hornsey.

The workhouse is managed by sixty trustees, who must all be assessed to the poor-rate at £30 per annum. They are elected annually at Easter. Mr. Cooper is at present clerk to the trustees.

The following is the dietary table of the workhouse, which is only varied four times during the year, namely, on Christmas-day by roast beef and plum pudding; Easter Monday, leg of pork and pens pudding; Whit Monday, shoulder of veal, and, in the season, beans and bacon:—

FOR THE ABLE-BODIED.

Breakfast.

Milk porridge, every morning, one pint.

Dinner.

Sunday.—Boiled beef, 6 oz. (when dressed), bread, 4 oz.; potatoes, 12 oz.

Monday.—Peas soup, 1½ pint; bread, 4 oz.

Tuesday.—Mutton, 6 oz.; bread 4 oz.; potatoes, 12 oz.

Wednesday.—Broth, 1½ pint; bread, 4 oz.

Thursday.—Boiled beef, 6 oz.; bread, 4 oz., potatoes, 12 oz.

Friday.—Peas soup, 1½ pint; bread, 4 oz.

Saturday.—1 lb. of suet dumplings.

Supper.

Bread and cheese or butter—cheese, 2 oz.; or butter, 1 oz.

In addition to the above, each man is allowed 1 quart of beer per day, and each woman, 1½ pint.

The diet for children under fourteen years of age, is as follows :—

Breakfast.—Bread and milk.

Dinner.—Sunday : Cold beef and pudding. Monday : Boiled mutton and potatoes. Tuesday : Roast mutton and potatoes. Wednesday : Cold mutton and pudding. Thursday : Roast mutton and potatoes. Friday : Boiled mutton, broth, and potatoes. Saturday : Baked round of beef and potatoes.

Supper.—Milk and water and bread.

Each child has half-a-pint of milk for breakfast, and a quarter of a pound of meat on an average, with the same quantity of bread for dinner. The puddings are made of rice or bread, and the beverage is toast and water.

Lewis states that a natural brother of King George II., was a pauper at Islington.

Churches, Chapels, &c.,

CHRIST CHURCH, HIGHBURY.

THIS beautiful church was consecrated for divine worship on the 16th of October, 1848, by the Bishop of London. From whatever point of view, the building presents a varied and striking form. It was erected at a cost of £6,000, from designs by Mr. Allom. It is built of Kentish rag, with Bath stone dressings. The plan is cruciform, the centre being an octagon carried by eight octagonal columns, supporting moulded arches, above which is the celestery, the windows being filled with stained glass of various patterns. The north, south, and west fronts have also each a stained glass window contributed by private individuals. The roof is of imitation oak, the lines formed by the intersection of the timbers having a very picturesque effect ; the organ screen is novel and beautiful, having two fronts richly carved in Caen stone. The pews are stained in imitation of oak ; the pulpit, reading-desk, and font are of Caen stone, carved very richly, and from the form of the church the whole of the congregation can hear and see the minister both in the pulpit and at the communion table ; the means by which this is effected gives a picturesque effect by the various intersections of the arches always so pleasing in Gothic structures. It will accommodate 600 persons. The Rev. M. A. Collisson is minister.

ST. ANDREW'S, THORNHILL SQUARE.

THE foundation stone of this building in Thornhill-square, was laid by the Bishop of London on the 2nd of October, 1852, and was consecrated on Monday, January 15, 1854. It will accommodate upwards of 1,500 persons, and was built at a cost of £6,000. Mr. Thornhill gave the site, and Messrs. Cubitt, Dennis, and Lord R. Grosvenor were the principal contributors. St. Andrew's church is cruciform in plan ; it is built of Kentish rag and Bath stone, and is of the middle pointed period of Gothic architecture. The pulpit of Caen stone, is correctly placed, adjacent to one of the piers of the chancel arch. The tower and spire are at the west end of the south aisle. Mr. Dove was the builder and Messrs. Newman and Johnson, architects. The incumbent is the Rev. S. Altmann, who has been so from the commencement. There are the usual benevolent institutions attached to St. Andrew's church.

ST MARK'S, TOLLINGTON PARK.

THE above church, which is a district chapelry of St. John's, Holloway, was opened for divine worship on Monday, May 22, 1854. It is cruciform in plan, and consists of nave, transept, choir, and chancel, with small side aisles to the choir. The tower is placed near the south-west angle of the structure, and stair turrets at the intersection of the nave and transepts, give access to the galleries. The chancel is paved with Minton's encaustic tiles ; and the windows of the choir and chancel are filled with stained glass. The whole cost was 5,000*l.* aided by a grant of 210*l.* from Her Majesty's Commissioners and 500*l.* from the Metropolis Churches' fund. The architect was Mr. Gough of the Strand ; the builder, Mr. Dove of Arundel-square. The Rev. John Lees is the incumbent.

OFFORD ROAD CHAPEL.

This chapel, situated in the road from which it takes its name, was opened on the 30th of November, 1856, the congregation first assembling for public worship in the school-room, on which occasion sermons were preached by the Revs. Dr. Bennett, H. Allon, and J. H. Godwin. It was erected after a design by Messrs. Lander and Bedells, of Great James-street, Bedford-row. The building is octagonal, and is a substantial structure of brick and freestone, ornamented in front with two short spires, and having a double entrance by two side porches. The interior is comfortably fitted up, the pews in the body of the chapel being of stained wood and cushioned throughout ; the galleries are also stained and ornamented with diamond panels. The cost of the whole was £3,000.

Previous to the erection of this building a church had been formed by a body of Christian people who came from a neighbouring chapel, and worshipped in a room in Twyford-street, Caledonian-road. Here, however, the accommodation soon proved insufficient for an increasing congregation and Sabbath school, and as the neighbourhood opened to them a much larger sphere of usefulness, they resolved upon the erection of a new congregational chapel. A committee, consisting of George Cuthbertson, Esq., H. W. Wilkins, Esq., and other gentlemen well known in the neighbourhood, was formed to carry out the undertaking, and the result was the erection of the present building.

Upon the completion of the building the Rev. Edwin Paxton Hood was called to the pastorate, under whose ministry both the church and congregation have rapidly increased, so much so, that it is in contemplation to erect another and much larger place of worship. Mr. Hood is the editor and proprietor of the *Eclectic Review*, a magazine devoted to the upholding of the principles of Nonconformity.

In connection with the chapel are Sunday schools, with an attendance of about 400 children every Sabbath; a Christian Literary Institute of nearly 300 members, a Band of Hope, Dorcas Society, &c.

BARNSBURY CHAPEL.

Barnsbury Congregational Chapel, situated in Barnsbury-street, was erected in the year 1835, at a cost of £2,300 ; it has, however, since that period been considerably enlarged and improved. It is a square brick-built edifice, and has in front a double entrance by two side porches, ornamented with pilasters. The school-room is in the rear of the chapel, and forms a continuation of the building. The interior is commodious and comfortable, and has spacious galleries, which, together with the body of the chapel, will accommodate about 1,000 persons. The Rev. Charles Gilbert was the first minister, after which the Rev. Theophilus Lessey occupied the pulpit. The Rev. S. B. Sloman is the present minister. Attached to Barnsbury Chapel are Sunday schools, an auxiliary to the London Missionary Society, &c., &c.

CROSS STREET BAPTIST CHAPEL.

Cross-street Baptist Chapel was opened for divine worship in June, 1852, at a cost of 3,483l. 1s. 7d. It is a handsome pointed structure, built of Kentish rag, with Bath stone dressings. There are two arched entrances, one on either side, having a short flight of steps leading to each. The interior is very beautifully fitted up ; a fine stained-glass window is situated at its western end, the pews are darkly-stained, and there is an elegant gallery supported on light columns. The ornamentation of the whole is strictly in keeping with the architecture of the building.

The first minister was the Rev. G. B. Thomas, who, on account of ill-health was compelled to resign in March, 1854. The church continued without a settled pastor until August, 1855, when the present minister, the Rev. Alfred C. Thomas, of Edinburgh, was appointed. There are separate day and Sunday schools, capable of accommodating 400 children, in the rear of the chapel, and many other valuable institutions are supported by the congregation.

ISLINGTON LITERARY INSTITUTION.

This institution was first founded by a few gentlemen fond of literary and scientific pursuits on the 29th November, 1832. After meeting for a time at a private house the present building in Wellington-street was erected at a cost of £3,500. The foundation stone was laid by the President, Charles Woodward, Esq., F.R.S., in April, 1837, and it was opened on the 16th of November the same year, the money being raised by shares of £10 each. The building is in the Grecian style, from designs by Messrs. Gough and

Roumieu, and is of a very elegant character. It has a reading-room, library, museum, class-rooms, and other offices. A theatre, which will accommodate 500 persons, is situated in the rear. The library contains some 5,000 volumes, and the handsome donation of philosophical apparatus given by Mr. Woodward and others, have greatly contributed to the success of the institution.

THE NEW CATTLE MARKET.

THE above market, situated between Maiden-lane and the Caledonian-road, was opened on Wednesday, June 13th, 1855. It occupies a quadrangle of about thirty acres, old Smithfield comprising little more than six acres. In its construction upwards of 3,000,000 blue Staffordshire bricks were used. It contains upwards of 13,000 feet of rail, to which 6,000 beasts can be tied comfortably, and 1,800 pens, affording accommodation for 35,000 sheep. The total cost of the market and its adjuncts was about £350,000. The thirty acres of the new market include not only separate sections for the sale of cattle, sheep, calves, and pigs, but vast rows of sheds for lairage, and a dead meat market. The buildings round the clock tower in the centre, are used as a bank, telegraph office, sale room, &c.

The opening of the market was inaugurated by his Royal Highness Prince Albert, attended by the Lord Mayor, the whole of the corporation, and a large circle of distinguished personages.

CONCLUDING SUMMARY.

SINCE the green fields, which once intervened between the *village* of Islington and the metropolis, have become covered with dwellings, the population of the parish has increased in a very rapid ratio; and from the extensive erections now going on in the neighbourhood of Holloway, Highbury, and Ball's Pond, it bids fair, before the lapse of the present century, to entirely lose all the rurality for which it was once so noted. Nevertheless, the general healthiness of its situation has made it the favourite residence of a large number of wealthy citizens, and its natural elevation will always secure a purity of air and a freedom from certain kinds of epidemics which low-lying districts do not possess. It is hoped, however, that the long-promised Finsbury - park will, before that period, have reserved for our use a few acres of open ground.

A new Agricultural Hall, on a large scale, is about to be erected in the Liverpool-road, which, in conjunction with the cattle-market will most probably make Islington famous in that particular line. The driving of cattle however, through certain streets, and the brutality of drovers, prove a serious nuisance to many respectable inhabitants, and it is sincerely to be hoped that a law will soon be passed abolishing slaughter-houses in the heart of the city, and causing all meat to be taken out in carcases from the market.

As regards educational and religious progress, Islington may be said to have met the wants of the increased population. Several new places of worship have only lately been erected, and two more new churches are determined upon by the Islington Church Extension Society, which we have not space to fully describe. A very handsome structure called St. Luke's, of which the Rev. Albert Rogers is the incumbent, and situated at the north side of the Cattle Market, was consecrated a short time since. There is also a temporary iron church in Arundel-square, (St. Clement's) of which the Rev. J. K. Harrison is incumbent; St. Bartholomew's is also a temporary church situated south of the Lower-road, in a densely populated district. St. Thomas, in Hemingford-terrace, is likewise a fine new structure, lately consecrated; the Rev. G. Allen is the minister. In addition to the above, services in connection with the Established Church are held every Sunday in Bishop Wilson's Memorial Hall, and other places.

Nonconformists have also not been behind in their exertions. A fine new Baptist chapel was opened a few years ago in the Camden-road, near the new City Prison, the Rev. Mr. Tucker, minister; the Baptists are also represented at Providence Chapel in the Upper-street, in addition to those mentioned. The Wesleyans have erected some substantial edifices, one in the Hornsey-road, another a very handsome pointed structure at Highbury, and there is a Methodist chapel in Frog-lane. The Congregationalists, in addition to those already mentioned, have erected a handsome edifice in Canonbury, called Hare Court Chapel; there is also a temporary Congregational church in the Ball's Pond-road, and another in York-place, Barnsbury, under the ministry of the Rev. M'Kewer Williams.

Attached to all the above places, of whatever denomination, there are benevolent institutions and schools of all kinds.

19 AU 62

CPSIA information can be obtained at www.ICGtesting.com
Printed in the USA
BVOW07s1643280214

346326BV00009B/309/P